LIVING MEMORY

SELECTED ESSAYS 1964-2014

LIVING MEMORY

SELECTED ESSAYS 1964-2014

Patrick Morgan

Connor Court Publishing

Published in 2021 by Connor Court Publishing Pty Ltd

Connor Court Publishing Pty Ltd
PO BOX 7257
REDLAND BAY, QUEENSLAND 4165

sales@connorcourt.com
www.connorcourt.com

ISBN: 9781922449573

Cover Design: Maria Giordano

Printed in Australia

CONTENTS

INTRODUCTION

A living memory of the weaknesses of the past can inoculate us to some extent from their repetition in the present. Understanding the 1930s, that 'low, dishonest, decade', provided a vantage point for me in the 1960s. One of the defining (and crippling) aspects of the 1930s was its belief in *politique d'abord*, politics before all else. Beginning with the Vietnam protest movement in the 1960s, this notion has become embedded in our psyches. Large segments of the populace are now hooked on the 24-hour news cycle, which provides us with our daily dose of indignation. T.S. Eliot said he didn't read newspapers because they were too exciting. Information overload has been accompanied by a narrowing of range. Instead of going out to report what's happening among ordinary citizens, journalists increasingly talk to and about themselves. The resultant flood of self-feeding commentary gives a misleading impression of the national mood.

These essays, which range over five decades, may throw some light on how attitudes have changed over that period. Coming from a tight religious background, one thing I found particularly attractive in the early 1960s was the liberal argument that all ideas should be heard, with free debate determining which were more persuasive. But the same liberals have turned turtle by today imposing restrictions on free expression, with words like 'Islamophobia' employed to shut down debate. With a longer perspective we can see they were arguing for tolerance when it was in vogue, and are now arguing for suppression for the same reason. As Shakespeare put it: 'The present pleasure, by revolution lowering, does become the opposite of itself'. This argument is developed in the article 'The Decline of Tolerance'.

I was brought up in a Melbourne Irish Catholic milieu, described in the essay 'Melbourne's North-West Suburbs', where belief rather than tolerance was pre-eminent. The religion we imbibed in the 1940s and 1950s was otherworldly, devaluing the things of this world and seeking immediate connections with the supernatural, like a bird trapped in a cage desperate to escape to its true realm. At university in the early 1960s I realized this was in Christian terms to play down the Incarnation, and to put premature emphasis on the Resurrection. In the 1960s the Catholic Church was, via the Second Vatican Council, discarding its Jansenist, anti-modernist attitudes. It is necessary to work through the materials of this world to bring it towards its completion, a sort of delayed gratification on a grand scale. There is no disjunction in this view between the world and the transcending of it. This began for me a transition away from thinking in purely religious terms.

Reading Denis de Rougemont's *Passion and Society* at the time revealed how Catharist notions of bypassing the material world and yearning to go straight to God the Father had infiltrated themselves into Christianity as an heretical underground via troubadour songs, and the Arthurian, Tristan and Isolde, and other legends. The 1964 essay in this book 'Doom, Innocence and Escape' argues that this impossible desire is in its extreme form a death wish. This realization cauterized me against current New Age and counter-cultural nostrums, which might otherwise have had greater attraction. The experience however left me with a lasting interest in folklore and myth. I had the inestimable good fortune of being raised in a tribal milieu – the last decades of the coherent Irish-Australian Catholic culture – which helped me appreciate how the folk mind operates.

In the 1960s the prominent Melbourne thinker Dr Franta

Knopfelmacher promoted the views of Eric Voegelin's book *The New Science of Politics*, which argued that Communism was a form of Christian heresy. A line of thinkers from Joachim of Flora on had predicted that Moscow would be the coming religious centre of the Christian world, the Third Rome. Communism, centred on Moscow, was a secularized variant of this belief, an attempt to establish a political kingdom of heaven on earth. Voegelin described Communism as a 'neo-Gnostic dream world', an unrealizable perversion of Christian belief. Voegelin's analysis fitted in well with views absorbed from de Rougemont: just as the Cathars claimed access to occult knowledge (*gnosis*) unavailable to outsiders, so Communists claimed to have special, unimpeachable insights into how the world and history operated. Both offered false hopes of premature transcendence. The New Age counter-culture, which later morphed into the Greens, was another, more domestic form of a religioid 'neo-Gnostic dream world'.

A year studying in London in 1980 added new perspectives, including understanding Australia better by experiencing the British and Irish cultures from which it originated. My Russian speaking wife Ann and I attended a course on Soviet and East European Politics at the London School of Economics chaired by Professor Leonard Shapiro. It was a tense year as Solidarity was mobilizing, and in response the Soviets threatened to invade Poland. Another course taken was on George Orwell at Birkbeck College with Professor Bernard Crick, then preparing his monumental Orwell biography. A third course was on the folklore of the British Isles at the City Lit, an adult education institution. New Age mythology, especially Celtic, was at its height, Glastonbury was gearing up for its annual festival, bookshops were full of tomes on ley lines, dolmens and ancient solar calendars. After a long period of hibernation the 'unhistoric' races of Europe were surfacing again, as foretold in the Arthurian and Ossian legends. My interest in folklore and mythology was quickened, particularly in the way underground cultures relate to the mainstream. These interests were strengthened by sojourns in two Celtic realms, Kerry, from where my maternal family originated, and the Auvergne, with a Celtic substratum still evident in its bagpipe music and its sites commemorating the Gaul Vercingetorex.

The notion that heterodox ideas could survive in non-explicit forms in literature and myth, below the detection apparatus of dominant regimes, led to an interest in political literature. In the 1960s one of the main political interests for many people was in totalitarianism, especially in its current form of Communist tyranny. I found that political literature produced more acute insights into the manipulations characteristic of totalitarian behaviour than political science typologies. Only by reading Koestler's *Darkness at Noon*, for instance, could one understand from the inside the tortuous rationalizations by which a Party activist could render himself complicit in his own execution. This led to an interest in the political literature of Russia and East Europe, which from the appearance of Solzhenitsyn's *One Day in the Life of Ivan Denisovich* in 1961 attracted world attention. The dissident writers of the Eastern bloc countries were forced to create a *samizdat* underground in which, like the troubadours, they could transmit their heterodox beliefs into the community in a way the political police were too obtuse to pinpoint. This is discussed in the essay 'Dissident Movements in the Soviet Union'.

We were interested primarily in the totalitarian virus, of which Communism was the most visible example. The essay 'Varieties of Political Catholicism' (1967) describes Communism and Fascism as variant forms of the totalitarian plague; as a consequence the view that left and right should always be seen as opposites was deficient. In the post-war decades Soviet Communism was the most virulent example of the virus, but less so than in its Stalinist form. Was it possible for such regimes to liberalize themselves? Orwell's *Nineteen Eight-Four* and Camus' *The Plague* introduced the further idea that a more 'normalized' or 'soft' form of the will to power was a possibility even in our Western societies, perhaps the next form of political organization.

These interests were strengthened by the influence in Australian intellectual life of Central European Jewish emigrés who introduced us to a way of thinking beyond prevailing Anglo-Australian parameters. Of these the one who influenced me most was Dr Frank Knopfelmacher; an essay in tribute to him is included in this book. Understanding the contemporary travails of Russia and East Europe helped put the disturbances of our Western societies in perspective – one took with a grain of salt the claim that student protesters in the West had some underlying similarity with the dissidents in the Soviet bloc. A disfiguring aspect of the 1930s had been the rise of fellow travellers of Communism (and Fascism); an unchecked utopian strain in their personalities led them to idealize distant societies of which they knew little. As Communism gradually lost its allure, radical dislike of our own Western societies, the other side of the same coin and equally debilitating, came to the fore; this phenomenon is discussed in 'Explanations of the Adversary Culture'. An extreme example of such self-hatred in Australia has been the accusation that our government's handling of the 'Stolen Generations' amounted to genocide, despite no one being killed.

The reasons for the collapse of Communism are explored in 'The Triumph of the Proles'. When this happened some commentators, including a few former anti-Communists, announced the whole problem was over, but concentration of political power continues to cause deformations in society. Over recent decades the totalitarian virus has mutated into new forms, being manifest in its *grand mal* form in the current Islamist insurgency, and in its *petit mal* form as 'political correctness'. Putinism is an eerie mixture of the two – the stolid Soviet KGB mindset bolstered by hi-tech disinformation and a post-modernist manipulation of concepts. During a six month teaching appointment at Charles University in Prague in 1994, my wife and I experienced the relief, and the chaos, which came in the wake of Communism's demise, described in the essay 'To The Kysak Station'. In contrast we were impressed two decades later by the startling improvement and underlying strength of East European countries when we visited Poland, Lithuania and Ukraine in 2013, a few months before the Maidan uprising. These experiences are covered in the essays 'The Borderlands of Europe' and 'The Ruthenians'.

I began to be interested in ideas in the sixties, a time which came to be known as the swinging sixties and the age of the counter culture. These movements had in common an ahistorical perspective – they comprehensively rejected the culture they had inherited, and claimed to be a new burgeoning of freedom and liberation, and a viable alternative (their phrase) to the materialistic, capitalist society of the West. Unfortunately over the decades society has tended to accept these proponents of liberation at their own evaluation, and as a result the misguided belief that our culture is damaged at the core has taken hold. In response political thinkers like Kenneth Minogue and Roger Scruton stressed the importance of inherited traditions. Disparaging the deep structures of our civilization is the cause of many problems.

In the 1980s a now forgotten guru named Alvin Toffler caused a flurry of interest when he demanded we pay attention to his world-shattering discovery that we now lived in a world defined by constant novelty and change. What was permanent about this brief apparition was not his message, but that we were in for a whole succession of Toffler-like prophets expounding 'cutting edge' ideas. As a result of this emphasis on the new, our society now severely downplays our common beliefs, and the continuities which bind our culture together. Post-war society did need change, but the one it got was not the one it needed. We don't have to take every new claim at its face value; we can embrace the benefits of modernity without falling for its excesses. Indignation and resentment have been elevated to the status of permanent public emotions. Protest, which should of its nature be episodic, has as a result become a constant feature of our times. In the West it has had a five-decade progression: 1960s student protest, 1970s counter culture, 1980s adversary culture, 1990s political correctness, and 2000s anti anti-terrorism (which superseded the earlier anti anti-Communism), each developing stage exhibiting a family likenesses to its predecessor.

Instead we have to step back and nominate our own topics. In the place of indignation and protest, which are negative activities, it's better to develop those communitarian virtues which enhance our way of life. One is to focus on civil society, the layer of communal organizations which mediate between citizens and government, and act as a cushion against too great top-down intrusion, against *politique d'abord*. It is this intermediate layer, not the political sphere, which should have our prime attention. A related notion is that individuals and nations are not, as they often present themselves, monochrome entities, but consist of layers or deposits of all the variegated inheritances which go to make up their identity. These two ideas are developed in the essays 'Private Breakdown and Public Remedies' and 'The Origins of Nations'.

A nineteenth century gentleman of means had the luxury of pursuing a great variety of interests. A university position in the humanities, with the salary-providing federal government playing the role of patron, similarly gave me the advantage of having the time and means to delve as widely as I pleased, apart from specific fields of teaching and research. From one perspective the essays collected here are a form of higher journalism, from another a popularizing of scholarly research. They inhabit a space between the two and connect them. Academic fields have so many layers of investigation these days that the general public often needs a way in; you have to know precisely at what point to place yourself on the intellectual 'great chain of being'.

My main field of study was literature, in particular Australian and political literature, but my forte was not doing pure lit. crit. on imaginative texts, of which there was a plethora already. Literary criticism can quickly become attenuated if not informed by some body of knowledge from outside itself. Leslie Fiedler's book *Against the American Grain* taught me how the close reading techniques devised by F.R Leavis and the American New Critics could be fruitfully adapted to fields wider than literature itself. Even though the essays here are presented under a number of different headings, history, religion, politics and culture merge with each other in social critique.

When I began studying in the 1960s the fields of Australian literature and history were booming. They have been sadly diminished over a half century by successive waves of theorists and their ilk. At Australian literature conferences we were told white Europeans couldn't comment on the Aboriginal experience because that would continue the imperial domination Aborigines had suffered, and that Aborigines had themselves been so deprived of their culture they couldn't meaningfully comment either. That didn't leave anyone with much room to move. Those who derided 'dead white males' because they constituted a canon introduced their own canon: women, Aborigines and the environment. A surfeit of such topics in high school and university courses has caused students to leave these offerings in droves. The new critics have swept the ground from under their own feet, to the detriment of our Australian heritage.

After first publishing in 1964, and in *Quadrant* in 1967, writing became a way of life, as these initial articles were followed at the rate of one a month by others ranging from book reviews to more sustained arguments, and eventually to books. Hannah Arendt pointed out in *The Human Condition* that a peculiar feature of power is that 'it does not survive the actuality of the movement which brought it into being, but disappears...with the disappearance or arrest of the activities themselves'. The same, I found, applies to the act of writing. You have to keep at writing to stay in the game; you can't take long breaks without a gruelling recovering period. The brain has its own rhythms, gearing and retrieval systems, which need to be kept in flexible working order. Visual systems like TV, videos, computer screens and ipads are easy on the eyes, but can, by blanking out other modes of perception, impair the recall of bodies of knowledge. Writing is much harder than talking. At certain junctures you may believe you have wonderful ideas, but a trip to the desk quickly deflates you, as they annoyingly reduce themselves to more mundane proportions. This is partly because prose, unlike poetry and music, sets out notions in linear, sequential form. You can easily draw together a range of disparate ideas as you speak, but it's much harder to simultaneously raise and relate them to each other in writing. Hence the saying 'talk is cheap'.

My interests developed over the decades in ways which were more cloudy than here described in retrospect; much necessary inchoate striving has disappeared in the process. A selection has been made of thirty essays, whose publication dates are spread fairly evenly over the five decades. A little over half were originally published in *Quadrant.* Some of the longer essays have been shortened, but with the central argument retained. In a few places a phrase in square brackets has been inserted to clarify the meaning.

Folkways

DIANA AS MYTHOLOGY

(1997)

*How could the extraordinary outpouring of public grief
occasioned by Princess Diana's death in 1997 be explained?*

Diana fascinates us because the trajectory her life took followed
the basic structures of myth, legend and folktale, patterns which
have always gripped human beings. Whatever her mixture of
personal virtues and frailties, she was increasingly swept along
by the momentum of events beyond her control. A larger-than-life
figure while alive, in death she is already moving into the realm of
mythology. We can understand her life in age-old terms:

The Fairy Tale. The Cinderella story: the third daughter who
meets and marries Prince Charming, who has rejected those higher
in the queue. She is going to be the next Queen, and then it all turns
to ashes. The archetype is here, even though she was of aristocratic
birth herself – in folklore structure transcends details.

Divisions in the Kingdom. Diana was a person of high degree,
whose actions and fate had consequences for the whole society. Most
myths begin with a division or feud in the realm, usually over love
or power or both. Here the feud was within the royal household, but
its complex conflicts over inheritance, the future rulers of the realm,
the constitution and religion, may ultimately have ramifications for
ordinary citizens who are watching or listening to the tale.

Fatal Attraction. The primary division was over love, involving

17

two triangular tensions: Charles, contested by Camilla and Diana, and Diana, contested by Charles and Dodi. Those love affairs set up deep fault lines, similar to those of the great love triangles of mythology: Arthur, Guinevere and Lancelot; Menelaus, Helen and Paris; Mark, Tristan and Iseult. This is fatal love, since there is always an impediment to final happiness. The pursued lovers must leave the realm; so Diana and Dodi escaped to the continent, or luxuriated in the sunny Mediterranean, like Odysseus and Calypso. Dodi was from another race, an outsider whose family had been rejected by the establishment, which ostracized the lovers, just as King Mark relentlessly pursued the doomed lovers Tristan and Iseult.

The Maimed King. The Grail story of the wounded Fisher King involved emasculation and inheritance. In her TV interview Diana, in saying that Charles was not suitable to be king, was administering the Dolorous Stroke, and denoting him the Maimed King. While this situation continued, there was speculation that the kingly role had to be passed on to his son, William, who is not sullied. Lancelot cannot acquire the Grail because he is not pure; the torch is passed onto his son Galahad.

The Trap. There was a feeling over the last five years that Diana was trapped by the whirl of events surrounding her, like a heroine in Greek tragedy. The stakes were always getting higher, the risks greater on all sides, and no-one could see a happy or successful resolution. Events had a logic of their own, a headlong rush to some unpredictable end.

Death and Fate. The end was sudden, random, unexpected, that is, tragic – the design of a malign but relieving fate. The death was not caused by either side in the dispute. An outside force stepped in to take a decisive hand, which the ancients called fate, the Gods, or destiny. The nature of the ending means that we, the onlookers, are relieved, having undergone our catharsis, though the underlying tensions have not been fully resolved.

Furies. The paparazzi who chased her to her doom were like the Furies of Greek mythology, who relentlessly pursued people to their death out of vengeance. Throughout the whole saga the media played the role of the bard, who tells the story to the public with endless variants and embellishments, but who also tries to shape the story as it is told.

Diana of the Flowers. Being buried on an island in an idyllic lake is an obvious reminder of King Arthur's end on the Isle of Avalon, where he moves to the sphere of immortality. Diana is also the Lady of the Lake, a spirit figure from outside our world, who in some versions of the Arthurian legends was assimilated to the Roman hunting goddess Diana. Diana lived by the lake with her lover Faunus, of whom she grew tired. When she died her body was put into the lake.

The Last Say. Momentous event demand a great funeral oration by a person close to the departed. Earl Spencer's speech was a final triumph over the establishment on behalf of his sister, who now lives on in the power of myth, though defeated in actuality. The speech showed the power of words, how a great speech can change things by appealing over intermediate structures directly to the audience, like the orations of Pericles, King Henry's Crispin's Day speech, or Leo Amery giving Chamberlain his marching orders during the second world war.

Diana was a flawed mortal, who might be considered not up to these grandiose comparisons. But mythology has a power of its own, independent of the trigger which gives it birth.

Adelaide Review, November, 1997

I admired the writings of the Perth author Hal Colebatch, whom I knew, which reflected a knowledge of the deep structures of mythology.

THE ORIGINS OF NATIONS

(2008)

*Instead of regarding divergent cultures as oppositions, they are
better seen as amalgams.*

Ethnic nationalism, the desire for one's race to be pure and to
exclude others from one's claimed territory, can in extreme cases
cause ethnic cleansing, as we saw in the Yugoslav civil wars of the
1990s. To think of ourselves as having a monochrome nationality,
a primary marker to distinguish ourselves from others, can result in
an antagonistic view of identity – British versus Irish, Croat versus
Serb, and so on. This can lead to nations, in the name of a false sense
of historical coherence, behaving badly.

The 'unhistoric races' of Europe were peoples who had hardly ever
ruled themselves, hardly ever owned their own territory, hardly ever
defined their own boundaries, and hardly ever gained international
recognition. (The Kurds and Gypsies are still in this situation today.)
As the nineteenth century progressed these subjugated races, for
example, the Czechs, Poles, Serbs, Croats, and other Slav nations,
Romanians, Hungarians, Jews, and various Celtic entities, saw the
creation of a national history for themselves as the first step on
the road to future nationhood. National feeling was generated by
Indo-European philologists, who republished early documents and
established a standard written language, and by poets who amplified
past national myths into modern form. Both wished to inspire
a passion for national identity in their people. Races yearning to

resurrect themselves desired the outward signs of nationhood: ethnic coherence, security, a defined area, their own language, culture, and their own rulers, free from imperial domination.

Creating a national history, though a necessary narrative, can become a danger if taken too literally. Nationalist leaders identified a time, usually in the period after the collapse of Roman Empire (c.400-900AD), when their people first arrived at their homeland and formed themselves into an identifiable unit. Historians rather portentously call this 'the moment of primary acquisition'; more colloquially it is the claim that 'we got here first'. Then some great defeat – Kosovo for the Serbs, Mohacs for the Hungarians, Camlann for the Romano-Celts in Britain, the sacking of temple in Jerusalem in 70AD for the Jewish people – was invoked to explain how the entity was dispersed, and led a subterranean existence for a millennium or more. Now they were awaking again, as in Arthurian, Barbarossan and Ossian legends of the sleeping once and future king.

Historians of the later Roman Empire, conscious of the disasters extreme ethnic nationalism have visited on the Balkans and other places, have demonstrated the misleading nature of many nationalist histories. To give one example: the word 'Croat' (*Hrvati*) was originally not an ethnic description at all, but a type of class or rank, and is found across Europe from Germany to Greece. In *The Myth of Nations: The Medieval Origins of Europe* (2002) the US historian Patrick Geary points out that many purported national histories:

> assume, first, that the peoples of Europe are distinct, stable and objectively identifiable social and cultural units, and that they are distinguished by language, religion, custom and national character, which are unambiguous and immutable...After these moments of primary acquisition, according to this circular reasoning, similar subsequent migrations, invasions, or political absorptions have all been illegitimate. In many cases, this has meant that fifteen hundred years of history is to be obliterated.

In reality European races are fluid, and the history of the continent has been one of continual migration, disruption and mingling, which continues today. Geary's book utilizes recent researches contained in two major books: Herwig Wolfram's *The Roman Empire and Its Germanic Peoples* (1990) mainly on western Europe, and Florin Curta's *The Making of the Slavs* (2001) on eastern Europe.

One of Wolfram's great insights is that when Huns, Avars, Lombards, Franks, Allemani, Goths and Visigoths, Vandals and others moved into parts of the old Roman Empire, they didn't bring with them people who were 100% ethnically Goth or Vandal or Lombard or whatever:

> The formation of a barbarian tribe was a political and constitutional process that involved the most diverse ethnic elements. When such a 'people in arms' migrated, an extraordinary social mobility prevailed in its ranks. Any capable person who had success in the army could profit from this mobility, regardless of his ethnic and social background.

Starting as a small tribe often with a charismatic leader, and a group of dominant males, the band gathered up on the way as it moved conquered people, camp followers, local inhabitants, female companions, adventurers, opportunists who wanted to be on the winning side, and so on, so that when for example the Vandals eventually reached Andalusia in southern Spain, there might have had only 10% or less ethnically Vandals, whatever that meant, among them. This was true even of the Huns, whose small bands may not have been closely related in the regions to the east from where they came. This explodes nationalist myths of racial homogeneity and purity. The novelist Anthony Burgess shocked everyone into realizing this when he pointed out that English is a creole language.

Curta's book shows that the notion of the 'Slav' was first popularized by writers from Byzantium, who named these tribes after one branch, the Sclavenes. There were many other 'Slavic' tribes such as the Antes, but all the local 'Slavic' tribes were bundled together from the Byzantine perspective as Slavs, though they themselves did not describe themselves as such, and may not have all spoken an early Slavic language. The description 'Germania' arose similarly, through Frankish and Roman use, as an umbrella term for the disparate tribes on the other side of the Rhine. Tribes were not ethnically pure, but consisted of a mixed group with leaders imposing their 'race' and customs on those they took over. Written accounts of the time often use an all-encompassing tribal label which hides the diversity underneath these newly forming alliances.

New races appeared on the edges of the old Roman Empire not usually because of invasions but because of sporadic raiding parties and migration, and even migration was often caused by simply mixing with adjacent peoples, intermarriage and assimilation. The scribes of the conquered peoples, like Gildas in England on the coming of the Anglo-Saxons, naturally wrote up the coming of a new people as a catastrophic invasion and destruction of all that they had known, but this was not always the case. We retain the image of terrifying Hun invasions. The Huns did invade, but they were not typical. A relatively small number of conquerors could impose their customs and language on local people, but did not obliterate them and were usually absorbed by them.

Curta shows that the Slavic homeland was not, as previously thought, in the marshes in southeastern Poland, from where Slavic invaders were alleged to have moved south over large distances in great forays. From Roman times there were Slavs just north of the Danube *limes*. The Slavs moved south into the Balkans more by migration and intermixing as citizens and mercenaries (*foederati*) than by direct invasion. A tribe would typically appear on the edge of the empire, fight a battle with the Romans, then sign a treaty (*foedus*) with them, perhaps to fight other tribes with Roman support, and with their warriors [to become] part of the Roman forces. As the empire disintegrated further these tribes set up within the empire as a state within a state. These processes over decades and even centuries produced new Romano-barbarian amalgams. Wolfram titles his book *The Roman Empire and Its Germanic Peoples* to make this point – he believes the Germanic tribes neither destroyed nor restored the Roman empire, but made a home in it.

Language and race did not always go together, as we have previously thought. 'Slavs' may not always have spoken a Slavic language. Those who spoke a Celtic language may not always have been a 'Celtic' people. Language is not necessarily the defining characteristic of a nation, as the 19th century language scholars thought, in comparison with locality, culture or religion. There are many examples of the non-primacy of language, for example, Serbs and Croats have a shared language, the crucial difference is religion. Conversely the non-Slavic Bulgars, originally an Asiatic steppe people, now speak a Slavic language which they have acquired. Geary concludes:

> The names of peoples were thus less descriptions than claims –
> claims for unity under leaders who hoped to monopolize and to
> embody the traditions associated with these names...The history
> of peoples in Late Antiquity and the early Middle Ages is not the
> story of a primordial moment but of a continuous process...It is a
> history of constant change, or radical discontinuities, and of political
> and cultural zigzags, masked by the repeated re-appropriation of old
> words to define new realities...The Serbs who came into existence
> in the decaying remains of the Avar Empire were not the people
> defeated at the battle of Kosovo in 1289, and neither were they the
> Serbs called to national aggrandizement by Slobodan Milosevic.

Those two well-known madmen of last century, Hitler and Stalin, were themselves devotees of 19th century ideas of race and nationalism, which led in their hands to ethnic cleansing. As well as eliminating the Jews, Hitler wished to clear the Slavs out of east and south Europe and settle Germans there, using as his excuse the fact that Germans had settled some of these areas historically. To give one out-of-the-way example which involves both dictators: Hitler was intrigued by the Goths of the Crimea, who had been there for 1300 years since the third century AD until they were diluted almost into extinction by the Ottoman Turks by the mid 16th century, though a Gothic language continued to be spoken for another 100 years. As Neal Ascherson explains in his wonderful book, *Black Sea*:

> The fantasy of an ur-German Crimea was retrieved by the Nazi mind – that drain-filter of broken, discredited and putrescent ideas – and recycled into a new version of pseudo-history and political legitimation. Crimea must be reconquered and the Gothic realm restored.

In 1941 Hitler planned the 'Gotland' project, in which Tatars, Jews and Russians would be cleared out of the Crimea, and Germans settled there to re-establish a Gothic Crimea. Sevastopol was to be called Theodorichshafen. But another annihilator had got there just before him. Stalin's specialty in the early days of the Soviet Union was as 'nationalities expert', a euphemism for ethnic cleanser. Half the Crimean Tartars had already been killed or deported by him via his 1930s famines and purges. So some Tatars naturally welcomed the arrival of the German army in 1941, though others opposed it. After the Russian army took over in 1944, the Tartars were unfairly accused of collaborating with the Nazis, and Stalin, like Hitler, continued his ethnic cleansing by expelling the whole Crimean Tartar population to central Asia. This is just one example of the murderous madness that 19th century ethnic nationalism eventually led to.

The second world war itself caused massive ethnic cleansing. Poland had a 40% non-Polish population before the war, but after it with Jews, Volksdeutch, Ukrainians, Ruthenians, Lithuanians, White Russians and others now gone, Poland was now much 'purer' – almost everyone was an ethnic Pole. This had not been intended by the Poles, but was caused by Nazi and Communist policies.

Similarly in the Czechoslovak lands. So the dangerous 19th century view of one 'pure' people on its own land speaking one language and governed by itself was actually coming into existence. After Tito's death the artificial supranational structure called Yugoslavia was quickly demolished in a frenzy of desire to create pure nations, for example the idea of a Greater Serbia to include all Serbs, including those in Kosovo, Bosnia and Croatia. At the same time a larger artificial supranational structure, the Soviet Union, disappeared with similar results.

The conclusions of historians working on continental Europe provisionally confirm the insights gained from using DNA in analyzing the populations of the British Isles. An example is Stephen Oppenheimer's *The Origins of the British: A Genetic Detective Story* (2006). The standard view of the populating of the British Isles is that Celts from central Europe invaded about the third century BC, and took over the original population. When the Roman occupation disintegrated, the Romano-Celt population in England was in turn taken over by invading Angles, Saxons and Jutes who decimated the existing population and formed a new entity, Anglo-Saxon England, until later Viking and Norman invasions.

The new view from DNA plus other evidence is that as a general pattern from much earlier times, the British Isles had two separate populations – all except the area we now know as England was settled by peoples coming from the Atlantic littoral of the Iberian peninsula. The province of England, as distinct from Ireland, Wales and Scotland, was settled by Friesians, Angles, Saxons, other Germanic peoples and Scandinavians, also from very early times. These people may have spoken an early Germanic language. There is no evidence for a great Celtic invasion of the British Isles about 300BC. Some must have come to transmit their language and customs, but the 'Celts' of the British Isles are not genetically related to the Celts of the central European Celtic heartland. Celtic was probably not spoken over the whole of England – there is no substratum of Celtic words in the English language, which one would otherwise expect, though there are Celtic place names in England.

New research suggests England was not invaded in the fifth century by massive waves of Angles, Saxons and Jutes who subsequently comprised much of the population. They came as a smallish ruling group and intermarried and imposed their language and customs on the existing local Germanic-Scandinavian-Friesian derived peoples. Thus the Anglo-Saxons may have come to an England already speaking some kind of Germanic language, though this is an inference which lacks conclusive objective evidence. They did not dominate and obliterate the local population, as written accounts had it but, small in numbers, eventually merged with it. The Celtic and Anglo-Saxon 'invasions' of the British Isles can now be seen to be more like the Roman, Viking and Norman ones: few came and though they ruled, the majority population remained the same and over time assimilated the outsiders. The revolutionary advances in research produced by DNA analyses, though fascinating, must at the moment be treated as provisional.

Just because present nations don't have the genetic continuity they believed they had should not deter them from celebrating their history and being attached to it in a sensible way. We needn't go to the other extreme – genes aren't everything. There has been over two millennia of continuous Celtic and Slavic and Germanic culture. This in itself is as great a determinant as genetics. Recent findings should also make us realize that there are few if any purely victim nations nor purely dominant ones – all have had their ups and downs, all have moved and displaced others and been displaced in their turn. In southern Spain, for example, Spanish Catholics under Ferdinand and Isabella finally took over from the Muslims, who had taken over from the Visigoths and Vandals, who had taken over from the Romans, who had taken over from the Carthaginians, who had displaced the original inhabitants. Seeking revenge for victim status has been the cause of bloodletting as well as imperial domination.

These findings are consoling in another way. We do not individually have a monochrome personal identity. We are all composed of many disparate layers, which have been deposited over time. In place of the conflict model of nationalism, it is much more fruitful to think of ourselves on the archaeological analogy of stratigraphy. Our personalities and our nation are like layers, each containing deep sediments going back over many generations and incorporating many diverse experiences. We may see only the top layer, the most visible and recent one, in our case the Australian one, but this is to neglect the variegated layers underneath. Jung described our personalities as like the storeys of a building, the upper storeys being the most recent ones and the basement going back to Roman times or beyond: 'everything is alive, and our upper storey, consciousness, is continually influenced by its living and active foundations'. Our task is to retrieve, as best as possible, remnants from deposits in our past, and to reconcile our multiple identities and allegiances into a meaningful whole, not to set them at odds with each other. Thus we each form our own private myth. But to exaggerate one strand and consequently diminish all the others is dangerous, and can lead to civil strife.

National identity is similarly an amalgam of all that has gone before it. With exclusive or oppositional nationalism, links to one country or one group are held to preclude links to any other. This sets up a false antithesis. Of course as citizens we give pre-eminence in our civic life to our country of allegiance. Below that we make our private adjustments and reconciliations. But just as we do not privilege the overt layer, nor should we privilege minority layers, the fatal mistake of multicultural ideology, which gives inner permission to immigrant cultures to assert themselves against the host nation.

Quadrant, June, 2008

HOW TRIBAL SOCIETIES OPERATE

(2005)

Another approach to understanding cultures different from our own is through an anthropological perspective.

Can failed states and devastated countries (like Papua New Guinea, Iraq, East Timor) be converted into viable civil societies? This pressing question is not just a matter of political and economic solutions – recognizing underlying cultural factors is crucial. One needs an imaginative reconstruction of how tribalized people think to try to get inside their minds, which are opposite to ours in many ways. We can begin by imagining in the remote past a wandering tribe of a few hundred families. In order for the tribe to survive, one man with warrior skills and innate leadership would by natural ability emerge as leader to ward off enemies, establish a hold over territory, and keep internal control so that food could be produced. This man also had to have great leadership qualities of a non-physical kind – charisma akin to being a god – to explain the meaning of things to his people.

Initially the king held all functions to himself, but he gradually sub-let some of them. The governing functions were split into law, administration and politics. The charismatic or magical sphere was devolved into the medicine man, the priest/shaman, and the poet/ seer. But the ruler still controlled all these powers and could retract his delegation, so no real separation of the different spheres occurred. He allowed no independent functions, no alternative centres of wealth or power to accumulate. Finally he did give these up. In the

English tradition, the second last to be given up was law, in late medieval times, and the last political power, from the seventeenth century onwards.

Tribal societies are not, as we might expect, a pyramid shaped hierarchy, but a flattened one with the ruler and his entourage on top, then a gap with no middle-ranging institutions, and with the atomised tribal members below. This was still evident in Indonesia in the 1950s, where Soekarno would receive petitions directly from ordinary people once a week on his verandah. Barons or lesser feudal chieftains replicated this structure, which was not a flexible or adaptive one. The death of the king, who was the lynchpin of the whole structure, rendered the society dysfunctional for a time – institutional longevity was not guaranteed. Today we talk of 'one bullet' regimes, meaning states, like Cuba or Libya, whose structure depends on one man. In the past they were 'one arrow' or 'one poisoned cup' regimes.

In the tribal perspective everyone is deemed a brother or an enemy. Nobody is deemed *neutral,* merely a neighbour, a citizen. Brotherhood is a bond by blood, the strongest tie of all, hence the sensible policy of nepotism. Or a person can take a blood oath, to make him like a brother. The tribe is something he would die for, and also kill for. The individual can perish but the tribe must go on. Tribal death, the possibility that the tribe might be wiped out, is always on the cards and is the great fear. The prime catalyst for change in these societies is a feud in the royal family, when the blood bond breaks down and treachery replaces loyalty.

The tribe is established by warrior power, and retains that characteristic, controlling territory and people. The instruments of violence, visible and permanent, are commonly used as a first resort. When might is right, it's winner take all. If an outsider transgresses, it's an eye for an eye. The instinct for revenge keeps everything on the same level – no reconciliation is possible, no hope of moving to a higher plane. It's always pay-back time. When Alphonse Gangitano was murdered in the Melbourne mafia world, his death led to a score of others. There was no way of ending the cycle, short of outside intervention. The New Testament injunction to turn the other cheek and love thy neighbour was a great advance in civilization.

Whereas our notion of time is linear, progressive and even transcendental, as in vertically inclined religions like Christianity, the tribal notion of time is horizontal and cyclical, a timeless world, where everything is destined to endlessly repeat itself. In *The Myth of the Eternal Return* Mircea Eliade shows how the primordial acts of the founding gods of the race, in the time before time, have to be ritually re-enacted for regeneration to occur. Imitation and repetition, not novelty, is the great, security-inducing task. There are three interconnected cycles:

DAY	YEAR	HUMAN LIFE
morning	spring	youth
midday	summer	mid life
evening	autumn/fall	old age
night	winter	death

There is an obvious problem here: the day comes back, so do the seasons, but we don't – one of these isn't really a cycle. The individual dies, but the tribe goes on – tribal preservation is the aim, serial immortality. This is personally not very consoling, hence the appeal of Christianity with its belief in individual immortality. Cyclical religions are a means of killing history, as no notion of progress exists. Heroes, larger-than-life deeds, the gods, existed in the past – we are lesser people. The tribe faces the past, not the future. Remote antiquity, hymned by the tribe's poet, is revered and the future feared as it may bring catastrophe or even annihilation.

To understand reality we categorize it by Greek philosophical dualisms, in contrast to seeing it as a timeless world animated by larger, controlling life-forces. The world is experienced as fluid, a continuum, with no strict boundaries between past, present and future; between here and the after-life; between humans, animals, plants and minerals; between earth, sky and underworld; between the living and the dead; between gods and man; between the material and the non-material world. Magic is the shape-changing catalyst which enables one plane of existence to morph into another. The world is synthetic, not categorized into discrete parts by cerebration.

We are ego-conscious, and we can retract ourselves into an almost hermetically sealed capsule of individuality if we wish. Individual consciousness as we experience it doesn't really exist in the tribal state; the living animistic world is the breathing, pulsating positive entity that carries life and creativity. We see the world as centring on our all-important ego, with which we act on things and try to affect them. In the older perspective human beings exist on the periphery of things, minor players, passive, whose only role is to recognize and merge into the great forces around them.

Religion then consists in obeisance to these larger forces, to overcome our fear and dread of the future. We are controlled by forces outside us, incomparably more powerful than us, which the ancients called Fate/Destiny/the Gods. We are bound, not free, we cannot control things, but we can by supplication align ourselves with these forces. Nature is regarded as the provider of bounty, but also as wild, awesome and capricious, with unpredictable catastrophes, like floods and storms at sea. It is to be propitiated rather than harnessed, with ceremonies like young couples making love in the newly ploughed furrows at seedtime as imitative magic to guarantee fertility.

The land was owned by the gods, and was the bride of the king. Later it was owned perhaps by the lord of the manor, but no individual ownership, much less freehold, existed. In Russian peasant society, according to Alan MacFarlane's *Origins of English Individualism*, the head of an extended serf family was only the temporary custodian of the land. Land was owned by the household; the family through time were the owners. The land could not be divided – there were no wills. No individual had a claim on the property as an individual. Yet in spite of this, there was great attachment to the place of birth, which often gave the tribe its name. You didn't move far from your place of origin, as you felt literally out of place away from it, as illustrated in Aboriginal songlines. The centre of your life was the hearth, fort, campfire, etc., where you felt safe – chaos reigned beyond. Only heroes ventured into the dark, alien world of the badlands where monsters and brigands stalked. A remnant of this attitude is felt in the word 'outlandish'.

The positive tribal virtues were absolute loyalty and obedience to tribe and king, and pride in their achievements. Negative virtues or emotions were dread (fear of death from accident, sickness, enemies or disasters), shame at transgression, and envy rather than trust. In his book *Envy* Helmut Schoeck points out that pervasive envy of others' wealth crippled the capacity for financial accumulation and therefore economic progress. People didn't think in economic terms – the unit of production was the self-sufficient household. In society as a whole, social control (including warfare) took precedence over increased production.

In modern civil society, which provides a striking contrast to traditional ways, the various realms – law, politics, economics, religion – are separate, and also subjugated, so one can't dominate or invade another. As Ernest Gellner puts it in *Conditions of Liberty: Civil Society and its Rivals*, the best recent attempt at comparing tribal and civil societies:

> What distinguishes Civil Society, or a state containing a Civil Society, from others is that it is *not* clear who is boss. Civil Society can check

and oppose the state. It is not supine before it…The broader sense of Civil Society…refers to a total society within which the non-political institutions are not dominated by the political ones, and do not stifle individuals either.

The state controls the elements of violence, but holds them in reserve – police are state controlled, the army can operate only externally; no private militias, like those which operated in Fallujah, are allowed. Society insists that disputes and power grabs be resolved not by force (might is right), but by resort to law, negotiation, elections, bargaining, tribunals and so on. Trust is essential, as killing has high transaction costs.

It is not necessary to have a pure democracy – Afghanistan is still a mixed part-tribal, part-democratic system. What is essential is a civil society with intermediate institutions and some form of elected representation. Such a society requires independent and equal citizens, who are engaged in production not warfare, who think economically, who internalize social structures and habits, and who do not to transgress unwritten rules. Institutional structures are hard to build up, and easy to destroy. Private ownership and an independent legal system, with transactions guaranteed under law, confer the security necessary for economic success and citizens' well-being.

Our society has no official beliefs, and is held together by no over-arching worldview. The New York novelist Chaim Potok has described the experience of moving from the 4000 year old Jewish culture of his youth – tight, controlled, belief-dominated, coherent, with everything imbued with meaning – into a secular, diffuse, free, recent polity with no shared beliefs. The danger is that myths can make a comeback because they have greater drawing power than anodyne democracies. We must, as Orwell said, defend the normal.

We are not so attached to place. The three great choices we make in life – where we will live, whom we will marry, what occupation we will take up – were not available in tribal societies. We have multiple choices, options, electives, scenarios: we are not bound. We act as though we can affect the world and our own destiny in a rational way. The new, not the known, attracts our active curiosity.

Tribal and civil society, described as ideal types, seem wholly opposed to each other. In reality it is not an either/or situation; today we live in a mixed society, where elements of both types of behaviour are present. Lady Diana now seems almost a figure from mythology. Leaders like General de Gaulle and Archbishop Mannix derived much of their power from their roles as tribal chieftains. The ALP has obvious tribal elements, true believers, heroes and villains, fascination with party history, the possibility of expulsion, whereas the Liberals are much more a modern secular institution.

Modern democracy is thought to be a secular, rational, Enlightenment project, but remnants of older values survive within it. The two different elements coexist in a healthy way in society, which each needs its own underground, its own unconscious. But malign combinations can arise. In *Modernity and the Holocaust* Zygmunt Bauman describes totalitarianism as a strange amalgam of sophisticated modern political techniques combined with old, dark, atavistic forces. It's important to insist that, overall, our world is better than the tribal one, an advance in human civilization. Otherwise we fall for the romanticism of designer tribalism, as Roger Sandall calls it in his book *The Culture Cult*. The intense conformity of tribal life can have a stultifying effect on the personality.

It is extremely difficult to consciously change from one type of society to the other, since culture is much stronger and of longer duration than politics – you can set up new structures and institutions, but thousands of years of habits, ingrained almost like a genetic code, soon come to the fore. The Aboriginal and Torres Strait Islander Commission (ATSIC) was a classic example. But there have been successes. Solidarity in Poland combined traditional

Catholic workers with modern intellectuals, who together worked out a sophisticated long-term, non-violent strategy of building a civil society within the carapace of the old regime, a more successful tactic than the atavistic strategy of the PLO/IRA/ETA kind. The East Asians economies, particularly Lee Kwan Yu's Singapore, have shown that elements of tribal society can be helpful in creating a successful modern state.

Quadrant, January-February, 2005

DOOM, INNOCENCE AND ESCAPE

(1964)

This 1964 article looks at the folk song revival, which presaged the New Age mysticism and regression to a simpler rural life which were to become fashionable as the 1960s and 1970s progressed.

We have all noticed that the folk song cult has assumed a quasi-religious role: it has its own rituals, services (hootenannies), faithful (purists), heretics (commercial compromisers), apparel, taboos (respectability), high priest (Ledbetter) and disciples (Seeger and Baez) to carry on the apostolic succession. Further, it is providing a worldview for interpreting the present; and since it is popular and taken seriously we'd better have a look at its values.

The folk singer is obsessed by one truth of our world – we feel it is getting out of hand, its final disintegration symbolized by the bomb. Baez: 'It's looming over your head. The kids who sing really don't have a future. I feel that we have just so long to live.' We can soften this reality by nostalgia for a more innocent age in the past. Folk songs have all these traits – doom, innocence and escape – and we can find plenty of evidence that people are projecting this vision on to today's reality.

The society in folk songs is earthy in the sense that it is rural (folksingers look like peasants), stratified, unmechanised (Singer won't listen to the radio), closer to subsistence level, where issues come out more sharply and tend to transform themselves immediately into physical terms. Hence the modern folk song: 'I'm gonna *hammer* out the love between my brothers and sisters', a strange but illuminating contradiction. So Seeger in the Public Lecture Theatre last year spoke as though society is stratified into two groups, bosses and workers, for whom there is only love or hate; as though physical Depression issues (keeping a roof over your head and food in your guts) were still the vital ones, whereas we know that intellectual rather than physical courage is needed for more of the problems we face.

The folk song society, because more primitive, is centered around basic drives, urges and emotion, where people act (rather than think) instinctively and unfailingly. (Baez: 'We were passionately, insanely, irrationally in love for the first few months.') It has an emotional and motivational range too simple for modern life: we know motives are rarely unmixed and that we can't locate good and evil, love and hate, purely in separate people. This Manichean polarization of elements shows itself on the few occasions when folk singers act publicly. Naive of the real subtlety of evil, they can select only issues with clearly divided sides, where they have the surety of locating right and wrong.

But these rare intrusions into public commitment are really anti-political, since they believe we are small men, ineffective in great movements; and all of us can find this fatalism and resignation reflected in the songs, which show a local, encapsulated, private world, where the protagonists have retreated into a small sphere where personal relationships are everything (love songs are by far the most popular and most numerous folk songs), where people act as individuals (the tragic hero), rather than as masses, where larger events intrude, not per se, but as agents of the lover's doom. So in this century of unprecedented murder and catastrophe, which demands some stance in explanation of it all, you abdicate, domesticating your fears into the cozy little world of private concerns, where instead of thinking, you can quietly emote.

Folk songs are not earthy in the sense of a bawdy Rabelaisian lust for life, for they dwell, not on birth and life, but on death and the otherworldly; they sing of the frailty of life and the imminence of death. Hence their sad, pessimistic, mournful tone, that diffused melancholy and overpowering doom, which induces the soporific and trance-like effect they have on us. The hero seeks an impossible goal, which must end in destruction: pursuing an ideal woman he can never attain; ideal in that she symbolizes a world of natural innocence (don't tamper with nature, says the folk singer): unattainable in that this is impossible on earth. This explains the unerotic love portrayed (the only trait which the cult has missed, or conveniently misunderstood); it explains their dream-like quality, disconnectedness, things left unexplained, that stately, graceful, pavane-like way they charm us away from reality.

Not all folk-song genre have every trait, but they retain the overall atmosphere. Political songs are concerned with broad issues, but the sentimentality in which they often indulge, especially in defeat, e.g. Irish Rebel Songs, contrasts strangely with the harshness of the reality they pretend to invoke. American Negro songs, though Christian, are uninfluenced by the nostalgic, pessimistic view of life, since they came through an African, not European, tradition; the second verse of 'When the Saints Go Marching In':

> Some say this world of sorrow
> Is the only one we need,
> But I'm waiting for that moment
> When the new world is revealed.

which is a direct quote from Paul (Romans: 8:18), explicitly condemns the Manichean vision. But the Negro songs are unsuitable as our métier because they describe a primitive, rural society: we don't face the problems of cotton pickin'.

Leaving aside these variations, the mystique is most intensely felt during long folk-singing sessions: in some dark, warm corner of a cafe we are sitting on wooden benches; in front, a folk singer, dark-clothed, eyes, closed, proclaiming by the limpness of his body his resignation to the buffeting that life has given him, sits singing quietly, lulling us with dulcet guitar chards. His singing is haunting and plaintive, through the stillness and smoke, we are gradually drawn into the spell, like the young Nazis at Hitler youth rallies where folk songs were sung; we still involuntarily murmur the choruses, but we are away, having dropped the drag of thinking; eyes, if open, gazing upward to the roof and beyond; anaesthetized into a world where we can lament over the great sorrow of life. We feel that somehow we are now in touch with those vague primordial things (whatever they are) which really matter.

The values of the folk-singing cult are remarkable in that they antithetical and inimical to everything needed to face life today. And it shouldn't be seen as an isolated phenomenon, but simply as a more obvious example of the temptations we all face quite often: to escape the complexities of our life. The mystique has been magnificently analysed by Denis de Rougement in *Passion and Society*, which shows how the troubadours of the 12th century took up the Manichean heresy of the world's evil, and spread it through Europe in folk songs, and how it has associated the whole Christian tradition with medieval fundamentalism, Puritanism, anti-industrialism, and all those other disfigurements which are publicly identified with Christianity.

But now, just as the Church is at last eradicating these heretics from its midst, their secular counterparts are arising, hitchhiking jongleurs come to strum again a high tale of love and death to a people caught up in a mess of money and machines. And today their arch-enemy who holds the other part of truth is not the Church but the scientific mentality which looks to the future not the past and, believing that all is manageable, wants to subdue the earth, not to escape from it, an ethic which for all it arrogance and complacency, is at least substantial. So Pete Seeger and Joan Baez compete with

Mark Oliphant as the culture heroes and high priests of our age, offering us their worldviews as the religion of our lives.

There is a widespread myth that the universities are places which encourage this apolitical vagrant view of life and that to acquire that limp look of resignation and disgust is the highest achievement of student life. The same myth persists about literature, but just as the great writings of this century are marked by their toughness in attitude towards current events, so it must be with us; and any retreat from this is a denial of all that we are here for.

Farrago, March 13, 1964

THE SECOND CELTIC REVIVAL

(2004)

The revisionist view of Celtic culture.

The first Celtic revival occurred in the last decades of the nineteenth century. It is associated in the public mind with people like Douglas Hyde, W.B. Yeats and Padraig Pearse, and with institutions like the Irish Republican Brotherhood, the Abbey Theatre, the Gaelic Athletic Association and with Irish nationalism in general. The 1970s witnessed a second Celtic revival which contrasted in many ways with the first.

*The 1890s emphasized Ireland alone (Sinn Fein) as the basic repository of Celticness. But in the 1970s the pan-Celtic nations of the British Isles (Ireland, Wales, Scotland, Brittany, Cornwall, the Isle of Man) were included in the perspective. More importantly the heartland of Celtdom was seen as central Europe, beginning with the Hallstatt and LaTene cultures, the time BC when Celtic tribes inhabited much of the territory of Europe, with the three Galicia provinces in Spain, Poland and the Middle East marking the outer limits of Celtic occupation.

*1890s Irish nationalists saw the fatal event in history which contaminated the present, the thing to be opposed, as the English invasion and conquest of Ireland, the perfidies from Strongbow and Cromwell to the Famine, and [the putting down of] the Easter Rebellion. But recent writing directs its animus at the much earlier Roman invasion and conquest of the Celtic heartlands of Europe as the root cause of Celtic dispossession and decline. Roman imperialism left remnant Celtic communities on the far western shores of Europe, which were later assimilated into the British sphere.

*1890s nationalists used poetry and mythology to construct their idealized view of Celtic history and culture. Propagandists rather than scholars, and operating largely in the English language, they selected what they found convenient in the misty past to confirm their partisan worldview. In recent decades however, Celtic studies has been led by scholars conversant with Gaelic languages and with early cultures, who use archaeology, history and other disciplines, and who scrutinize ancient texts in a critical and detached way.

*The first Celtic revival regarded Celts in a romantic and fanciful way as fey, ethereal, imaginative but ineffectual creatures, always downtrodden and oppressed victims (the dying Gaul), inhabiting a Celtic or pre-Raphaelite twilight. Recent writing depicts them more realistically as a tough and prosaic warrior race who themselves conquered many other races, such as the original inhabitants of the British Isles, and established ruling civilizations.

*In the 19th century there existed a somewhat tenuous Catholic-Celtic amalgam, based on the belief that Catholicism had superseded older pagan superstitions and was the natural religion of the Irish, and that the British had imported an alien religion, Protestantism, into Ireland. Newer research has opposed Celticism and Catholicism as two rival religions, one based on horizontal nature worship and the eternal return of the species, the other on vertical transcendence. Catholicism is seen as itself an imperialistic force which denied Celticism its breathing space, just as the Roman and British conquerors had. Catholicism and Celtic studies have now gone in quite different directions.

I have for the purposes of contrast made a sharp differentiation between the two revivals. There were of course elements of the second in the first (as we can see with, for example, Douglas Hyde), but on the level of popular perception the differences are marked. In music the change is clearly seen in the move from the Clancy Brothers and the Dubliners to the Chieftains. One forerunner of the new movement was Daniel Corkery's incomparable *The Hidden Ireland* (1924), since augmented by Thomas Kinsella's translations in *Poems of the Dispossessed* (1981). Frank O'Connor's *Kings, Lords and Commons* (1959) was an earlier attempt at a similar thing. My introduction to the new view of the Celts was Myles Dillon & Nora Chadwick *The Celtic Realms* (1967) and Alwyn and Brinley Rees *Celtic Heritage* (1961), but there were many such books. Popular compilations by Barry Cunliffe, Brian de Breffny, Proinsias MacCana and others summarized the new findings on the subject. The Welsh writer David Jones offered his own unique contribution.

At school in the 1950s we learnt in Roman history that at one stage Rome, attacked by wild tribes, was saved by the squawking of geese, with relief that Roman civilization, whose side we were implicitly on, was saved. I was amazed to find out, decades later, that these tribes were Celtic ones, trying desperately to recover their lost patrimony. By some grand feat of amnesia their ethnic identity had slipped off the historical radar. The Irish Catholic tradition, in which I was raised, did not acknowledge that we were descendants of them as much as of Roman culture. The Romans were having another victory, two millennia later.

We all have our own personal views, our own private myths, on these matters: it's a question of how far we want to take the new findings as rules for current living. Some have drawn the conclusion that in our culture the Roman virtues of discipline, rationality and political rule have been magnified at the expense of the more Celtic ones of imagination, intuition and inspiration, but we now recognize that all civilizations need a balance or tension between the two.

Religious implications have caused the most angst. Some

have taken the Christian-Celtic tension to mean that the two are incompatible, and have usually, in choosing to embrace some variety of New Age Celtic mythology, felt that Christianity has to be jettisoned, or at least discounted. In my view, this is not necessary: one can fruitfully participate in both cultures.

Since the second Celtic revival, a new development is that DNA studies reveal the Celts of central Europe and those of the British Isles are not genetically connected, so that Celtic culture, language and religion may have spread by trade and contact rather than by discrete tribal invasion, as was thought in the past.

Táin, April-May, 2004

A MELBURNIAN'S MEMORY OF RAFTERY THE POET

(2010)

One of the last of the travelling Gaelic-speaking bards in Ireland was the blind poet and fiddler Anthony Raftery (1784-1853), known as Raftery the Poet. Like his predecessor, the blind harper Turlough O'Carolan, Raftery wandered the roads of Ireland staying at houses where he sang for his supper. Raftery's poems are well known in Ireland and are still taught in schools. In 1902 an 80-year old Melburnian, Martin Hood, revealed that he had known Raftery in his youth when the poet visited his parents' home in Ballylee, Galway. Hood came to Melbourne in 1854 with his wife and children.

The catalyst for Hood's disclosure was the publication in Melbourne's Catholic paper *The Advocate* (April 19, 1902) of a Raftery poem set in Ballylee, 'Mary Hynes'. The poem appeared both in the original Gaelic and in an English translation by Dr Nicholas O'Donnell, Australia's foremost Gaelic scholar. In the opening stanza the poet meets Mary Hynes one Sunday morning:

> Going to Mass by the heavenly mercy,
> The day was rainy, the wind was wild;
> I met a lady beside Kiltartan
> And fell in love with the lovely child;
> My conversation was smooth and easy,
> And graciously she answered me,

"Raftery dear, 'tis yourself that's welcome,

So step beside me to Ballylee."

(Frank O'Connor's translation has been used here.)

Raftery falls in love with her. The poem is a paean of praise to the girl's beauty which the blind poet cannot see. In the next issue of *The Advocate* Martin Hood published his letter of reminiscence:

Ballylee

Sir, I was much interested in the Irish song, "Ballylee", printed in the "Advocate" of last week; not more because of the clever translation by an Australian native (Dr O'Donnell) than that the author was personally known to me in my early years, and that I was born and brought up within a few miles of Ballylee. I remember Raftery paying one of his itinerary visits to my father's house – I think about 1834 – when he remained a few days. He had with him as a guide a boy of about 14. He was of course blind from his early childhood and learned to play on the violin. He was in the habit of paying periodical visits to the houses of the gentry and well-to-do farmers. He was welcome anywhere he called, and, I may say, his poetry was more appreciated than his music. He had other favourite ladies besides Mary Hynes. His song "Briget Vasey" was more popular and more generally sung in my native place than "Mary Hynes". He composed a remarkable dirge on the "Cholera Morbus", a scourge that committed fearful ravages in 1832, and this was one of his best known productions.

Raftery had great command of the Irish language and a good knowledge of history. He had frequent altercations with kindred poets – one in particular named John Burke. Their recriminations were frequently recited at the firesides on long wintry nights. As indicated in "Ballylee", Raftery was by no means indifferent to an abundant cellar.

Ballylee is in the parish of Kiltartan – a parish that takes in the northern portion of the town of Gort – a town well known to His Grace Archbishop Carr. If the departed spirit of poor Raftery could take any interest in mundane matters, he would view with satisfaction the feelings excited by Dr O'Donnell in the recitation of his eulogy of "Mary Hynes" at the other side of the globe, and which was in Raftery's day a recreation ground for the kangaroo and the emu. – Yours etc. MARTIN HOOD.

Melbourne's Archbishop at the time, Thomas Carr, was born in Galway and was Bishop of Galway when appointed to the Melbourne See in 1885. Raftery wrote poems berating rival poets – his poem on Shawn a Burke (John Burke) imagines Burke being hunted through the countryside as punishment for his poetic transgressions.

Raftery's poems were not committed to print during his lifetime. Oral versions were later collected and published in 1903 as *Songs Ascribed to Raftery* by Dr Douglas Hyde, a leader of the Gaelic Revival movement. Hyde says of Mary Hynes: 'She was the handsomest maiden, they say, who was born for a hundred years in the West of Ireland.' An old fiddler remembered her: 'Mary Hynes was the finest thing that was ever shaped. There usedn't to be a hurling match in the country that she wouldn't be at, and a white dress on her always.' Another man said: 'If she went to a hurling match or a gathering the people used to be running on top of other to lay their eyes on her.'

Raftery's most famous poem was occasioned by someone asking who the blind fiddler was:

I am Raftery the poet,
Full of hope and love,
With sightless eyes
And undistracted calm.
Going west on my journey
By the light of my heart,
Weak and tired
To the end of my road.
Look at me now!
My face to the wall,
Playing music
To empty pockets.

Ballylee is near the town of Gort. The Gort-Kiltartan-Ballylee area in south Galway has many associations with W.B. Yeats, who bought an old tower in Ballylee in 1917, as he tells us in his poem 'To Be Carved on a Stone at Thoor Ballylee':

I, the poet William Yeats,
With old mill boards and sea-green slates,
And smithy work from the Gort forge,
Restored this tower for my wife George;
And may these characters remain
When all is ruin once again.

In Yeats' poem 'The Tower' the blind poet is Raftery. As Yeats recalls, Mary Hynes herself and Raftery's poem celebrating her had not been forgotten in the neighbourhood:

Some few remembered still when I was young
A peasant girl commended by a song,
Who'd lived somewhere upon that rocky place,
And praised the colour of her face,
And had the greater joy in praising her,
Remembering that, if she walked there,
Farmers jostled at a fair
So great a glory did the song confer.
And certain men, being maddened by those rhymes
Or else by toasting her a score of times,
Rose from the table and declared it right
To test their fancy by their sight.

Martin Hood in Australia was one of these who remembered the Raftery poem set in his home town of Ballylee.

Hood was a stalwart of Melbourne's Irish Catholic community for over fifty years. He was a founder and six times President of the St Patrick's Society which staged the annual St Patrick's Day procession and fete from 1857 onwards. Though a teetotaler he worked in a wine and spirit store, and later as manager of a brewery. He was a prominent member of many organizations: the Melbourne

Athenaeum, the Benevolent Asylum, the Mutual Society, and the Irish National League which campaigned for Home Rule for Ireland. He died in 1909 at the age of 86.

Dr Nicholas O'Donnell, who was President of the local Gaelic League and also a leader in the agitation for Home Rule, published a column in Gaelic in *The Advocate* during the first decade of the 20th century. He had persuaded the management of the paper to import type with a Gaelic font. Each week he published a text in Gaelic with his own translation into English. In the issue of May 21, 1904, O'Donnell disclosed he had been able to buy a number of handwritten manuscripts in Gaelic, which included a text of Brian Merriman's long poem 'The Midnight Court', and a 250 page version of the most important ancient Irish epic, the 'Táin Bó Cúailnge'.

It is remarkable to think that a century ago Melbourne harboured ancient Gaelic manuscripts and a man who knew Raftery the Poet.

Tinteán, March, 2010

The Public Realm

PRIVATE BREAKDOWN
AND PUBLIC REMEDIES

(1999)

How citizens should relate to civil society.

The Jaidyn Leskie saga at Moe shocked Australian public opinion. It was not just the unsolved mystery of the baby's death, but more the background pattern of events which it revealed: serial relationships, child abuse, drunkenness, parental irresponsibility, anti-social behaviour – a terrain of unrelieved societal disintegration. There seemed no way out of the impasse for the participants, no way back into society and normal modes of behaviour. Nobody wanted to take the blame. Latrobe Valley leaders said their area was being unfairly targeted, and the metropolitan press ran Moe horror stories as though this sort of thing never happened in Melbourne and Sydney. But the underlying pattern, the endemic social dislocation which lies behind these outbursts, is more common than commentators admit. It occurs as the background in many reported cases of child abuse by stepfathers.

We notice both social isolation and its apparent opposite, messy serial relationships in a fluid state of disruption. There is a type of young male who never finds a pathway into society, much less employment. Instead he moves into himself, removed from external influences and undisciplined by internal ones, and with no rituals or structure to his life. It is sometimes the most sensitive and intelligent who go this way, cutting themselves off gradually from the world of jobs and social mingling. Their parents having themselves imbibed anti-authority and anti-assimilation attitudes, there are few role models of people who make the move into employment and society. The successful are derided by derogatory designations like 'yuppie' and 'young fogey'.

Society appears tight and formidable, unable to be cracked. The young have the added stress of finding jobs in hard times and money to buy a house, as well as starting up their lives as their parents did, but with the burden of greater financial strain. The younger generation, with less employment, savings and housing, may have to subsidise the wealthier older one (for example, paying for superannuation and government debt), which will increase the imbalance in the future. If natural outlets into the wider community are not available, individuals are forced back on themselves, and the family becomes a beleaguered haven in a heartless world, a society substitute. But it can't stand this pressure: it too must link itself to wider institutions. In *Reinventing Australia* Hugh Mackay identifies a major problem in contemporary Australia: working wives have two jobs, as they in fact take responsibility for the household chores, whatever the formal arrangement with the husband. This frequently leaves such women stressed, without enough time for everything, particularly the children, causing strain on the marriage.

Elements in the education system encourage lack of self-discipline and anti-authority attitudes. Students are taught (by example as much as in class) to despise ambition, business, success, profits, discipline, drive and enthusiasm by some teachers. There is nothing one can appeal to (for example, honour, shame, self-respect, camaraderie) to influence or change them. In the arts, the romantic notion (seen in extreme form in Brett Whiteley) that the outsider/ artist/thinker is somehow a modern hero, unfairly neglected and derided by the society he does not want to enter, still holds sway.

The tremors of modernity cause us all existential angst. We are now plunged into a world where there is no accepted belief system, no overarching worldview, no communal or national culture which makes things coherent for us. Society is often seen as a kaleidoscope of impressions and sensations bombarding us at a great rate, and out of our control. Objects have lost not only their sacred quality, but have often been evacuated of meaning. Ernest Gellner says we look out on the world as though we were in a submarine with multiple periscopes, taking in at random a great many scenes but without being able to put them together. We see the world as hard-edged and increasingly outside ourselves, having an almost schizoid separation of our reflecting consciousness from the world outside us. Imprisoned in our own egos, from which there is scant relief, we relentlessly ask the question: 'How am I going?' This leads to free-floating anxieties, personal fragility, widespread low-level depression, the feeling of being stripped down and without adequate resources. We yearn for some relief from this treadmill. Incapacity to cope with this condition can lead to tragedy.

Endemic problems have to be recognised below the level of violent outbursts. Governments can't solve these personal problems by themselves, nor are they meant to. But they can help by attempting to remedy distortions in our society which inhibit assimilation. A properly working civil society has three levels: the private sphere of families and individuals, the intermediate area of voluntary, [business] and communal organisations, and the level of government. The intermediate and private levels co-operate to prevent autocracy; one function of the intermediate level is a cushion against the cold impersonal hand of the state. We rarely deal with government directly. A healthy society has a strong middle realm which acts as a transmission mechanism in both directions between rulers and citizens. The state should support the intermediate level so that citizens can get full benefit out of it. We are socialised, part of society, if we react constantly with the intermediate level. 'Social capital' designates the good will and trust that community organisations generate in a properly functioning civil society. Societies with high levels of involvement in voluntary groups (like choirs, service clubs and sporting bodies) have greater social cohesion, and fewer problems such as crime. Social capital is a precious commodity, the lubricant which smooths the running of society and prevents friction between the three levels.

Some societies do not fit this model, having a weak or absent middle level, notoriously Russia where it hardly exists, and southern Italy where, as Peter Robb shows in *Midnight in Sicily*, the mafia fills the vacuum between citizen and state. Western societies today have deformations of a different kind. Firstly, over recent decades the composition of the intermediate layer has changed: voluntary organisations have declined, to be replaced by large, government-funded top-down ones, for example, universities, welfare agencies, semi-government tribunals. Quangos have pushed out private organisations, for example in welfare where parish-based groups have been replaced by state community services. Our problem is not the absence of a middle level, as in countries like Russia, but its enormous growth and change in character.

Secondly, the relationship between the three levels has changed. There is now an alliance or nexus between the government and intermediate areas. Governments have until recently expanded greatly, moved into new areas, and created mendicant organisations at the middle level. They infiltrate this level with their own supporters, and then listen to his master's voice played back to them by interminable committees. Inhabitants of the quangos, who benefit from this arrangement, and their supporters like Eva Cox in her 1995 Boyer Lectures, naturally welcome a dominant government-quango nexus. Welfare workers, for example, can become the recipients of public largesse, rather than the disadvantaged for whom it was intended. This is exactly the opposite of how a civil society should work, where the private and intermediate areas combine to protect citizens from dominance from above. The middle level, far from protecting citizens from the state, can thus itself become a mechanism of control by government. An elite-versus-ordinary-people gap develops, now noticeable in Australia. This means the middle level faces the wrong way, towards government rather than towards the people, whom it renders societally mute. It prevents a real national conversation. Notice the vicious and relentless treatment of One Nation voters, who were rendered societally *persona non grata* by the elites.

Society, represented by the middle level we deal with, therefore presents itself as in part opaque and resistant, a barrier hard to overcome. Bob Browning in *Bad Government* (1995) has documented a pattern of incestuous networking in many semi-governmental areas in the 1990s. Essentially private and community activities are being stymied by quasi-government organisations. Ordinary people cannot relate fully to society which they feel is run by an elite apart from themselves. We need to allow people in, to stimulate voluntary organisations and rein in the quangos. The private sphere, which should attract much of society's focus, has languished from neglect, not having high social mobility. The young in their bleaker economic situation are more likely to turn to government bodies for handouts. Those with problems cannot effectively negotiate with the intermediate sphere, if that realm is facing towards the government and acting against their interests. The public focus has to be shifted from the government-quango nexus, where all the energy of lobbyists and press reporting goes, and instead focus on restoring the links between citizens and voluntary/community organisations. This is the key relationship which must be in good working order for a society to function properly.

How did social dislocation occur and the middle level change? The 'Me Decade' ushered in narcissism as a society substitute. We were encouraged to foster and coddle our own identities, to do own thing, to develop self-esteem (which means never feeling shame).

This view saw the world as a vast cornucopia of opportunities from which the rampaging and ever-expanding ego could pluck as it pleased. The individual personality was a hermetically sealed capsule of opportunism, a missile ready to set out on its task of engorging hubris. With decline of belief in the afterlife and the restraints that belief imposes, a modern version of hedonistic living-for-the-present set in. We were being lectured on the evils of the authoritarian personality just as it was going out of fashion, and another style of behaviour emerging. Plunging into the chaos of modernity, people embraced the wild, the dangerous, the anarchic, even the demonic as the interesting elements in life and culture, in opposition to perceived bourgeois stability. This was the *vita periculoso* (living dangerously) of Mussolini deriving from Nietzsche.

This changed personality had a different attitude to institutions, which were no longer treated with deference. There was no need for a period of apprenticeship, there was no self-identification with institutions which produced feelings like pride, honour, loyalty, leadership and so on. An instrumental attitude to institutions emerged. Our role, we thought, was criticise and dismantle authoritarian structures and to embrace the daring and the new. This was, in retrospect, a mistake. We didn't see that the modernist world we now inhabited was swamped with angst, and lacked structures and beliefs, so applying liberal solvents, appropriate to a rigid world already gone, exacerbated existing trends towards disintegration. The adversary culture's attitude to institutions is to corrode their authority systems by ridicule, entryism, power seeking and other means originally described as Leninist tactics. It destroys the group allegiance and sense of common endeavour which is essential to the running of any successful enterprise. It kills off accumulated social capital. The adversary culture is the dominant mode of the new-class quangos.

As institutions forget their aims and surrender their beliefs, they become ripe for takeover. They lose a sense of the purpose for which they were initially created, and become directed towards survival. They work for their constituents, not for their clients. All energies eventually go on internal power struggles and on continually imposing new agendas. Nowadays not argument, debate and tolerance, but bureaucratic decisions without discussion, and regulation through 'equal opportunity' and 'affirmative action' and the like, is the way things are going. Finally the goal becomes simply power, and the original aim of the organisation withers away. For these reasons these new institutions, which have replaced the older type of communal organisation, don't work very well. Where once school parents went to working bees organised by parents-and-friends groups, they now argue over the politics of education on a formally constituted school council.

New Class bureaucrats pretend to talk on behalf of the wretched of the earth, whereas in fact they have great power. This is a peculiar modern paradox – power is not wielded directly but anomalously on behalf of the powerless, those awarded victim status. Governments once tried to artificially redistribute income, now they are in the business of trying to redistribute status. Because of their adversary origins, they can never admit they are wielding power openly; they can never acknowledge their own authority. So one gets the peculiar mixture of people in power assuming a dissident stance, for example, two-income trendies empathising with unemployment, a characteristic example of double-think. Large, well-funded public institutions persuade ordinary people they are victims of social injustice. These people then become vexatious complainants, join the grievance system and apply to these same bodies for financial compensation. This causes spiralling disaffection and spiralling costs, which makes solutions more unlikely. Ordinary people get sucked into the quangos' *modus operandi*, rather than having natural and fruitful relations with the intermediate level. They are forced to remake themselves, for their own short-term benefit, as victims of the system, rather than citizens of society.

Combating government intrusion and over-regulation in the economic sphere has been an important issue over the past two decades. That battle has largely been won, at least at the level of ideas. The next and analogous step is to resist government intrusion in mediating institutions. In Poland, Solidarity set up replacement institutions, as the official ones were so bankrupt; here the need is mainly to renovate institutions. As well as encouraging voluntary communal organisations, middle-level bureaucracies must be consciously reduced. These will not voluntarily dismantle themselves, as their clients are often their employees, not the public for whom they were set up. There is a need to make them face back to help ordinary people. In *Double Take* (1996) Les Murray writes of the creation in Australia of 'an unelected para-government made up of the media, humanities faculties in the universities and a system of semi-governmental boards and authorities'. This para-government, the public voice of the quangos and the new establishment, is the conveyor of the current mindset to the wider public. This public-opinion-forming alliance creates a misleading impression of what public opinion is; it conducts a false national conversation. Carrying out the behests of the government-quango nexus, it acts as a diversionary mechanism in the intermediate area. Its real role should be to listen as well as transmit, but it has ceased listening. As a result the state cannot hear its own citizens.

When tragedy occurs, families today have to deal with large, impersonal quangos, which are less likely to solve their problems than privately based, local, self-help welfare groups, which are more effective and efficient. The social capital which exists when there are well-oiled links between families and voluntary community organisations means there is less likely to be tragedy, and when it occurs it can be better handled. Families can't exist by themselves, they can't be the solution. A healthy relationship to a properly functioning middle sphere is crucial to keeping both us and our society in good working order. Below the level of tragedy we need release from constantly living inside our own minds, release into communal activity where we are subsumed in a larger venture and the boundaries of our egos begin to dissolve.

Quadrant, November, 1999

THE DECLINE OF TOLERANCE

(1990)

Over the last decade the pendulum has swung noticeably against freedom and tolerance, and towards interference by government bodies. The various bans on smoking are a sign of things to come – people don't know what is good for them, and have to be compelled to quit. In New South Wales an Anglican believer was fined by the Equal Opportunity Tribunal because he would not let his flat to a de facto couple. UNESCO promotes social rights (an Orwellian euphemism for state control) over individual rights. Though economic deregulation is in vogue, we have a new era of socio-moral regulation.

Controversial issues spawn not so much argument as quasi-government tribunals; in areas like race relations, human rights, equal opportunity, health issues, sexual discrimination and multiculturalism, public guardians hand down their judgments. In this atmosphere litigious behaviour flourishes. Affirmative action is a pleasant-sounding alliterative phrase, but it actually means that some people are now more equal than others. The principle of political equality, dear to us for good reasons, has now been ditched, and a new set of privileges are being enforced under the guise of levelling off. Liberalism is now identified with inegalitarian policies, and those who speak out against these developments are not argued against but threatened with the gag, or worse still, with penalties. Rael-Jean and Eric Isaac have named these new custodial zealots in the US the 'coercive utopians'.

How different from three decades ago, when in thinking circles it was an axiom that truth was arrived at by open argument, and that tolerance of different viewpoints was the key Enlightenment virtue which led to an open society. Every week, TV's 'Meet the Press' enshrined Voltaire's motto in the popular culture: 'I disapprove of what you say, but will defend to the death your right to say it'. Henry Mayer edited *Catholics and the Free Society* to show that established institutions could no longer rely on prestige and privilege, but had to defend their case in the open marketplace of ideas. The separation of Church and State was necessary to prevent governments imposing species of morality on the populace. What is also striking is that it is the erstwhile liberals who have become the new coercers. As soon as he became a Minister, the eminent civil libertarian Gareth Evans sent planes snooping over Tasmania, an equal partner in the Federation, whose rights were not respected. Scratch a student radical of the sixties and you may now find an authoritarian bureaucrat, who reaches for a regulation as soon as he/she hears the word freedom. Opponents are disqualified by legislative fiat or by bureaucratic manoeuvring or a combination of both. Consider the change the phrase 'civil liberties' has undergone. Whereas once it meant freedom to express one's views, now it can mean almost the opposite. In the Combe-Ivanov affair, Combe's supporters argued that you couldn't have an inquiry into his actions because his civil liberties would thereby be infringed.

Some years ago Henry Fairlie of the *New Republic* argued that conservatives were now the only true liberals. By this he meant that in the Vietnam debates the original liberals quickly accepted the radicals' proposition that the free exchange of ideas and striving for objectivity were establishment tricks to prop up the status quo. It followed that action, not discussion, was paramount, and that people with different views were to be characterised as the enemy, to be harassed, humiliated and exposed, but never to be argued with. The liberals, swamped in the sea of vitriol they had caused, had betrayed their origins and it was left to the conservatives to occupy the vacant middle ground, arguing the traditional liberal position of allowing all sides to be heard. Why did the liberal position collapse so quickly? Basically I think because some forms of pluralism and tolerance disguise an absence of beliefs. This was the essential first step which made today's atmosphere of enforcement possible.

It is true for obvious reasons that one can never be objective or dispassionate. This insight was twisted into the notion that it was therefore fraudulent to strive for as much objectivity as possible, an essential feature of which is sympathy for evidence which may be contrary to one's own inclinations. It was argued that history is always subjective, the result of the historian's own viewpoint as much as the evidence itself. Any interpretation can be argued, and is invariably politically motivated. In literary criticism an analogous view developed: any reading of a literary work is valid, and is created as much by the reader as by the author. A poem means what the reader believes it to mean. By such means prejudice took on the kudos of scholarship. Groups like the Labour Lawyers, the New Journalists and the Concerned Asian Scholars sprang up. All were determined to press a partisan position at the expense of their professional codes. Such partisanship is not only now acceptable but has also been taken a step further: governments are back in the old business of enforcing the morality of various influential pressure groups.

A difficult and permanent tension always exists between clinging to one's own strongly held beliefs and tolerating the existence of views that diverge from them. (The introductory chapter of Allan Bloom's *The Closing of the American Mind* is a powerful statement of the contemporary form this dilemma takes.) In the Salman Rushdie affair, we all wanted him to be free from the dreadful threats made on his life by Muslim fundamentalists. That was the major point at issue. But in a minor key his swingeing attack on deeply-held Muslim beliefs was worrying. Notwithstanding that, here was a case where the community correctly opted for tolerance, not banning. An example of prohibition is the ban on IRA statements on the BBC and Irish media, on the grounds that physical force nationalism could destroy the community. Not so clearcut was an incident in the US last year when a citizen publicly burnt the US flag. Many Americans, including President Bush, believed it should be illegal to defile the symbol of their nation's beliefs. Civil liberties groups supported flag burning as an example of freedom of expression protected by the First Amendment. In my view the latter argument gave a privileged status to those who have no beliefs and who wished to hold in contempt the beliefs of others.

In Britain in the mid 1980s the National Council for Civil Liberties split over two issues which involved the same fundamental tension. During the miners' strike, some members of the Council argued that the freedom not to strike should be defended as strongly as the freedom to strike. They also argued that (facetious) requests from the National Front to defend its right to be heard should be accepted. The Council split because in both cases the liberals agreed to these requests, while the Marxist bloc in the organisation did not. For the latter, a political agenda took precedence over a professed desire to protect civil liberties.

At the same time as the new emphasis on government regulation, there has been a resurgence of arguments based on 'choice'. The proponents of abortion, euthanasia and ending the lives of deformed babies all use 'liberal' arguments based on the notion of choice. This harks back to the liberal catchcry: 'I can do whatever I like, so long as it doesn't hurt anyone else.' This was the original 'choice' argument, always in my opinion a pathetically inadequate one, since all actions, no matter how apparently personal and private, change us and so affect others. The slogan revealed that one of the mainsprings of liberalism was moral narcissism: tolerance for oneself and an absence of beliefs (anything goes) were its key features. This slogan is not used any more, since in the cases of abortion, euthanasia and infanticide, another party is being grievously hurt. And it can't be mentioned in the new coercive climate either. Today's slogan is the opposite: 'People don't know what is good for them, and have to be guided.' Marcuse began this line of thinking by arguing that people didn't really know what they wanted; they were deluded by society's 'repressive tolerance' into thinking they are free and happy, and didn't recognise they lived under thrall. By breaking down the opposition between repression and tolerance, Marcuse gave his followers the inner permission to establish the bureaucracies (based on their own version of 'repressive tolerance') with which we are familiar today.

Many of these disturbing currents of thought meet in the great contemporary polemicist Noam Chomsky. Chomsky has always been a vigorous supporter of freedom of expression for those who claim there was no Holocaust or Cambodian genocide, yet when an English commentator wrote that such views lessened Chomsky's credibility, Chomsky exerted a lot of pressure to have these comments removed (and succeeded in the US edition of the book in question). What happened to the right to free expression of Chomsky's opponent? Chomsky's method is not a clear statement of his own beliefs but the application of massive, sustained scepticism to the findings of others. Impeccably liberal arguments are deployed to non-liberal ends, such as support and comfort for the No-Holocaust lobby. As Dostoievsky understood, what 'starts from unlimited liberty ends in unlimited despotism'.

The difference in the public treatment of smoking and AIDS is intriguing. Smoking, which is not contagious, is subject to many restrictions, but the response to AIDS – a lethal, contagious disease – is one of tolerance and lack of coercion. These cases seem to be examples of contrasting public reaction, but they do have something in common. In both instances lobby groups which did not represent mainstream public opinion, struck a deal with government bodies to get their own way, to ban what they did not like (smoking) and to legitimise what they tolerated (behaviour which could lead to AIDS). Looked at this way both cases follow a pattern: majority viewpoints are thwarted.

How can this development be explained? Twenty years ago groups associated with minority, radical and unpopular causes were peripheral to the power structure, so they defended their causes with liberal, civil liberties arguments. Today many representatives or supporters of these adversarial groups have come to power in government and bureaucratic positions. Even in power their animus is directed against the earlier, conservative viewpoint. They still employ an old embattled rhetoric as though they were a minority group fighting larger foes, never admitting that they now constitute a powerful Establishment themselves. Anomalously, they keep their adversarial anti-authority attitudes even when in power, trying to retain the advantage of identifying with victim or minority groups. Brecht, among others, noticed this anomaly in Hitler. At one moment he would be threatening everyone with his power; at the next he would be painting himself as one of the poor downtrodden of the earth, set upon and victimised by larger forces.

Iconoclasts in power support those who have no beliefs and punish those who have strong beliefs. What the new elites want is deemed a 'choice' issue, and what they don't like is subjected to government regulation. Previously these groups fulminated against the old Establishment; now they are legislating against it. So a new version of a familiar political agenda (in favour of radical groups and against mainstream opinion) is now being implemented under the guise of dispassionate, official policy.

A gap exists in our society between the beliefs of the new elites (public opinion formers, academics, media personalities and government functionaries) and the views of ordinary people. Most of the new policies are never spelt out in public, as their supporters would lose the argument, and public opinion would not support them anyway. Instead pressure groups and government bodies get together and exert influence by bureaucratic means. At the same time, public opinion is manufactured from above, by public education campaigns financed by governments themselves and directed against an initially unwilling population. These 'consciousness raising' exercises are based on the principle that the public does not know what is good for it. Obfuscation and euphemisms are used to disguise goals that cannot be clearly stated. Equal opportunity quickly changes into something quite different (affirmative action) which actually means preferential discrimination for some. 'Dying with dignity' means legalised state killing. The proposed Bill of Rights would have removed those rights which it did not explicitly endorse.

Influential educationists want every student to pass every subject as a means of social readjustment. But this aim is rarely expressed. Sometimes the vague and harmless-sounding phrase 'equality of outcomes' is used, but mostly a series of complicated, minor changes is made to the whole education system to achieve this aim without parents being able to pin down what they suspect is happening, that is, the disintegration of education as such. In the food industry, consumer groups are lobbying the government to stage a repeat of the anti-smoking campaign: what can be sold will be determined not by the market but by regulations to stop the multinationals ruining our health. These lobbies are themselves sponsored by the governments they purport to influence, a cosy and undemocratic relationship.

Once the new tribunals and the coercive atmosphere have been established, groups can use this by subtly going beyond the original intention of 'evening up'. Instead of simply accepting the advantages which affirmative action confers on them, putative victim groups can use their privileged status to attack others, relying on the emotional and legal levers of their 'disadvantage' to render them immune from challenge. In New York, two years ago, Tawana Brawley, a young black girl, disappeared and was found some days later in a very distressed and dishevelled state. She claimed to have been abducted and assaulted by a group of whites. Her case was taken up by black leaders like the Rev. Al Sharpton, who claimed a cover-up was in place to protect the perpetrators, and called for arrests. A white District Attorney was publicly named as a suspect. The case continued at fever pitch in the media for many months. It subsequently turned out that Tawana had invented the story to escape punishment from her step-father. Because of the history of black deprivation over many decades, black leaders and the media were able to run this baseless anti-white story for many months without challenge.

In Cleveland, England, doctors, alleging widespread sexual abuse of children by their parents, removed, with the active consent of welfare workers, the children from their families to institutions. In some cases mothers were forced to separate from their husbands to get their children back. Later the evidence for the claims was found to be practically baseless. The doctors and welfare workers had claimed that the children were the victims, the parents the aggressors, and that they were protectors of the victims. In fact the doctors and welfare workers were the aggressors, and the parents and children the victims of this outrage. The doctors and welfare workers used certain reasonably based fears to conduct a witch-hunt against which (at the time) there was no redress. The lesson we learn is that those who claim to be protecting victims may in fact be damaging them.

We are getting the worst of both worlds. The best situation would be one of strong beliefs and a strong tradition of tolerance. Today we have a situation of no beliefs and declining tolerance. In the past the danger was from beliefs that were held too strongly, especially if they had government backing. Today the danger is of a regime of non-belief dressed up in liberal guise getting government support.

The new zealots want to suppress and even eliminate the beliefs of others while imposing their own vacuum on society.

Quadrant, September, 1990

The incidence of litigious zealots penalizing those they don't like has increased a lot since this piece was published 30 years ago.

EXPLANATIONS OF THE
ADVERSARY CULTURE

(1983)

Why some sections of Western societies began to exhibit a deep contempt for their own cultures.

From 1914 to 1945 Europe was traumatised by a succession of shocks – wars, depressions, revolutions, dictatorships and mass slaughter; unimaginable terrors were likely to occur at any time. We still don't understand these events, and we can never wholly come to terms with them. In the later years of the second world war, it was commonly expected that Europe would continue in some similar state of domination and disruption for the foreseeable future. But something quite different happened, which shaped the contours of the post-war world. Except for countries under Soviet control, the abnormal world of the previous three decades did not continue. The surprising thing is how quickly European and Western societies became normal again, with stable and prosperous economies and without internal or external threats. This is also something we haven't fully come to terms with yet. For four decades now our societies have had a remarkable record of routine, democratic equanimity. This is so obvious that it literally goes without saying. Goldstein's analysis in *Nineteen-Eighty Four* has proved correct. Skirmishes and wars keep erupting on the edges of the three superstates' spheres of influence, but the populations of the metropolitan hinterlands remain relatively unscathed. Repeated predictions of the imminent collapse of capitalism have not proved true.

The contrast between conditions before and after 1945 was extreme. It was very hard for intellectuals to de-escalate quickly from this fevered, 'larger-than-life' time, when meaning stared out at one from every incident. Thinkers have a natural attraction to crisis situations brimming with 'significance'; ingrained habits of thought persisted into the post-war decades, long after the conditions which caused them to arise had disappeared. Post-war societies, were, moreover, peculiarly difficult to analyse by the accepted methods, being relatively monochrome and predictable. They lacked obvious symbols and turning points which analysts could latch on to, and through which the society could be understood. Lack of perspective makes it hard to realize how special one's situation is. Our societies are unusual because they are normal.

Anyone who lives, thinks and reads today lives in two different worlds. We absorb the disturbances of modern literature, and we learn about the horrors and violence of the wars, camps and regimes of the decades when Europe went mad, and then we look out the window of our studies at our own quiet and sane world. The contrast is so great that there seems no connection between the two. After the war people believed that Dachau and Hiroshima exemplified, in intensified form, the essentials of the contemporary condition, but we aren't sure now that the relationship is so simple. The precise connection still eludes us. Both worlds are undoubtedly true, and at different times we emphasise one or the other. But we can't put them together – each seems to drain meaning from the other. But if we have to choose, the apocalyptic world of the past usually gets priority.

Since the Enlightenment, the emphasis in our culture has been on the new, the original and the different. Like the scientist, the academic analyst is admired if he has something unique to say, some distinctive thesis which revalues previous beliefs. You don't get an article out of saying that nothing has changed. Revisionism is all the rage. Conversely, pressures to undervalue everyday life exist. Since the Enlightenment, intellectuals have, in the name of liberty, seen it as a pre-eminent task to criticise the tyrannous tendencies of their rulers. Rulers often denied their citizens material freedoms (the right to live above subsistence level) and spiritual freedoms (the right to one's beliefs and their free expression). Such thinkers' defining role was to be resisters, dissenters, an opposition – I criticise, therefore I am. Both the Romantic and the avant-garde modernist movements reinforced this supposed antagonism between the thinker and society.

But changes in the world have outpaced the analysis of them. Today's Western societies, more than any in the past, allow their citizens to live free from tyranny over their lives, over their physical survival and over their beliefs. This needs acknowledgement, which it often doesn't get. The role of thinkers is not just to criticise, but to say what is true, which sometimes means criticising and sometimes affirming, and usually some mixture of both. But many analysts still automatically adopt an adversary stance and never look at what they are commenting on. The valuable tradition of liberal critique of tyranny can, if continued as unthinking dissent, turn full circle and erode the freedoms it was inaugurated to protect.

Today both going to university and coming to an interest in ideas are often accompanied by a physical move away from the suburbs to a more bohemian existence around the campus. Although there is no necessary connection between the two, this awakening to ideas is thought to be connected with moving away from one's past life. The new ideas taken up reflect this, and will tend to downgrade ordinary life. A transference of loyalties occurs, so that it becomes demeaning to return to the life one came from. A thinker today believes he can break clear of his own culture; by understanding it, he transcends it and is exempt from its exigencies. In traditional cultures, the wise men of the tribe preserve and pass on an inherited wisdom, which they embody and with which they dare not tamper. The job of today's wise men is to expose the taboos. In a review of a Cyril Connolly novel about an artists' colony in France, Orwell described the characters as waging a 'ceaseless war against decency...But this, you see, only amounts to a distaste for normal life and common decency'. In Orwell's view the novel was based on the false dilemma that you must either be a bohemian rebel or conform to the modern rat-race, and he concludes: 'The fact to which we have got to cling, as to a life-belt, is that it is possible to be a normal decent person and yet to be fully alive'.

The vogue word 'meaningful' betrays a yearning for events that yield plenty of meaning in a world short of these. Sensibilities attuned to great expectations find our everyday world even flatter than if really is. Something, they feel, is missing. There are no heroic contests or challenges left to pit oneself against. Yeats lamented that the contemporary scene provided 'no second Troy' for Maud Gonne. Man's genetic structure evolved over millions of years, during which time we needed to be aggressive and active to survive. Suddenly we are idle and we feel misplaced; ideas that don't end in action cause frustration. Our kind of society doesn't provide moments of sudden insight, and it blocks off avenues of transcendence. Revelation is a scarce commodity. Resentment at ordinary life combined with attraction to the 'great days' of the recent past has badly skewed contemporary analysis. We have to understand what endures in our societies more than what changes. Peace hath her victories no less renowned than war.

Take the commonly heard expression 'the system'. Now it is true that totalitarian systems strive, as far as inhumanly possible, to set up an all-encompassing structure to which all activities relate. When independent activities are eliminated and society functions as an internally articulated whole, it is fruitful to speak of a 'system'. But this notion has been applied as an analytic tool to Western societies. Neil McInnes has explained the evolution of this idea:

Lukacs had argued that society was a concrete, dialectic totality that has to be taken, and could only be changed, as a unit. You must keep your eye always on the big picture, the total dialectic system, which you could then aspire to revolutionise at one fell swoop. This notion funded the 'critical theory of society', a philosophical school of sociology. It was adopted by Marcuse in the essays lately resurrected under the title *Negations* and it re-appears in his condemnations, e.g., in *One Dimensional Man*, of all partial, empirical, positive social studies, which simply distract attention from the whole and thereby encourage timidity and surrender. It is the same theory that Marcuse uses to condemn tolerance and to justify violence in his influential essay 'Repressive Tolerance': 'According to a dialectical proposition, it is the whole which determines the truth…in the sense that its structure and function determine every particular condition and relation'.

This idea was wrongly applied, as our societies have multiple centres of power, and independent viewpoints (like Marcuse's own) are not suppressed. While not denying some coherence, it is ludicrous to say that our society is an interlocking 'system', and that we have a clear-cut choice of working 'within the system' or 'outside the system', as the modish distinction of a few years back put it. Because our society is not unidirectional, we constantly make a great variety of decisions about adaptation, compromise, rejection, tolerance, acceptance, etc. on a whole range of matters. Only in very rare cases does it become a case of making the grand refusal. We are immersed in our society as in the sea, and our choice is how we swim, not whether we get out of the water or not.

Fantasy and reality are reconciled by the Marcusian notion of repressive tolerance – the capitalist authorities are too subtle to openly oppress people, so they have highly developed the art of internalising their own violence. Thus the very absence of visible violence and repression becomes the knockdown argument in favour of their existence. This is known as dialectics. In such cases contradictions are dressed up as paradoxes. Having set up the notion of a 'system', it can be conveniently scapegoated, as all discomforts and hatreds are externalized on to society at large, which is considered innately malign. This leads to a grossly exaggerated view of the gloominess of the world, where from the Franklin River to the SALT talks, disasters lurk in every nook and cranny. Little can be done about it because of the iron grip of the system. Tinkering at reform is useless; only radically altering the structures of society will do any good. Meanwhile the attitude adopted is one of comprehensive disgust.

The reaction in the decades after 1945 was to identify with the victims of oppression. But as the European horrors recede into the distance, another attitude has emerged. The victor-victim distinction has diminished to be replaced by a morally undiscriminating desire to undergo the total experience in some surrogate form, in the belief that it is more 'real' than our own dull sum of littleness. What is sought today is the transcendence the experience provides rather than the moral championing of the victims. We can see a movement in this direction in the later poetry of Sylvia Plath. She yearned to undergo a great experience of death and rebirth, and she thought she had found this by identifying herself with Jewish concentration camp inmates. But she wanted to go through the whole experience: she could 'turn the violence against herself so as to show that she can equal the oppressors with her self-inflicted oppression', as Alvarez noted. In 'Lady Lazarus' she revels in the experience of dehumanisation rather than opposing it. She vicariously experiences oppression in order to feel 'real' and to gain an identity. This is a false way of applying the lessons Europe's traumas to our own lives, and it doesn't provide an identity at all. It is a manipulation of the sufferings the concentration camp victims to use them for one's own ends. The ultimate indignity to the victims, which involves a terrible inversion of priorities, is that their sufferings should be used to bolster *us* up. It does not redeem them; it demeans them by reducing them to the level of our 'identity' problems. It takes away the meaning of their fate.

The student invasion of buildings in the late 1960s was apparently causeless and motiveless. How could society's most liberal institution, the university, be a symbol of an oppressive society? It was the absence of problems that was really unbearable. The protestors were nourished by two diets, firstly the literature of the last hundred years, chaotic, demonic and primal, as Lionel Trilling described it, and secondly, an imaginative identification with the wars, tyrannies and violence which have created real worlds far more terrible than anything imagined by Dostoievsky or Kafka. Yet students had experienced nothing of this. With minds attuned to the apocalyptic, they felt let down by a society which provided none of this. Hence the need to create a heightened and frenetic situation in which they could act out their desires. Normal society, for example, produced few visible signs of oppression. But if a demonstration was staged, police breaking it up were a visible sign of oppression. Thus the argument that society was repressive became self-fulfilling. Changing reality to fulfil one's beliefs is one essential mark of the adversary culture.

The teach-ins show this most clearly. An unnaturally tense, hot-house atmosphere was generated by long hours in the same lecture room. Ordinary life was suspended and outlets to the outside world of sanity and normality were cut off. Everything was politicized. Participants, exhausted after sleepless hours, were open to hysteria and hallucination. Universities were subjected to a form of show trial. During these endless exhaustion sessions, interrogation and denunciation of opponents ruled the day; in a characteristic inversion, this incessant hectoring went under the name of a 'free speech movement'. The teach-ins were little capsules of self-induced totalitarian frenzy, trial runs for the future. Though not victims, student protesters had to appear so, since it is a mark of the adversary culture that it must always put itself in a dissenting stance no matter how powerful it is; it must never appear as an authority system in its own right.

This mixture of heightened events and simulated anger makes the world seem much worse than it is. In *Encounter* December 1982, Professor Helmut Schoeck shows how in West Germany TV features endless pictures of the destruction of forests, and long discussion programs on youths' reaction to this. One young student said:

> I have to say that I see the future of our society and our world as rather black!...First of all, the insane destruction of the environment. If one considers how much of our countryside gets built upon, how much gets destroyed, then I choke up so much I can hardly breathe!

Schoeck contrasts this with the facts: 86% of West Germany is fields, woods and waters, whereas only 6% is taken up by urban housing and business premises. The media makes the world much worse than it is, and society is blamed. Schoeck describes a closed circuit effect on youth: they hear this incessant propaganda, and they notice how important those who protest become in the public eye. The educational and cultural atmosphere prepares them for dissent:

> Never before in our history have we seen the spectacle of politicians, and pastors, pedagogues and best-selling writers, teachers and hit-songsters, all vying with each other to impress our children with the ugliness of the prospects facing them, with the horror (partly real, partly freely made-up) of all of life's problems that will soon overwhelm them disastrously.

As an example I have in front of me a Form 12 Australian History syllabus, whose core section has always been admirable. Options have been added, which include women, Aborigines, migrants, the dismissal of the Whitlam government, and violence. The first three topics are on many other courses, and the Kerr controversy is hardly historical. But consider the topic of violence in Australian history. We have been one of the most tranquil and undisturbed societies imaginable, but there is no option on 'the quiet continent'. Once again, the minor fact is being promoted at the expense of the major, and the abnormal at the expense of the normal. The anomaly is overcome by the following statement:

> A definition of violence should be arrived at, which should be broad enough to include physical violence, class and racial violence, violence done to political institutions, to the environment and to social institutions.

In other words, students don't have the choice deciding that violence has been minimal, since they are directed towards an extremely elastic definition of the term. To cap it off, students are reminded that 'violence may have positive as well as negative consequences'. Ah, we knew it would come to that!

Consciousness raising courses are now imposed on society's putative victims. Ordinary Australians are not visibly dissatisfied with their condition; migrants don't feel they are slaves; housewives aren't organising protest movements. Most Australians are 'enjoying the world around them without too much interference from others'. The victims aren't screaming. This is appalling. Poor benighted Australians of all kinds are wandering around under the delusion that they are enjoying things. This has to be changed. They need the benefit of a consciousness-raising course to take their enjoyment from them. Marcuse has reached the suburbs. The new apostles of praxis have a duty to stir the victims out of their lethargy. If this succeeds, the original contention that change is the most important feature of our society becomes self-fulfilling.

Quadrant, August, 1983, abridged

THE PLAYTHING OF
THE NEW ELITES

(1999)

Arguments opposing the 1999 referendum on an Australian republic.

New class elites in Australia have foisted the republican case on to us. It is a tenth order issue for which there was no natural groundswell. Behind the manipulation of cultural symbols is a grab for power and influence by an unrepresentative minority who consider themselves different from ordinary Australians.

The term 'new class' was invented to describe a new strata: bureaucrats and those in the knowledge industries who today inhabit the interstices of public organizations. Milovan Djilas noticed their proliferation in the Tito Communist government, where they exercised great and maleficent power. He named them in order to oppose them. In Western societies James Burnham described the managerial revolution, the rise of those inhabiting intermediate structures which did not produce anything, but were needed to connect production with power. New class elites oil the wheels of business and government. They cannot be described by the old designations of lower, middle and upper class, nor as part of the traditional professions, nor as part of the primary, secondary or tertiary sectors. They are typically academics, public opinion formers, political operatives, journalists, denizens of community, welfare and environmental bureaucracies, appointees to quasi-government tribunals, and such like. They tend not to have strong beliefs – power is what activates them. They wield influence on behalf of themselves and of the power group to whom they give allegiance.

The rise of the new class is a natural evolutionary development, and not necessarily anti-democratic or retrograde. But when new class operatives turn themselves into a power group in their own right, cut themselves from the citizenry to whom they feel superior, and entrench themselves in power in a cosy corporate state arrangement, we have a problem, a new class in the pejorative sense of the term. They then act as a 'prophetic shock minority', imposing their unrepresentative views on to an indifferent public. The new class is an unelected elite, which believes it has the right to elevate its own prejudices to the status of public policy preferences.

The new class in Australia is behind the push for a republic. Ordinary people have little enthusiasm or even interest in the issue. The pressure for a republic is strongest in the nexus between intellectuals, the media and the public opinion forming sectors. As commentators from Hancock to Encel have pointed out, Australians are anti-government in attitude, which allows bureaucrats much more space for action – they fill the political vacuum. The result is that paradoxically they have great influence here. A good example is the number of quasi-government tribunals which have been set up in Australia. The new class, having no strong basis in the society, considers itself a protected species. In spite of its rhetoric of tolerance, its mind is wholly closed to views outside a narrow range of politically correct causes which it endorses.

The new ascendancy is a contemporary update of the older notion of 'armchair socialists'. The latter phrase expressed the contradiction of wealthy people supporting working-class causes. Today trendies who themselves are addicted to a hedonistic style of life feel obliged to display social concern. The sight of a privileged group adopting a victim posture is not an edifying one. Their original motivation came from adversary politics, and even when in power they cannot abandon this stance. Previously groups in power exulted in it – today it is fashionable to apologize for it. People can't openly admit they want to run the show, which is thought too authoritarian, so it is now done in more covert ways. The republican posture is one of the injured victim – we have been imposed upon too long by British structures, and wish to liberate ourselves. Chardonnay and social concern, or having it both ways, is an illuminating if contradictory mix.

The republic campaign is a typical grab for influence and power by the new class. Polls are used to give the impression there is great public support for republican beliefs. They are employed to increase support, not to measure it. The new class knows that the Australian people won't elect them to power, and if they do, as with the Whitlam government, they will soon remedy the mistake. So they like to dabble in symbolic politics to achieve power in this way. It is their republic, they keep nominating their kind (like Janet Holmes a Court) as suitable potential Presidents. The old structure, which did not give them easy access to power, will have to be dismantled.

The republicans keep saying their republic is inevitable. It is the wave of history, and we must get with the strength. Where does this idea come from? Partly from the Marxist notion that the believers are on the side of light, and all others must be consigned to the dustbin of history. But there is also an Australia component. Late last century thinkers believed they were in touch with mysterious currents of feelings of the times. They believed a new Australia was about to be born, it was just around the corner, they were waiting for the start. This would be a clean break from the past. The year 1900 was a good one for such a start. Now the coming year 2000 is being enlisted in the same cause. Republicanism is being presented as like a new spray-on tan to make us prepossessing and fit to face the new millennium. This is the new class in its role as managers of the historic moment. They can't let the republic come about naturally with the effluxion of time. They have to artificially intervene, and push the chariot of time on to its destined course.

Like all future oriented visionaries, the republicans are very conscious of their place in history. They see themselves as like the founding fathers of the 1890s. Generations yet unborn will be taught to revere the name of Malcolm Turnbull as a nation builder, the equal of John Curtin, Simpson and his donkey, Weary Dunlop and Don Bradman. They even have a founder's book to be signed by unwary Australian citizens. This reveals the very elevated view they have of themselves.

Australian nationalism last century was based on the false view that to be an Australian you had to reject other nationalities, pre-eminently the British. This is a conflict model promoting exclusive or pure nationalism, which has led to much trouble, as we can see in the Balkans. Today's republicans inherit this outmoded conflict model from last century, which stirs up animosity between different groups. In her recent book on Federation Helen Irving rightly says that 'it is now more or less accepted that a person may have simultaneously and authentically more than one cultural identity'. This more intelligent approach sees being an Australian as incorporating into one's personality all the heritages which come for one's ancestors. The republican's view of nationalism is a regressive one.

The republicans of the 1990s are the direct descendants of the nationalists of the 1890s. Both represented less than half the country, but got to centre stage by self-acclamation. Both insisted that unless you took up their cause you were somehow outmoded. Both claimed to be the mainstream voice, and had amnesia about the actual majority which did not agree with them, or treated the majority with derision. Both claimed they were victims of vestigial British rule imposed as an alien force on this country. In both the Irish Australian element was prominent. In our times Thomas Keneally and Paul Keating in Sydney, and the late Dinny O'Hearn and Eddie McGuire in Melbourne, have paraded their Irish Australian credentials to perpetuate the 1890s myth that the anti-British tradition found a natural home in Australia. In this way old antagonisms are being resurrected long after they have lost their vitality.

Bu there is one great difference between the nationalists of the 1890s and the republicans of today. The nationalists were insular, believing in an Australia isolated from the rest of the world. In those days it was the conservatives who were the internationalists. They had a geo-political outlook based on the British Empire, and Britain's string of colonies around the world linked by trade, defence and common institutions. Today's new class are strongly internationalist with a cosmopolitan outlook. They admire overseas more than Australia and look to overseas models for precedents and guidance. On the other hand, ordinary Australians today are more likely to be insular nationalists, believing in a fortress Australia, Australia as the best country in the world, and so on. This has been a great changeover since last century – the two groups have changed sides. John Howard backed 'mateship' in the constitutional preamble, but for the new class it is an outmoded concept. So the great anomaly at present is that in the republican debate New Class commentators are donning the colour of nationalism. They have been pushing strenuously for involvement with Asia, they favour us signing international treaties which abrogate some of our rights, yet they pretend to be 'born again' nationalists.

The first great enduring hero of the New Class was Gough Whitlam. In his term as Prime Minister he tried to bring into existence the new kind of Australia they wanted – progressive, permissive, internationalist, run by people like themselves in public positions of power and privilege, a far cry from the old dowdy, suburban country they believed we had been until Gough's galvanizing influence. But Whitlam's government staggered from crisis to crisis and bungled the vision. They look back on Gough as their long lost king, the icon of the true believers. The man who formally stopped Gough in his tracks was Sir John Kerr, a fellow participant in NSW Labor politics. The present republican campaign is a major prong in the strategy of revenge on Kerr and the rehabilitation of Gough. The proposed republican model has an amazingly easy mechanism for dismissing the President, virtually at the whim of the Prime Minister. This is just the latest in a series of moves attempting to reduce the almost zero powers of the head of state. In the 1970s it was the attempt to de-authorize the office by personal attacks on Sir John Kerr and by 'maintaining your rage'. In the 1980s it was by a series of constitutional conventions with the same end. Now in the 1990s it is the sacking powers in the new bill.

The republican push stems partly from this internal wrangle among the right of the NSW ALP. This explains why the republican debate has been so Sydneycentric. But the nationalist movement has always been strongest in Sydney. *The Bulletin* began there last century, and Sydney was much more closely in contact with great outback plains than Melbourne was. Geoffrey Serle has pointed out that the bush mateship type was not as common in the Victorian countryside as in other states. Convict free Melbourne was founded by, in Paul de Serville's phrase, 'Port Phillip Gentlemen', whose connection with Britain was explicitly maintained. John Docker has traced these two opposing traditions in his book *Australian Cultural Elites*.

But though it is a Sydney-centered movement, the republican cause fits into Australia's beltway, the south-east triangle of the continent where New Class ideas are strongest. Since Whitlam's days, Federal election voting patterns have revealed a new split in the electorate. The closer you are to the big cities, and to the south-east corner, the more likely you are to vote Labour. The further you are from the cities and the remoter the state, the more you are likely to vote for the Coalition. This pattern is being repeated in the republican referendum.

This is a sub-set of the phenomenon Katharine Betts in her recent book has called *The Great Divide*. Betts demonstrates a growing gulf between new class groups and ordinary Australians, those John Howard calls the battlers or the mainstream. Many commentators on Australia have shown a decidedly un-Australian cast of mind, despising us for being a country behind the eight ball. *The Age* journalist Geoffrey Barker wrote in 1980 that we as a country 'have a dark side. We are xenophobic. We fear the outside world...we have a broad streak of racism...All in all it is a sweet swinish life... We glorify the ocker, we wallow in his vulgarity and celebrate his crassness as a triumph of Australian culture.' On Phillip Adams' Lateline show during the last federal elections, Margot Kingston of the *Sydney Morning Herald*, referring to the Hansonites, said what are we going to do with *these people*, as though they should be outside the Australian polity. This is a dangerous and unnecessary embryonic split in Australian society, which the republican camp is exacerbating with its rhetoric.

From *The No Case Papers* (1999)

The vote was 55% to 45% against the republic, which was not, as it proponents claimed, inevitable. Polls had been employed, as this article says, 'to increase support, not to measure it'. The false version of public opinion evident in this case was replicated two decades later when Brexit, Trump and Morrison triumphed against the pollsters' odds.

VARIETIES OF POLITICAL CATHOLICISM

(1967)

The series of confusions caused by the Catholic Church's belated acceptance of modernity at the Second Vatican Council.

European political history of the past few centuries divides itself into two fairly distinct periods: that between the French Revolution and the First World War, and that since. The first period, which can be called the period of modernity, is characterized by the struggle of the ideologies of the traditional Right and the traditional Left in Europe. The most important thing about the Traditional Right is that it had a cultural, not a political worldview: it envisaged an ideal society held together by religio-cultural bonds. Its closest terrestrial embodiment was the ordered, feudal, pre-industrial society of the medieval synthesis, hierarchic, aristocratic, reverent, where everything, including the supernatural, had its appointed place in the organic harmony. It treated national culture as the highest good, a delicate thing to be preserved at all costs. It believed, accordingly, that social change is effected culturally, that is, by first changing each individual's dispositions; it called typically for a 'change of heart', usually in a superior, authoritative and heavily moralizing language. This emphasis on personal responsibility as determining factors in earthly events complemented its generally fatalistic tone, blaming God's design and providence for the inevitable injustices and sufferings of those who inhabited the vale of tears. Its theology derived from the stern Augustinian complaint against the vanity of earthly endeavour, reinforced by a subterranean current of heretic Manichean yearning for the immediately transcendent. This mentality (of which Jansenism and Puritanism are national derivatives) is often called 'otherworldly', and it illustrates the withdrawal of the religious sensibility from the real areas of concern in the 19th century. It detached itself, and gave paramount importance to explicitly religious questions.

Because of its cultural basis, the worldview was profoundly anti-political. However, it had institutionalized itself as the ordained view of the ruling class, and it is in this sense that it can be spoken of the worldview of the European traditional Right. Those in power tried to preserve the traditional values of European civilization, in which they had a vested interest, by maintaining the established order based on submission to authority, the authority of the foundations of society, the monarchy, the aristocracy, the Church and the army. Hence the Church was an integral part of the traditional Right, and completely identified with it as an important bearer of Western culture.

The traditional Left had its origin in the belief of the Enlightenment thinkers that the world could be known by rational exploration alone, and without recourse to outside explanations, for example, Revelation. It was above all interested in what was happening on the face of the globe, believing in social justice, brotherhood, equality, and freedom for the underprivileged, who were the majority of the inhabitants of the earth and with whom this view identified itself. It saw things in terms of class (not racial or national) divisions. Its worldview was a political one, based on the assumption that environment, not personality, was the determining factor in social change, that it was only the encrusted structures of society, erected by time and the ruling classes, which prevented man from displaying himself in all his pristine purity. Looking to the future, not the past, it was optimistic about human nature, and about the chances for an improvement in the condition of man by his unaided actions. Activist by disposition, it came increasingly to call for a radical change in the nature of society, and it saw as its chief obstacle the entrenched ruling class which prevented this humanitarian revolution coming about. The *ancien regime*, it claimed, preserved the feudal slumber of the population by an ideology of superstition, mystification, and appeals to a religio-cultural heritage, and by its fatalistic, shoulder-shrugging explanations of earthly calamity, all designed to cover up the hypocrisy and greed of its own class. Marx's 'religion is the opium of the people' is simply the most famous statement of this Enlightenment charge of the socially stabilizing use of religion.

Conversely, the traditional Right saw these new ideas as totally subversive. It used its entrenched power to defend itself as a last bastion holding out against these attacks, the first and greatest of which was the French Revolution. It developed a siege mentality which rejected the whole modern venture, and came to be defined by what it was against: anti-modernity, anti-progress, anti-industrialization, anti-democracy, anti-science, anti-Enlightenment, etc. It became literally conservative, trying to preserve what it had, the status quo. The Church too acted in its own area to defend the values of the traditional Right against these incursions. Ridden with a dualistic terminology, it tried to assert its teachings by complete emphasis on the explicitly religious, and it opposed what it called the 'secularization' of the world. Its comprehensive condemnation of the Enlightenment is contained in that unholy trinity of anathemas *atheistic, secular and materialistic,* both the staple and the standby of the Sunday sermon ever since. Anything that was not religious was worldly, and therefore wrong. For these reasons the Church did not encourage all forms of intellectual inquiry, and was against the scientific investigation of the secrets of the universe as a blasphemy against the mystery and beauty of God's creation. It mounted a religious struggle against the two great ogres of the 19th century, Darwin and Marx.

Perhaps the two most notorious, yet somehow typical, examples of the identification of the Church with the European traditional Right were:

(a) The Syllabus of Errors (1864) and Vatican Council I (1870) which set the face of the Church officially and authoritatively against the modern, liberal world. The Syllabus contained such 'errors' as 'That man is free to embrace and profess that religion which, in the light of Reason, he should consider true.'

(b) The Action Française, which the Catholic Church got itself caught up with in its early days in France before the First World War. It was a militant movement, run and led by a cultural ideologue, Charles Maurras, to defend the glories of the traditional, Catholic, French, national heritage against the invasions of cultural decadence unleashed by the Third Republic.

It was a time in history when two sharply defined and dominant ideologies opposed to each other in every respect. The failure of the Church in this period was that it supported the less preferable ideology, leading it to withdraw from areas of concern which occupied the thinkers of the traditional Left like Marx and which should have occupied and engaged the Church.

The second period, however, that since the First World War, is very different. Its newness and uniqueness lies in the fact that it produced a world in which totalitarianism was possible, and in some cases actually happened. The change can be summarily described as follows: 1. The totalitarian Right (Fascism) and the totalitarian Left (Communism) were more than simply ideologies or collections of ideas. 2. The totalitarian Right and Left did not, fundamentally, derive from the traditional Right and Left. 3. In their totally institutionalized forms (the regimes of Hitler and Stalin) they were more similar to each other than different. The words 'Right' and 'Left, therefore, have quite different meanings in the different periods.

The totalitarian personality amalgamates a worldview of the earlier period with the special life-style, ruthless and nihilistic, now possible in the contemporary world; and it is the second that is ultimately dominant. Lenin was a combination of Marxist ideas and the Nechayevist revolutionary tradition. What was not clear until recently is that, in the same way, early Fascist leaders were an apparently contradictory combination of the ideas of the traditional Right and a ruthless Bolshevik personality; and, unlike the old Royalists, in a pinch they considered the old ideas expendable. In this way, the totalitarian Right and Left became similar, since their original ideas came to matter less and less. The totalitarian regimes institutionalized in power this new personality type on a nation-wide scale. For Communists this was no problem, but the traditional Right had always been anti-political. The Fascists made the crucial step of moving into the political arena to enforce their cultural aims. In power, it is known that Hitler and Stalin admired each other and nobody else. It did not really matter if they said that they believed in race or class respectively, because it amounted to the same thing in the long run: similar regimes founded on the terror of the secret police and the concentration camps. In this period, therefore, the old basic framework of a struggle between two opposite ideologies is no longer correct.

Many of the traditional Right and Left were deceived into sympathy with Fascism and Communism respectively because, using this outmoded framework, they mistakenly saw them as their counterpart, simply an institutional extension of their own traditional beliefs. Thus some of the liberal Left of the Western world welcomed Stalin's 1936 Constitution as the highest embodiment of enlightened rule (which on paper it was) at a time when the great purges were in full swing. Much of the traditional Right of Europe welcomed Fascism as the protector of the old order, that order which Fascism proceeded to destroy as soon as it had power. Similarly, the traditional ideologies each opposed its opposite totalitarian regime for the wrong reasons. Hitler was seen as the tool of big business and capitalism, and Bolshevism as another threat of an invasion by the barbarian hordes from the East out to destroy the European way of life. Neither understood the newness and the historical uniqueness of totalitarianism, because that would have meant opposing it in all its forms, not seeing one form as a saviour from the other.

The Catholic Church made the same mistake as the traditional Right, and became, not Fascist, but a fellow traveller of Fascism, as Guenter Lewy's *The Catholic Church and Nazi Germany* (1964) shows. The Vatican signed Concordats with Mussolini and Hitler thinking, in its explicitly religious way, that they would preserve the institutional integrity of the Church. In the old oppositional terms, the Church utterly opposed 'godless' Communism for the same reasons as it opposed the Enlightenment and the whole traditional Left: it was atheistic, secular and materialistic. As a corollary of this, it mistakenly thought that the Soviets, like the Enlightenment, attacked the Church only for reasons of atheism. But the Communists attacked the Church (as Hitler planned to attack it in Germany after he won the war) to destroy it as an alternative focus of loyalty, power and authority. It was a political move.

By the time of the Second World War the Church was making a double error: it was two stages behind. If the criterion of pro-modernity of the traditional Left was insufficient for understanding reality in a totalitarian world, how much more insufficient was the criterion of anti-modernity? The Church, like the traditional Right, was still waging a last-ditch struggle against a modernity which itself had long since been superseded. It seems to me that the only feasible position is from the point of view of the traditional Left to oppose all forms of totalitarianism for the same reason: to oppose Communism not because it attacks God but because it attacks men, and to oppose Fascism not because it supports God but because it attacks men.

Camus ends *The Rebel* with the charge that 'Historic Christianity postpones, to a point beyond the span of history, the cure of evil and murder which are, nevertheless, experienced within the span of history,' What was traditionally held against Christianity was that it imposed upon men an unnatural pattern of life. But from Berdayev to Camus the most coherent interpretation of Communism has been as a terrestrialized analogue of the Christian archetype, which shows (though Christians can hardly be flattered by it) that when men freed themselves from Christianity, they proceeded to act of their own accord in exactly the same way – so the Christian pattern was not so unnatural after all.

The recent Vatican Council II was partly obligatory, given the low prestige of the Catholic Church in post-war Europe over its political accommodation with the regimes of the totalitarian Right. But, contradictorily, what the renovation amounts to in political terms is a sloughing off of the embarrassing paraphernalia and beliefs of the traditional (not the totalitarian) Right, and acceptance of Enlightenment Left values (secularization, liberalism) as salutary, even incarnational, a process which Malcolm Muggeridge has described as the Church's 'selling out its Heavens for what they were worth and buying in Earths on a rising market'. Vatican II is an explicit repudiation of the atheistic, secular and materialistic anathemas of the Syllabus of Errors and Vatican I: the Catholic Church has correctly changed sides and embraced modernity. If this is what is meant by those who say that the Church must be Left today, then well and good. It is hardly time for self-congratulatory gestures when you correct the errors of 100 years ago. For Vatican II was in no literal sense an 'aggiornamento': it brought the Church only into the period of modernity, and that ended half a century ago. In politics, the Church has only overcome the first of drawbacks. Vatican II was a necessary step, a preparation for entering the post-1914 world.

Peculiar confusions are caused by the adoption of a position 50 years after it was adequately applicable. It means that the Church now has different errors and different reasons for them. Vatican II has not entered into the problems of the totalitarian world, so the old criteria of opposition between Left and Right are still applied, only the sides are now changed. So non-opposition to the traditional Left (including Marxism) is mistakenly implied to entail non-opposition to Communism, which is seen as the highpoint of modernity; and opposition to the traditional Right is mistakenly taken to entail opposition to Fascism (and so clear the Church's name in Europe). Withdrawing the atheistic, secular and materialistic slogan from Communism does not get you very far, as it was erroneously applied under anti-Enlightenment auspices in the first place anyway. The result of it all is that the Church has reversed her condemnations, instead of (if the nature of totalitarianism were really understood, that is, that it is inherently depriving and ultimately murderous) condemning it unequivocally in all its forms. The way the Catholic Church should assuage her guilt at placating one form of totalitarianism this century is not by placating the other.

The Church was two stages behind: she has caught up one. What has happened is that many Catholics, coming 50 years too late, have telescoped the two processes into one. Armed with their newly discovered modernity ideas, they go into the world thinking they are entering modernity itself, when in fact they are entering a new, potentially totalitarian world, and they get things disastrously wrong by using criteria which do not apply any more. They would consider Nechayev's 'All is permitted' a liberal statement. They lack discrimination in judgment because, thinking that all modern and secular things are good, they therefore think that all (except the old Right) is good in the world, which unfortunately is not the case.

The two most important questions relevant to this subject in

Europe at the moment are the dialogue between Christians and Communists, and the attempted rapprochement between Church and State in Eastern Europe. The much more important question is the East European one because, unlike dialogue, it actually affects human lives. The Russians are now prepared to make easy concessions not only to the new Left Church, but even to the old traditional Right one, like Yevtuschenko's appearance at Fatima, a devotion which has been used by the Church since 1917 for anti-Bolshevik purposes. It is a strange time for the Catholic Church to start making concessions now when the élan of the Soviet Communist experiment is at its lowest ebb in 50 years, and when there are appearing for the first time in Easter Europe individuals who have got outside of the whole Left totalitarian mentality, and all of whom (Tarsis, Sinyavski, Mihajlov, Svetlana Stalin) claim, significantly they are Christians or identify themselves with Christianity. What must they think of the Western Christians to whom they look for support being so eager to get on with their jailers? Muggeridge has said that 'Christians were funny enough when with crazy gallantry they tried to defend the book of Genesis against Darwin's panzers; they are even funnier now that belatedly they have decided to join the army of progress just when it is in total disarray, if not in headlong retreat.' From the point of view of the East European anti-Communists, it must seem more appalling than funny.

The second half of this article applied this analysis to various Catholic groupings in Australia.

Quadrant, September-October, 1967

DR FRANK KNOPFELMACHER

(2002)

A contribution to a volume of essays in memory of Professor Patrick O'Brien of Perth.

Patrick O'Brien attended Melbourne University as a mature aged student in the early 1960s. There he encountered Dr Franta (Frank) Knopfelmacher, whose influence at the University was then at its height. For those emerging out of a Catholic Irish-Australian background, like among others Paddy O'Brien and myself, the ideas Dr Knopfelmacher brought to Melbourne were a potent mix. His thinking processes were not formed by the Anglo-Australian mould then prevalent. Trained in the German philosophical tradition from Hegel and Marx to Weber and Arendt, he had absorbed not just their specific ideas, but the whole habit of mind associated with them. This many of us at the time found refreshing, as this way of thinking seemed better able to explain the complex world of Europe in the aftermath of Hitler and Stalin. Many similar central European Jewish social critics had emigrated to the USA, where they exercised a profound and fruitful influence. There were only a few in Australia – in addition to Dr. Knopfelmacher, Professor Hugo Wolfsohn from Melbourne University's Political Science Department, Professor Henry Mayer of the University of Sydney, and Professors Eugene Kamenka and Heinz Arndt of the ANU. Richard Krygier of Sydney, the founder of *Quadrant*, came from the same background.

Born in 1923 to a German-speaking Czech Jewish family, Dr

Knopfelmacher was raised in Kromeriz and Brno in Moravia. The family were in trade, mainly as distillers, with connections in Bohemia, Moravia and Vienna. As an adolescent boy in the mid to late 1930s he sensed, unlike the rest of his family, that the Nazis meant business, that is, extermination, and emigrated to Palestine. He had some natural, intuitive understanding of the totalitarian mentality. Virtually all his relatives were murdered in the Holocaust; about a dozen Knopfelmachers are memorialized in the Jewish museum in Prague. In Palestine he joined the Free Czech army when the second world war broke out, and was for a short period a member of the Communist Party. But reading authors like Arthur Koestler, Franz Borkenau and George Orwell, as well as his own experiences, turned him into a democratic socialist. Transferred to England, he fought in France and then returned to Czechoslovakia. But while studying at Charles University in Prague, he noticed the pre-coup behaviour of the Communist Party was eerily reminiscent of Nazi behaviour of the previous decade. When the Communists took over in 1948, he fled from a totalitarian regime in his own country for the second time in his life. He studied at Bristol University for a Ph.D. in experimental psychology in the early 1950s, at the same time renewing his admiration for the fundamental freedoms, tolerance and decencies of the English way of life. He came to Australia in 1955 when offered a Lectureship in Psychology at the University of Melbourne. His own summary of his life and what he learnt from his experiences can be found in his autobiographical article 'My Political Education', *Quadrant*, July-August, 1967.

To young Catholics, Communism had been demonized as primarily atheistic because it attacked God. To Dr Knopfelmacher it was reprehensible not because it attacked God, which many modern philosophies did, but because it attacked human beings. Pope Paul VI issued an encyclical stating that false philosophes, like Marxism, were to be abhorred, but that their end products, like Communism, may be tolerable in practice. To Dr Knopfelmacher this was to get things exactly the wrong way round. Marxism was an illuminating, if debatable view of the world, but its descendant, Communism, was murderous. From Marxism and the German tradition, Dr Knopfelmacher passed on the practice of demythologizing institutions, by looking, for instance, at their economic bases, and at the *realpolitic*, rather than the stated, aims of politically active individuals and groups. From Freud he learnt to be suspicions of arriving at conclusions convenient to one's own outlook. Relentless and ruthless critique of society to destroy illusions was the role of the intellectual sociologist. 'Some of the greatest womanizers and atheists in history believed in defending their country' he would say, to shock those who believed that sexual and religious morality must lie at the basis of political morality, and to break the nexus between them.

The struggle between the traditional left and right in Europe, who saw each other as opposites, had been superseded by the new phenomenon of totalitarianism, which Dr Knopfelmacher explained using the classic studies of Arendt, Orwell, Koestler and Borkenau. It was an enemy of both left and right, who had to see that the new divide was between the totalitarians and all others. Totalitarianism was in its Russian version a combination of the ideas of the European chiliastic left and the tactics of Russian revolutionary movements, as exemplified by figures like Nechayev. These two currents came together for the first time in Lenin. One of his favourite books at the time was Eric Voegelin's *The New Science of Politics,* which focussed on these ideas: Communism was a neo-gnostic dream world, the traditional religious notion of Moscow as the third Rome secularized into an earthly political paradise. Another favourite book was Phillip Selznick's *The Organizational Weapon,* which explained the tactical side: techniques of institutional entrism, subversion and take-over had been perfected by trained 'prophetic shock minorities', and conscious counter-organizational strategies had to be employed to prevent this. Anti-Communism was simply part of the larger strategy of anti-totalitarianism. One could easily be anti-Communist without being a conservative, or a supporter of the Tory/Liberal parties. Democratic socialists were in fact usually the most successful anti-totalitarians.

Connected with this analysis was Dr Knopfelmacher's belief in the extreme fragility of human personalities and institutions. He had seen people's self-identity shatter under the first pressures of Fascism. Institutions were held together by morale, assent of members, and internalization of their mores or unwritten rules. Freud understood that we had a thin veneer of civilization, under which we were seething volcanoes, who could easily crack under pressure. Dr Knopfelmacher had seen two catastrophic eruptions in his homeland in his own lifetime, the Nazi and Communist takeovers of Czechoslovakia. Based on his training in psychology, he opposed the notion of the 'authoritarian personality' devised by Adorno and the Frankfurt School. This he considered a damaging, 'sophisticated' neo-Marxist claim that Western middle-classes were irredeemably right-wing, even proto-fascist, based on the bygone right-left distinction. If accepted it would weaken our societies by eroding their morale. Marcuse's theories of the 1960s and 1970s, which claimed media and sexual saturation dulled the innate revolutionary drives of Western citizens, he saw as a revamping of the discredited Marxist-Freudian amalgam of the German thinker Wilhelm Reich. He emphasized what Jean Francois Revel later called 'the totalitarian temptation': fellow travellers and left liberals worshipped political power vicariously, and their activities could lead to the subversion of existing democratic institutions. This had nothing to do with the traditional right or left.

The Soviet Union was for most of his life seen as the principal source of these political problems. In the last decade of his life, however, after returning for a time to his native Czechoslovakia, Germany became the principal threat, as it was beginning to economically dominate the former Soviet satellite countries of central and eastern Europe. These views partly reflected the traditional central European suspicion of the two great powers which had historically threatened them. Dr Knopfelmacher brought with him to Australia a living sense of central Europe as a highly developed and sophisticated civilization in its own right, the central Europe of Mahler, Schindler, Weiniger, Kraus, Freud, Roth and others, all of whom he often talked about. This stimulating world of central Europe had been hidden from our view by the disasters which had befallen it. Joseph Roth lamented the collapse of Austro-Hungarian rule in his novel *The Radetsky March*. Interestingly the novel has in it a character called Knopfmacher, who, like Frank, came from a Brno Jewish family. His homeland was at the cutting edge, tragically, of world politics. Lessons for the rest of the world were to be learned there. He liked quoting Karl Kraus that it was a training ground for the end of the world. Much of the greatest literature of our time has emanated from this region.

So we in Melbourne, because of this influence, became in our turn fellow-travellers of central and east Europe. It was as much our spiritual home, our source country, as Australia or England or Ireland were. We saw the future there and why it didn't work. Dr Knopfelmacher often talked of Hans Fallada's popular novel *Little Man, What Now?*, whose hero was always struggling and always battling against the big battalions. Dr Knopfelmacher adopted the stance of the embattled dissident. Later when the United States became the big man, he reacted against it. He did not take up the Marcuse or *The Greening of America* critiques of the US, which he thought flawed. He saw the US as corrupted by money and the easy life, devoted to upward social and status mobility. Anti-Communist rhetoric was just another, subtle form of upward status mobility. The anti-Communists believed in it, but they used it to get on. He particularly targeted in this analysis some of his own fellow European Jewish intellectuals like Henry Kissinger and Sidney Hook (I found this unfair). He was very taken by J.M. Cuddihy's *The Ordeal of*

Civility, on the problems Jews and Irish encountered in assimilating in Western WASP societies, which he took as a documentary proof of what he had always impressionistically maintained.

He was also, like many central Europeans, a profound Anglophile, though his mind didn't operate in the English mode, and in some quarters his behaviour was considered not *salonfähig* or respectable. He believed the English had given the world the great gift of representative democracy as a bulwark against tyranny, and this system should be defended against subversion. In addition the English had naturally internalized civil liberties and freedom for the citizenry. He had seen, by way of contrast, people in east Europe being treated like cattle. He was greatly influenced in this direction by reading George Orwell's pamphlet *The Lion and the Unicorn* soon after it was published in 1941, and he noticed how unpanicky and practical the English were during the second world war. When he came to write a column in *Quadrant* in the 1980s, he named it after Orwell's Tribune column 'As I Please'. In Melbourne this Anglophilia inoculated people like Paddy O'Brien against a certain prevalent anti-Britishness, which stemmed from a remnant romantic Irish nationalism among many of Melbourne's Irish Australian Catholics.

The title of Dr Knopfelmacher's book *Intellectuals and Politics* expressed his interest in the connection between these two activities. He admired Weber's writing on this subject, and what he wrote on Weber could be applied to himself:

> There is nothing in Weber's work which could be shaped into a redemptive key to the universe and there is a plurality of methods and devices, explicitly acknowledged as a plurality. This then is the first important feature of Weber's sociological work: methodological and pragmatic pluralism and a complete absence of potentially chiliastic pronouncements. There is a tremendous passion in Weber's writing – he is certainly not a 'mere' academic – yet it is a passion for unconditional sobriety.

Intellectuals should engage in critique and also act in politics. Democracies were fragile and vulnerable to subversion, as he had witnessed in central Europe. Orwell was right that totalitarian ideas were most likely to take hold in the minds of intellectuals everywhere. Universities then were particularly important areas of political action. Objective critique must be applied to them, as well as from them. But normally universities exempted themselves from rigorous self-scrutiny as to motivation, and so made themselves sanctuaries of protection. They were often places of upward status mobility and in addition were inclined to the totalitarian temptation. The Political Science Department at Melbourne University was a particular cause of concern for Dr Knopfelmacher. As Ian Milner, who defected to Prague, was involved in its founding, and Dr Lloyd Churchward, a Communist, gave lectures saying the Soviet Union of the 1960s was a kind of democracy, he had reason for his worries. Recent revelations on Ian Milner as a Soviet spy, uncovered by Dr Peter Hruby of Perth, seem to have confirmed his worst suspicions. He gave a series of lectures for some years on political philosophy and practice from Hegel to Mao as a countervailing influence to the Political Science Department.

Dr Knopfelmacher took active steps to prevent subversion in the student and intellectual body, by forming a group of democrat socialist students of mainly Catholic and Jewish background. He wrote at the time:

> Australian Catholics play a key role in Australian politics...an important section of the Australian Catholic community awoke much earlier than other Australians from colonial slumber. While the others still slept, they were already responding in an alert and intelligent manner to the political signals from a new and dangerous world... when I debated issues which interested me the people who were attuned to what I had to say, who were 'on the same wavelength', tended to be, more often than not, Catholics. This was for reasons probably quite unconnected with religion as such.

With James Jupp, Vincent Buckley and others, he revitalized the Melbourne University ALP club, of which Paddy O'Brien was an influential President in the mid 1960s. The Labour situation at Melbourne University was different from that prevailing in either Victoria or NSW. After the split in Victoria, the centre and left of the Labour forces formed the ALP, and the right the DLP. In NSW all three groups stayed in the ALP, with the centre and right holding dominance. At Melbourne University in the fifties, the centre and right had split from the extreme left, the Labour Club, to form the Melbourne University ALP Club. Hence the MUALP Club differed radically from the then Victorian ALP, and worked with the NSW ALP and Gough Whitlam to diminish the influence of Bill Hartley and his pro-Communist 'unity ticket' clique.

Dr Knopfelmacher's personality was striking. He showed no deference to institutions as far as their status was concerned, though he was a keen defender of their institutional authority. His critique of universities was particularly stringent, and he was not subdued by institutional self-regard. He used material from a wide range of sources which he put together in a stimulating mix. He aimed to shock as a form of pre-emptive strike, and to be somewhat unpredictable and unrespectable. What he was thinking came tumbling out of his mouth, so that his listeners could see the processes of his mind at work.

To what extent was Paddy O'Brien influenced by Dr Knopfelmacher? The debt is most clearly seen in Paddy's first book *The Saviours*, which castigates the Australian intellectual and political left for succumbing to the millenarian fantasy of earthly redemption. In that book Paddy O'Brien uses the image from Konrad Lorenz of the greylag goose, which forever loyally follows the animal it first meets after leaving its parents. Dr Knopfelmacher was probably the first great intellectual influence on Paddy, but Paddy was no greylag goose. He developed his own ideas and arguments as he lived and went along. He had his own fresh inputs, like his own ancestor Sir Henry Vane, whose writings he used in *The People's Case*. In addition, the move to Perth meant that his contacts with Dr Knopfelmacher and Melbourne circles gradually diminished, however much he kept in touch during visits.

However we can see the influence of Dr Knopfelmacher on Patrick O'Brien in many of the matters discussed above. People saw Paddy as quintessentially Irish Australian, but Dr Knopfelmacher appealed to the English and German strains in his background. Dr Knopfelmacher was in social and class terms a mixture of demotic popularist and cultural aristocrat, a combination Paddy also embraced. Paddy's early articles on totalitarianism come from Dr Knopfelmacher's influence. Paddy was stimulated late in his life by his time in Poland, the east Europe to which Dr Knopfelmacher had introduced him. Both had no deference to institutional mythos, and severely criticized universities. Both came up with a unique blend of ideas from disparate areas. They poured out a stream of ideas in such a way that their thinking processes were transparent – you could witness them developing ideas on the spot. Both were Anglophiles who believed in British institutions, as we see in *The People's Case*. Both saw their task as combating the prevalent fashions of their time, in particular the trendy liberal mindset, one tenet of which was that the left and the ALP could do no wrong. Paddy believed that taking this position did not make you automatically a Liberal supporter, as his book on that party shows. In connection with the WA Inc. affair, Paddy demonstrated that democratic institutions are fragile and can easily be perverted, and that intellectuals should act in politics by critique and action to remedy this, thereby preserving civil freedoms.

From *Power and Freedom in Modern Politics,* eds. Jeremy Moon and Bruce Stone (2002)

Australian Literature

SUBMERGED CULTURES IN AUSTRALIA

(1987)

Australian culture is not, as it was once portrayed, unidimensional.
Not only the Aboriginal presence, but a range of European cultures
are at least subliminally present here.

Australian writers have been preoccupied with the difference between Britain and Australia: how much of our British heritage did we bring here, and how much of an Australian heritage did we invent? We endlessly debate the supposed antagonism between the two. Until recently it was thought that immigrants brought with them a monochrome identity, and that the Australian personality was similarly unvariegated. There has also been a focus on how invading imperial cultures suppressed local, indigenous cultures – in our case the European suppression of the Aborigines.

But the invading culture itself was not uniform: it contained suppressed deposits within it, its own 'internal colonialism', of which the Celtic one was pre-eminent in the British Isles. One colonialism was engaged in two quite different, though simultaneous, suppressions, and there were a number of subject cultures, one indigenous and the others imported. People came to this new continent for liberation from some restriction that impeded them in the old world: the Irish to get away from English rule, the nonconformists to set up a 'paradise of dissent' in which the established church did not rule the roost. Like the rabbit, your type would proliferate, released from the hereditary enemies and predators who had kept it in check at home, and with no new rivals here. But did ideas and cultures that remained underground in the British Isles actually release themselves here and flourish, or did they remain suppressed, or even die out, in the new country? The great hope of liberation, it seems, was rarely realised in Australia.

In his essay 'Feeling into Words', Seamus Heaney writes that in contemporary Irish literature we witness the 'tail-end of a struggle between territorial piety and imperial power'. Older cultures grew out of an indefinable attachment to a specific place, forming a natural unity of locality, religion and race. But they were often taken over by more extensive cultures that relied on imposed power, instead of fidelity to one particular place. The Roman Empire and the Christian church, for example, both eliminated religions that worshipped in the open, in natural settings like hilltops, groves and wells.

Larger territorial agglomerations in Europe suppressed earlier cultures (like the Etruscans and the Basques). Marx and Engels called these 'the unhistoric races' of Europe, as they had no official story. While much of their culture did die, such races continued to exist in shadowy forms. As they went under, they sought to keep themselves alive through the power of myth, in compensation for the actual power they were losing. Yeats used the phrase: 'Things reveal themselves passing away'. Les Murray writes in his poem 'To a Jacobite Lady': 'Your Cause grew literary as it died'. These races prepared themselves for long periods of hibernation. They developed myths of surviving underground in vast mountain fastnesses, and of revenant heroes – Arthur, the Irish Ossian, the Welsh Cadwallader, Barbarossa on the Continent – who would re-emerge blinking in the clear light of day many centuries later, bemused at the ways of the new society. Similarly, at the end of Peter Weir's film *The Last Wave*, the Aborigines say: 'We have lost our dreams, and when they return we don't know what they mean'.

Many of the ideas of earlier cultures were subtly infiltrated into the consciousness of the conqueror, so the underground cultures did not wholly die. The Arthurian legends, for example, kept in circulation heretical notions of love which were subversive of medieval Christian belief. Earlier ideas sometimes not only survived, but had their revenge. Recognizing this, scholars have now begun to argue that all civilizations need an underground, the mystical, suppressed side of themselves. The constant tension between the two is fruitful, in a way analogous to how our own unconscious works, affecting us even in our waking state.

The various nationalisms of Europe held together quite disparate regions and cultures. During the nineteenth century new nations appeared on the continent. These nationalisms devised an ideological rationale to justify themselves. They had to invent a coherent past (Wales' medieval separateness, for example, is never mentioned in British mythic nationalism). They had to create an artificial national culture that transcended older regional and race attachments, and in which no variations could be admitted. To accomplish this, nationalism took on a quasi-religious aura, with its own ceremonies and symbols (Jubilee celebrations, Nelson, Waterloo and Westminster in the British imperial pantheon). Such nationalist ideologies replaced regional loyalties, which could no longer appeal to the whole. Nineteenth-century nationalisms were uneasy federations of disparate parts, concealed by the 'religious' rhetoric of unification.

Given centuries of takeovers, we now realize that European cultures and people consist of many deposits or strata, only the top one of which is visible. Freud referred to the 'city of memory' as 'a mental entity...in which nothing once created has perished, and all the earlier stages of development have survived alongside the latest'. An Irishman coming to Australia last century would have had an overlay of British culture, an Irish identity to which he gave allegiance, various deposits of both Roman and Irish Christianity, and inside it all some remnants of the original Gaelic culture. An internal colonial struggle was being waged within the individual. But which aspect would be preferentially released by coming to Australia?

In the second half of the nineteenth century, when migration to Australia was heaviest, the Victorian consensus was being threatened. At the very time when nationalism and imperialism seemed at their height, cracks began appearing in the confident facade. British imperialism and Christianity both found it difficult to keep the lid on things. 'Loss of faith' appeared at the time of Arnold's poetry; all overarching world-views began to loosen at their foundations. Law and order disintegrated in the mind before it did in public places. As a result, a range of small, dissident, avant-garde ginger groups arose to challenge the established ways: spiritualists, theosophists, vegetarians, occultists, sexual emancipists and devotees of magical, mystic and esoteric religions. These constituted an underground movement of freethinkers. Among these islands of advanced thought, were groups advocating political liberation (utopian socialists, agrarian reformers and so on), from whom Australian nationalism derived many of its ideas. Connected with this was the resurrection of various 'unhistoric' races like the Czechs and Hungarians. Europe witnessed their rise to consciousness and, eventually, to nationhood. These groups became interested in their remoter racial past, no matter how chequered their actual history might have been. Poets resurrected or invented language, myths and culture as a necessary prelude to political identity. People at the time thought in terms of races rising and falling and rising again. Australia was ideologically settled under the auspices of such ideas. Going into the remote past was also linked with going into one's own personal unconscious. Freud made the connection in *Totem and Taboo*, where contemporary neuroses and the customs of 'primitive peoples' were interpreted in the light of each other. The discoveries of Darwin, Marx, Frazer, Freud and Jung destabilised the dominant culture. It took some time for their implications to set in, but they did probe the weaknesses of the Victorian consensus.

In this reappraisal, the discovery of the Australian Aborigines and the recording of their customs were central. They were seen as living examples of those older races who were attracting so much attention and admiration in Europe. The works of Howitt and Fison, and Spencer and Gillen [on Aboriginal customs] were extensively used by thinkers like Frazer, Durkheim, Freud and Jung. At the very time of their suppression, for a moment before going underground, the Aborigines supplied vital material to undermine the dominant culture. There is some scant evidence that the Aborigines realized they were going under, as in this poem from the 1850s, attributed to a Western Victorian Aborigine called Peter:

One time
Death visited the Blackfellow so seldom
That we hardly knew him,
And hardly dared to look on him.
But now
He stands behind every gum-tree
Hides in every flower;
Floats in the passing breeze,
And rides on the storm clouds.
He is everywhere;
At all seasons and at all times,
In every hour...
Gathering in the Blackfellows
As a stockman gathers up his herd
And he will not relax
Until he has yarded them all
In the grave.

The Aborigines themselves had their own ideas of going underground and achieving resurrection. The Tasmanian Aborigines believed the souls of their dead went to an island in Bass Strait, where they survived in the guise of white men. The Tasmanians gave England the name 'Tini Drini', the island of skeletons, thinking that the whites were revenant figures of their own race. The Aboriginal notion of a white spirit beyond death was conveniently fitted into the contemporary Victorian mythology of the revenant figure. The early Australian feminist writer Caroline Dexter commented on these matters in an article called 'The Corroboree', published in Melbourne in 1861:

> A deep significance, deeper than they dream of, lies in the universally received belief among them that immediately one of their people dies, he returns to earth and awaits a resurrection, when he is to reappear in the form of a white man. 'Lie down black fellow – jump up white fellow', is the thought which gives them most consolation when bereaved of friends or relations. If not true of man, it is of races. It seems a decree of nature, that if the conquered race has not strength to rise and mingle with the conqueror, they must yield place to him, and at length become extinct.

Caroline Dexter here espouses the conventional Darwinian notion of an indigenous race being extinguished by a stronger invading force. But things were not so simple. Jung later came to learn, by studying the Australian Aborigines themselves, that these processes work both ways:

> Certain Australian primitives assert that one cannot conquer foreign soil, because in it there dwell strange ancestor-spirits who reincarnate themselves in the new-born. There is a great psychological truth in this. The foreign land assimilates its conqueror...Everywhere the virgin earth causes at least the unconscious of the conqueror to sink to the level of its indigenous inhabitants.

The imperial power does not have it all its own way; in the long run it's an even, and maybe a losing, battle. In Seamus Heaney's terms, this is an example of territorial piety surviving the onslaught of imperial power, and even subjugating it.

In demographic terms, Australia was settled last century by a British Isles population skewed disproportionately to the suppressed areas: people from the south-west of Ireland, some Scots from the Highland clearances and a proletariat that the Schedvins have called 'the nomadic tribes of urban Britain'. How did these components rearrange themselves when they came to Australia?

A striking fact about the biographies of many Australian authors is that they were catalysed into writing not so much by the fact of Australia as by that convulsion called 'loss of faith': the erosion of the certainty of personal immortality, and its supersession by hopes for the immortality of one's race. The withdrawal of certainty was reinforced by the fact of living in a new country where many traditional support systems did not exist. The Celtic Twilight writers of the *Bulletin* were affected by these currents. Like O'Dowd and Lindsay, many lesser writers between 1870 and 1930 populated the Australian landscape with nymphs, water sprites and faery daemons. This fey mysticism was the Victorian age's attempt to recreate the old religion of the 'God in the tree'. These strains in Australian literature were as powerful as the nationalist urge, with which they are connected, but, as in England, they remained subversive enterprises which never gained respectable mainstream status.

A related strand in radical thinking was the move towards political and social freedom. This too was often connected with disillusionment with traditional religion; various secular political utopias acted as a balm against personal uncertainty. Australian nationalism picked up these ideas, which were common in England in the later decades of last century. But here there was one big difference. Whereas in England they remained isolated oases of ferment, here, released from past restraints, they flourished. This is one example of a liberation movement being successfully released on coming to Australia. But in expanding to a position of dominance so rapidly, Australian nationalism took on the attributes of nineteenth-century European nationalisms. It imposed an artificial mystique on the continent. It emphasized unity, and allowed no variations or regional differences; it had no sense of a specific place (Australia for Brunton Stephens was 'one continent-isle of Emerald'); it created a monolithic national type, with no subtlety or layers; like European nationalisms, it ignored the presence of a subject race, in this case the Aborigines. There were to be no ancestral voices or mystery here: everything was to be clear cut in a land Bernard O'Dowd called 'the sunniest, and the least fey land in the good green globe'. Though it believed itself to be breaking away from British colonial rule, Australian nationalism used the forms of the imperial culture.

As one of the more mystic variations on the nationalist theme, however, a new conceit was developed. Australia itself was seen as a long-submerged culture. It had lain dormant down the aeons of time, while the fabled empires of the past had risen to their glorious heights and then declined. They had had their turn; now it was ours. We were about to emerge from obscurity and rise to greatness, the culmination of all previous history. The *Bulletin* balladist John Farrell expresses this at the beginning of his poem 'Australia':

> O Land of widest hope, of promise boundless!
> Why wert thou left upon a dark, strange sea,
> To wait through ages fruitless, scentless, soundless,
> Till from thy slumber men should waken thee?

Joseph Furphy, in his wonderfully discursive way, re-creates a sense of the epic proportions of the wait:

> Pause and think how she has waited in serene loneliness while the deltas of Nile, Euphrates, and Ganges expanded, inch by inch, to spacious provinces, and the Yellow Sea shallowed up with the silt of winters innumerable – waited while the primordial civilizations of Copt, Accadian, Aryan and Mongol crept out, step by step, from palæolithic silence into the uncertain record of Tradition's earliest fable – waited still through the long eras of successive empires, while the hard-won light, broadening little by little, moved westward,

westward, round the circumference of the planet, at last to overtake and dominate the fixed twilight of its primitive home – waited, ageless, tireless, acquiescent, her history a blank, while the petulant moods of youth gave place to imperial purpose, stern yet beneficent – waited whilst the interminable procession of annual, lunar and diurnal alternations lapsed unrecorded into a dead Past, bequeathing no register of good or evil endeavour to the ever-living Present.

Poets like Victor Daley and Bernard O'Dowd immersed themselves in various ancient mythologies. Sometimes, as in O'Dowd's poem 'Australia Mavourneen', we find the belief that Australia has superseded past lands. But in others Australia embodies a past civilization come to light again. So in O'Dowd's 'An Ode to Sydney', Australia is depicted as the paradise or afterworld of Celtic legend:

Whither in trance
Long, long ago
Lured the White Doe
Oisin? And whither Arthur did they row?
Surely to the tarn of queens
Over whom like lover leans Sydney,
As a jonquil dreaming, Sydney!

In a curious piece of prose, 'My Little Kingdom', O'Dowd fancifully places ancient Irish legends in an Australian setting – the Ballarat district where he came from – to show they have not died:

I fancy I have sat many an hour, beneath a mullock-heap among the 'yam-holes' near the present site of the Eureka Stockade monument at Ballarat, with him and Lord Edward and Cuchulain and King Arthur and Conn of the Hundred Battles and Niall of the Nine Hostages...and three black swans flew by towards Lake Burrumbeet to bide the time of the loosening to human form again of the enchanted Children of Lir, and the Son of Tuirrean blew his defiant horn on the forbidding and forbidden Black Hill, and Amergin drafted Arbitration Acts and framed No-Rent plans of campaign in consultation with the shades of the Eureka rioters, and Finn hunted the giant kangaroo through the spectral gums towards Buninyong, and Oisin himself with his hounds, Bran and Sgeolan, followed the white flying doe that led him past Baal-fired Warrenheip to the wonderful Tir-n-an Og beyond.

Norman Lindsay also populated the bush with figures from ancient mythology.

If, by and large, Australia was stony ground for underground cultures, one individual is a notable exception: John Shaw Neilson. He is a freak occurrence, a throwback to the remote past. No sociological or demographic account suffices to explain him. A much earlier form of poetry was released here in him, in some quite inexplicable way. Various deposits from the past exist in his poetry, and at the base is a Celtic one, clearly if only partly present. The Scots Gaelic tradition had missed the main turning points of European civilization since medieval times – the Renaissance, the Enlightenment, the Industrial Revolution, Romanticism and Modernism – and living in Australia may have continued, for Neilson, this lucky isolation from influence.

Neilson's poetry has something in common with the earliest Celtic nature poetry, which Seamus Heaney has written on in his essay 'The God in the Tree'. The pristine clarity of vision in Neilson has nothing in common with the fey mysticism and wispy melancholy of the Celtic revival poetry, influenced as it was by late Victorian sentiments. Nor does Neilson think like us at all. A Celtic way of experiencing things is present, as Chisholm points out, in such Neilson phrases as 'Fear was upon me' instead of 'I feared'. There is no discrete, egoistic 'I' at the centre of his poems. The natural world is at the centre, and its aura permeates us:

Near by me was a lover lad
And the sweetness was on him

Nature is the active, originating and animating agent that rules everything; all we can do is to be receptive to it. We are on the periphery, at the edge of the world's joy.

Neilson put aside the hard god of his mother's Calvinism, but this had been only a superficial imposition, as he does not compose his universe in terms of the hierarchical Christian cosmology of incarnation, redemption, transcendence, and paradise after death. His is an older view of the world, cyclical, seasonal, dying, rising, coming to glory, fading, and so on. Like the seasons, each day and each human life has its dawning, midday, evening and close. In the world of nature, the natural cycle recurs each year: Spring returns revenant after the death of Winter. But with us it doesn't: the individual dies and disappears, though the species and the whole natural world go on. As well as the exultation of the 'green singer' motif, there is in Neilson's poetry the constant other theme of sadness, sorrow and the fear of death. This seems only minor at first, but the more one reads Neilson, the more the 'old man in the autumn' moves to the centre of the stage. More and more we notice how Neilson emphasizes the ungraspableness of things, how unsatisfied and unfulfilled our experiences are:

> The song will deceive you, the scent will incite you to sing;
> You clutch but you cannot discover: you cannot go down to the Spring.
> It is at the edge of a promise, a far-away thing;
> The green is the nest of all riddles: you cannot go down to the Spring.

This theme does not exist in early Celtic nature poetry. The strong sense of exile that later emerges as a strain in Celtic poetry does not appear in Neilson either; no lost homeland is invoked in his poetry, so the sorrow cannot come from that source. The sadness that comes from the realization that life is indirect and does not reveal itself may be linked to a feeling that his whole culture and way of approaching life has gone. Our new way of direct, cerebral grasping doesn't work. But the old culture of sensuous apprehension of nature is not available either. It has passed on, and what remains is the unbridgeable gulf between the two.

In this century, as the imperial culture has gradually broken down, views that previously were underemphasized have become more prominent. We see this in the increased focus on specific locations here, an interest pioneered by D. H. Lawrence, who sought the old dark gods in Cornwall, he tells us in *Kangaroo*, before coming here to search unsuccessfully for them. We are now aware that, after their arrival in Australia, suppressed peoples such as the Scots Highlanders did not feel fellowship with the other suppressed culture, the Aborigines, but acted as a dominant group. Les Murray prays that:

> We too, the Scots Australians, who've been
> henchmen of much in our self-loss
> may recover ourselves, and put off oppression.

We now also recognize the successful adaptation of the Aborigines to the continent over millennia. Jung noticed that Americans in the USA were slowly and subtly adopting customs like the Red Indians, through similarity of habitat. There are some small signs of an analogous process of assimilation here. In the folklore of southern Victoria, for example, farmers say that the sight of black cockatoos portends rain, just as the Aborigines believed.

Recently quite a few writers in Australia have become conscious of the descending layers of their past, and of the hidden Europe in the white Australian consciousness. Philip Martin, like Seamus Heaney, has written poems of ancestral voices and early cultures in his collection *The Bone Flute*. The writings of Les Murray and Vincent Buckley reflect the influence of the new outburst of scholarship in this field. Both believe that their forefather cultures have survived here, but barely. As Murray says, 'There are all these tiny gestures that remain from the past, they're not words, they're habits of mind'. But in his 'Elegy for Angus Macdonald of Cnoclinn' he is more pessimistic:

> A genus of honey bees has died out
> A strain that came to us from the lost world.

Vincent Buckley writes of himself: 'I know this [Irishness] in myself, and in recognizing the signs of it, I feel the stirring of that insight, whether memory or guess, that links me with the psyches of long dead ancestors'. But he also recognizes the failure of the transmission process when he speaks of how 'most of these things could not be brought to Australia. What remains is the ache of their absence'. Many of the poems in his book *The Pattern* reflect these thoughts, as does the later poem 'Two Half-Languages'.

David Malouf's *An Imaginary Life* and Randolph Stow's *The Girl Green as Elderflower* are comparisons between 'higher', dominant civilizations, and an earlier, pre-imperial, pre-ordered world. Other recent novels that include occult and mystical experiences include C. J. Koch's *The Doubleman*, Nicholas Hasluck's *The Bellarmine Jug* and David Foster's *The Adventures of Christian Rosy Cross*. In Malouf's novel the Roman civilization of Augustus is 'solemn, orderly, monumental', dull compared with the earlier world in which Ovid finds himself in exile. Writing of the two half-languages that Ovid uses, Malouf gives expression to the urge that underlies so many of our writers' attempts to connect with that bottom layer of their culture, the suppressed, non-rational language of the unconscious:

> When I think of the tongue that has been taken away from me, it is some earlier and more universal language than our Latin, subtle as it undoubtedly is. Latin is a language for distinctions, every ending defines and divides. The language I am speaking of now, that I am almost speaking, is a language whose every syllable is a gesture of reconciliation. We knew that language once. I spoke it in my childhood. We must discover it again.

Meanjin, Winter, 1987

WAITING FOR THE START

(1968)

The Australian habit of constantly announcing an imminent national 'coming of age'.

'We live in the most exciting time this country has known. For so long in the past we were not a nation as a whole, but this has all changed dramatically,' said Mr. Gorton last month at Moorabbin, during his appeal to Australians to develop a new sense of nationalism. Was the Prime Minister asking for something really new, or was he engaging in one of the oldest habits of those who talk about Australia and its future?

Australian nationalists have continually been engaged in drawing attention to some crucial event or period whereby, they claim, our nation decisively came to birth or maturity, when independence (either political, social or economic) was attained, and we became one, autonomous and identifiable as such for the first time, so that a national identity and culture were securely founded. In all cases, a national 'coming-of-age' is invoked; at some stage a take-off point was reached; we had crossed the threshold, there had been a revelatory opening into a new world of our own, on which a fruitful developing process could be pursued through subsequent time. After this real start, one had one's own history: there is a tradition, a continuity which can be traced from the start through to the present day. Such is the pattern of these claims.

Of the many attempts to pinpoint the time when things first got off the ground in Australia, the most persistent and publicised has been that usually referred to as the 'Australian tradition.' It falls roughly into three parts:

*Eureka and the gold rush decades were looked back to by the 1890s optimists as the time when it all started – the beginnings of the spontaneous democracy of the brotherhood of man, the eight-hour day, social legislation, the gaining of freedom by the diggers. It was thought that this start was being brought to fruition and maturity in the 1890s. For those already disillusioned, it was seen as a past Golden Age, which had now been entirely subverted, and a 'new start' (for example, in Western Australia or Paraguay) was needed. Professor Manning Clark has documented these attitudes in his article 'Rewriting Australian History' (1956).

*In the decades after the gold rushes, there was a widespread feeling that this national birth was imminent, e.g. Brunton Stephens' 'The Dominion of Australia' (1870s):

> She is not yet, but he whose ear
> Thrills to that finer atmosphere...
> Hears in the voiceful tremors of the sky
> Auroral heralds whispering 'She is nigh...
> She waits the incorporating word
> To bid her tremble into form.

and Henry Lawson's first poem, the 'Song of the Republic' (1887):

> Sons of the South, your time will come –
> Sons of the South, 'tis near –
> The "signs of the Times," in their language dumb,
> Foretell it, and ominous whispers hum
> Like sullen chords of a distant drum,
> In the ominous atmosphere.

Stephens is the first of that line of poets (Stephens, Lawson, Arthur Adams, Daley, Gilmore, O'Dowd, Furnley Maurice) who can be called the poets of prophetic-rhetorical gestures of nationalist wish-fulfilment. A quotation from O'Dowd's 'Poetry Militant' (the title is indicative of the nature of the enterprise) shows this: 'The fact of evolution and the fact of Australia make Australian poets, if they will, essentially poets of the dawn, poets whose function it is to chart the day and make it habitable – marching poets, working poets, poets militant.'

The combination of this strain with utopian dreams transferred to a rural bush paradise setting produced the nationalist 'coming-of-age' outburst of the 1890s, which is, of course, the paradigm in Australian history of all attempts to locate the start of national independence. As with the 1850s, the 1890s was resurrected as a Golden Age by some of the disillusioned radicals of the 1940s. Others, like Brian Fitzpatrick and Ian Turner, saw conscription, the IWW, and industrial Labor during the period of World War I as the start of the 1940s movement.

*The third stage in the nationalist myth was the attempt in the 1940s to take over the nationalist-mateship sentiments in order to produce a new utopia, the industrialised Socialist/Marxist/ Communist paradise; this mateship-socialism was directed to quite different ends than the 1850s and 1890s ventures from which it claimed continuity.

As the writer of the article 'The New Nationalism?' (*The Bulletin*, October 5) says of Mr. Gorton's speech: 'The idea of ourselves as a nation of bushwackers became demographically unbearable and no one convincingly retranslated the rhetoric of mateship into new terms.' As a contemporary viable world-view, the 'Australian tradition' has been seen to have lapsed for at least a decade. It never had the continuity of a genuine tradition. At each stage it gained support by combining the attractions of a new form of utopia with a cashing-in on the prestige of the previous utopian vision, a vision quite contradictory to the present one. And, moreover, what appear to be attempts at pure historical assessment and interpretation within this tradition are also, and more importantly, retrospective creations of a national birth or coming-of-age.

The Australian tradition was the main attempt, but there have been many others in the compulsory activity of spotting the time when things really started here:

*The deeds of the bronzed Anzacs.

*The watershed in many areas in the later part of the 1930s after the Depression. Professor Crawford says of this period in his *An Australian Perspective*: 'Rarely indeed is one given the means of dating the coming-of-age of a new nation so precisely as they are given in this case.' Descriptions of the appearance of modern Australian intellectual, literary, and artistic life in this period are common.

*The break from Britain, as expressed in Curtin's famous wartime speech on December 27, 1941: 'Without any inhibitions of any kind, I make it quite clear that Australia looks to America, free of any pangs as to our traditional links of kinship with the United Kingdom.' As well as this, there was the fervour and purpose in getting the economic structures of the country planned and moving during the war, of which Colonel Alf Conlon became to some writers the somewhat bizarre symbol. W. W. Rostow says in *The Stages of Economic Growth* that the decisive economic 'take-off' toward full industrialisation in Australia occurred during World War II. Professor Partridge has said of the period in *Australia* (ed. Greenwood) that 'for many years it had been a cliche of Australian oratory that Australia achieved nationhood through the exploits of her troops at Gallipoli in 1915. It could be argued that World War II brought about a much more decisive advance toward national maturity; (it) led to a broadening of attitude of mind among a considerable proportion of Australians.'

*An increased intellectual sophistication in the later 1950s in a number of interconnected areas with the implication that we were now part of the world community; the fruits of this can be seen in Peter Coleman's symposium *Australian Civilisation.*

*The awakening of Australia to the world by the effects of the three As, Art, Affluence, and Asia in the 1960s. Craig McGregor's *Profile of Australia* is an example of this claim.

All these accounts are based on an independence of some sort, a break-through to freedom. They write from the point of view of the exclusive, militant group which is just on the point of success. Australian history, the past, consists of the struggle of the small, vitalising group in a hostile environment which is never defined. This follows the pattern set by Lawson:

> Sons of the South, aroused at last!
> Sons of the South are few!
> But your ranks go longer and deeper fast,
> And ye shall swell to an army vast
> And free from the wrongs of the North and Past
> The land that belongs to you.

This causes the poverty of general social critique in this country. The Australian myth interpretation, because of its exclusive interest in the existence and progress of the mateship man, completely ignored those Right-wing, Liberal, middle-class, respectable people who have been the majority group in Australia all this century at least.

In contrast with the past, the present is seen as the period of the triumph of the group; or sometimes it is seen as about to triumph; that is, the retrojection of future expectations on to the present. Thus, Mr. Gorton is reported to have said in his speech that the slow rate of change which had taken place up to and during World War II had now given way to an explosion. Each claim denies (correctly) that the ones before it were successful; this has the effect of perpetuating the vacuum. Hence, today's starters, like McGregor, denigrate and devalue our first 50 years this century (correctly) as bourgeois, conformist, and dull. But they don't describe the period in detail; their only interest in the past is to trace the embryonic activities of the lonely movement which has now burst into fruition. Each sees the period before only as a revelatory opening to a higher level, and all developments afterward are incorporated as a development of the claimant's tradition; e.g. Professor Crawford absorbs the movements of the forties and fifties into his interpretation, though they themselves claim autonomy. In each case, the future is seen as dependent on the present breakthrough; so Mr. Gorton said: 'These developments will so transform this country that in another ten or 15 years we will be more than able to play a full role in the world around us.'

The Australian myth interpretation of the vitalising role of the Labor forces in Australian life is simply the stereotype, the first and best known of all these claims. Said Randolph Bedford: 'And then I saw my first copy of *The Bulletin* and thereby entered a new world it was...Australian, whereas all the daily papers of Sydney were English provincials.' This claim also tries to assimilate later turning-points, for example, the Anzacs. When the nationalist venture failed, alternative ventures were indulged in, but the habit of announcing the start and seeking a coming-of-age, which the nationalists saw as their primary concern, continued and has gone on ever since. One inverted form of this is described by the writer of 'The New Nationalism': 'Australia was taken to have come of age to the extent that it ceased to be like itself and became instead like some other place – a mythical "Overseas".'

Recent popular books on Australia, true to the pattern, all emphasise that a significant change is just around the corner. George Johnston ends the text of *The Australians* by claiming vaguely and impressionistically that 'the smell of imminence, of things yet to happen, pervades the air'. Don Whitington in *In Search of An*

Australian hopefully detects the beginning of the new Australia in, of all events, the annual *Meanjin* v. *Overland* cricket match at Templestowe: 'Here, in the crucible of Templestowe, there could be the embryo of the Australia of tomorrow. Here, and in half a hundred, half a thousand hamlets like it around Australia, the iron is being thrust into the flames to produce a new national type.' McGregor's last sentence is: 'Australian society has become complex enough to embrace the extremes and contradictions its own strength has generated, and perhaps it is in this field that it has achieved the maturity which writers on Australia, nationalists to the last man, have forever tried to thrust on their once-colonial country.' McGregor is a nationalist himself here, though I doubt if he is the last one. Though conscious of the pattern of announcing the breakthrough, he indulges in it himself at the same time. His breakthrough, he believes, is being effected: the new, young, cool, detached, professional generation is taking over from the old, Right, conservative, illiberal, reactionary, amateurish mass.

All these claims have failed to set up something permanent and continuous in Australian life, and also to provide some continually fruitful interpretation of it. The mateship beliefs have collapsed; the Labor Party has failed in its aims; so has the meaning of Anzac. The Crawford watershed hasn't produced the goods and the directions of the Coleman symposium have not been extended. As for the current talk of the McGregor variety, it mistakes change for a new start. Of course we will be very different now from the thirties and forties: change is easy, ever-present, and inevitable. But a real tradition is something that doesn't so much change but is modified and enlarged. The mere facts of art-booms, affluence, and Asia won't necessarily make a difference. It's only if their radical ramifications are grasped that anything permanent will be effected, and there aren't many signs of this at the moment. In another ten years it will be something else.

Because of this, what we have here all the time is simply

change and nothing else. This gives Australian life its ephemeral, disjointed and dissipating quality: our history becomes a series of isolated parts, each rejecting the ones before as unsalvageable, but substituting an alternative venture of the same kind in place of it. For instance the intellectual arguments of the 1940s seem quickly dated and unrelated to the present when read now; on the other hand, the impression is given that the same sort of fruitless debate was going on then as now, that there has in this sense been no progress. The simple fact of change only is evidence against the existence of a tradition, nor for it.

In an article in *Quadrant* (2/1968) called 'Images of Australia', R.W. Connell detects similarities in all accounts of Australian life, and implies plagiarism in the authors; but it is not a matter of culpable or fraudulent borrowing, but simply of working on the same basic pattern. When Mr. Gorton claims: 'There has been a sudden explosion in this country, which has not yet reached its heights. All our old conceptions have to be reassessed,' one is entitled to wonder if this is the latest in the long line of similar pronouncements, and whether it will have the same fate as the others.

Leslie Fiedler called his book on apocalyptic movements in American literature in the past half-century *Waiting For The End*. Our position can still be called 'Waiting For The Start.' It's not that the sentiments behind the call for a new nationalism are wrong; it's that it is not likely to come through the announcement of a sudden explosion or breakthrough to a coming-of-age. In *Such is Life* Tom Collins exclaims: 'O Virgin continent. How long has she tarried her bridal day.' She may have to wait much longer than Tom Collins ever imagined.

The Bulletin, November 2, 1968

AUSTRALIAN LITERATURE THROUGH TIME AND PLACE

(1994)

A talk given to the American Association of Australian Literary Studies conference at the University of Texas in Austin.

This paper shows how different types of topography were discovered and then incorporated into Australian literature over time, and also how the idea of location was itself abandoned at a certain stage. Australia has a puzzling geographical position: is it the world's largest island or smallest continent? It is in fact a large island situated off a continent; the only analogous situation is Greenland, not an inviting comparison. Australia has little physical connection to its region. There is nothing but ocean to the south and west; the islands of the Pacific to the east are too tiny to have any meaningful relation to Australia's vast land mass, so the only link is north via New Guinea and the Indonesian archipelago, through Asia back to Europe. How did Australians, and in particular thinkers and writers, respond to this situation?

Figure 1 — Australia in Context

Fig. 1 Australia in Context

Australians first tried viewing their country as an island, and looked east, outwards towards other islands. European settlement was founded on a roughly north-south line from Brisbane to Hobart. Australia was first seen as part of a paradise in the South Seas, which was itself viewed by Europeans as a place to get away from the Old World. The beachcombers of the South Pacific were dropouts from European culture. Many nineteenth-century books on romantic adventures in the South Seas are listed in Morris Miller and F.T. Macartney's *Australian Literature: A Bibliography*. But no easy affinity existed, so the connection was dropped reasonably early – the nationalist instinct triumphed over the internationalist one in Australia during the first one-and-a-half centuries of European settlement.

Instead Australians began to see themselves as inhabiting a self-contained continent. In place of looking outward, Australians reversed the way they faced and looked inward from about the 1820s onwards. This orientation lasted for almost 150 years. Figure 2 is a diagrammatic representation of Australia's major topographical regions. We did not think of it like this today, because people came to believe in the false dichotomy, 'Sydney or the bush', as though only two types of location existed and as a result these internal differentiations were later obliterated in the Australian consciousness. But the diagram shows how different landscapes were in fact successively encountered. In addition, the outback, being as much an imagined as a real place, cannot be properly represented as a discrete geographical entity.

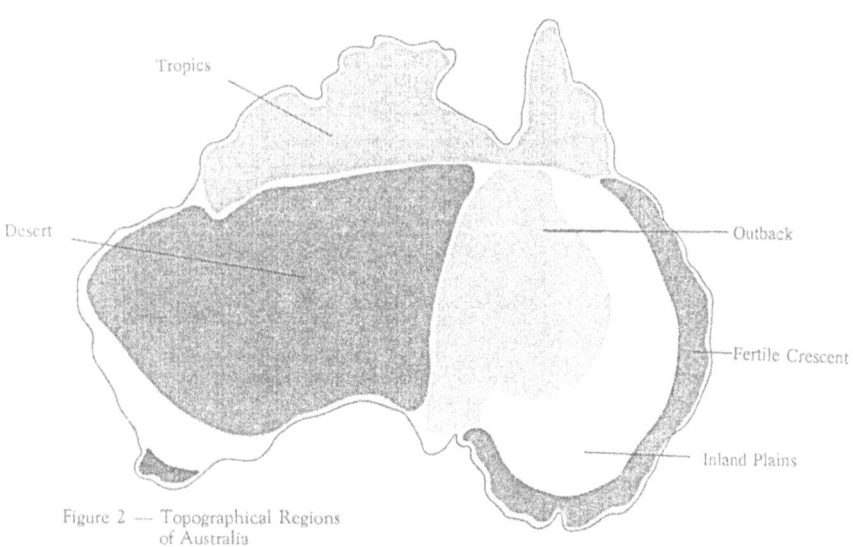

Figure 2 — Topographical Regions of Australia

Fig.2 Topographical Regions of Australia

The first region of settlement was the fertile crescent from Cairns to Adelaide, including Tasmania and the south-west corner of Western Australia. This coastal strip stretches about 100 miles inland, and, having mountains, fern gullies, and some semi-cleared areas, is very green and fertile, unlike the rest of the continent. It was familiar to the European gaze, but was seen as 'inverted' and an ancient form of the familiar. It fitted in with the ideas of the early Romantics, as we see in the poetry of Charles Harpur and Henry Kendall, a tradition which has continued but has not been in the forefront.

From the 1830s people began setting up large squatting properties, wide and independent, on the inland plains; they had not yet reached the outback. These plains were open, lightly timbered country. The gold rushes, which took place on the margin between the fertile crescent and the plains, occurred in the middle of the squatting development. Gold, which was connected with adventure, and squatting, which was connected with hard work, were temperamentally opposed developments. These tensions are apparent in some early squatting novels, such as Henry Kingsley's *The Recollections of Geoffry Hamlyn*, which is incongruously set in the fertile crescent to accommodate the romantic predilection for adventure tales that gold, bushrangers, and mountains provide.

Figure 3 — Mining and Selection

Fig 3 Mining and Selection

When alluvial gold ran out from the 1860s the diggers had a choice between settling down on selection blocks or moving on to search for gold. Some continued the life of goldfield camaraderie by becoming prospectors and fossickers, restlessly following the rush that never ended. The 'lone hand' who moves on to places like the Queensland goldfields or Kalgoorlie in the Western Australian outback, pursuing a roving life without fixed responsibilities was highlighted (perhaps dubiously) as the true Australian. Such people attained mythic status, though they were numerically not the most representative group.

Selection was the widespread movement from the middle of the 19th century onwards for ordinary people to select small blocks and establish self-sufficient family farms. It took place on the margin between the fertile crescent and the open plains. Figure 3 indicates the general area of selection in the eastern part of the continent, with the southern goldfields marked within the selection area. Those who left mining to select small farms near the diggings – the other group[apart] from the 'lone hands' – underwent an extreme psychological change; they gave up the prospect of a quick fortune amid the feverish fellowship of the goldfields, and resigned themselves to a life of long, hard, and solitary work. This majority who farmed took on a much less dramatic way of improving their lot; but as this went against the folkloric current, it was played down. The quieter life of the selector did not lend itself to romantic adventure fiction. For these reasons the yeoman farmer family was not portrayed as heroic the way it was in American literature.

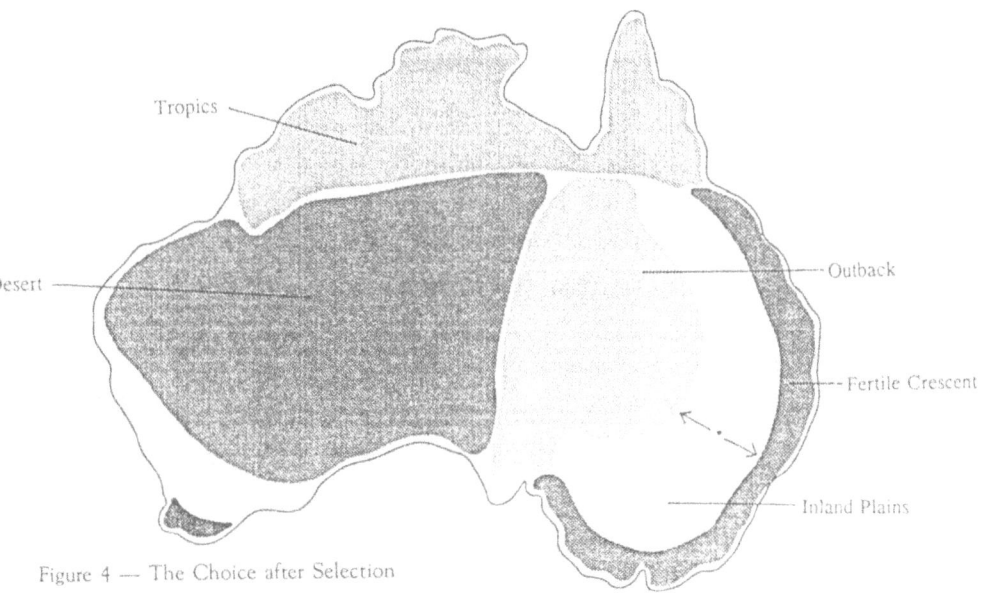

Figure 4 — The Choice after Selection

Figure 4 The Choice After Selection

Literature became involved in the great crisis when the small farms began to collapse from the 1880s and thereafter. People now had to choose to go physically in one direction or the other (see the arrows in Figure 4). We witness again a psychological choice between restlessness and settling down. The selector's sons were tempted to move out beyond the settled districts to take up the nomadic life of outback workers, and in addition to take up the bush mateship legend to compensate for their displacement. In contrast with this heroic minority, many people moved in the opposite direction toward the seaboard and continued their settled family lives in town and city, but this was less noticed. The minority reaction, freedom on the wallaby, was again highlighted and made heroic, and the majority one, settling down, was underplayed. To the extent people indulged in restlessness, they were likely to enter Australian literature. On the other hand, those who settled down were likely to enter Australian history as part of the society recognizable today.

Australians at this juncture made three crucial choices: they moved back toward the coast and the cities and settled down; they expelled the fertile crescent area, which symbolized failure, from their consciousness; and they made heroic the outback and its aura of restlessness. As Banjo Paterson wrote in 'Clancy of the Overflow': 'For the drover's life has pleasures that the townsfolk never know.' The outback was different from the plains and the fertile crescent. It was not an inverted form of the familiar, but was altogether strange. What resulted from this is a literature of tension between plain and outback, as Henry Lawson's character Mitchell and the dialogue in 'The Banks of the Condamine' reveal. Here were those who moved further out, the flotsam and jetsam left over after the collapse of the small farms. The new literary vogue of realism was able to accommodate this still, monotonous, unadventurous life much better than previous romantic modes.

The outback came to mean moving further away, further out, beyond, inward. It was moving towards nothing, to a place where people, places, nature, objects thin out. Unlike the United States, there is no east-west connection on the Australian continent; nor, except for the fertile crescent, is there a north-south one, as the failure of the Burke and Wills expedition revealed. The outback is, as Lawson pointed out, an endless expanse of ragged, stunted trees, which provides no point on which to focus. It became an image of nothingness. But for the restless minority, it represented a physical movement inward and away from the restrictions of civilization. For most Australians in the cities it became a matter of psychologically escaping, the old South Pacific ideal now applied internally. The initial migratory urge to drop out continued, but was now applied not just to Europe but to life in Australia itself. The outback became, not a location, but any place that was farther out, beyond the Black Stump.

The result was that Australians lost a sense of location. They saw their country as a blank, except for its outline. Schoolchildren had plastic

Figure 5 — Australia as Outline

Fig. 5 Australia as Outline

maps of the continent, which were used to draw an outline, without Tasmania. These maps had written on them: 'Note. Tasmania to be drawn free hand'. That is because the image had to be symmetrical, enclosed, in a vacuum. There could be no Papua New Guinea either. This outline became a national icon. The continent has a beautiful shape, irregular yet balanced, and roughly symmetrical about its north-south and east-west axes. Its two more angular protuberances to the north pointing to the rest of the world are balanced by the flatter bottom ones on which it rests. The continent was imagined as having no internal configurations or relations; it was monolithic, uniform, unvaried in the imagination. It was enclosed by its outline, and there was no opening to the outside world. It did not orient itself to adjacent land masses. It floated in a vacuum, cut off from the north and the rest of the world by an ocean, as in the line from

Australia's national anthem: 'our home is girt by sea.' This was the final national form of escape. Its personal analogy was the deflating, self-deprecating humour of the bush. This comparatively recent obliteration of internal differentiation was also projected onto the past, as though it had always existed.

By the 1940s and 1950s the outback had become an overplayed image, and more remote and exotic areas – the tropics, the desert, and the south seas – began to appear instead in the work of Xavier Herbert, Ion Idriess, Frank Clune, and Olaf Ruhen, and in painting as well. The inward-looking spell was broken by the 1960s, and Asia, the north, became the new place that was both exotic and defeating for Australians.

Antipodes, December, 1994

THE CAMARADERIE OF NOT CARING

(2007)

Henry Lawson's life and writings reveal a picture at some odds with his received image.

The legend of Henry Lawson which arose after his death was that of a man who had been there at the birth of the nation in the great days of the *Bulletin*, and who had partly created it himself. It was Lawson the depicter of rabble-rousing republicanism, of back-blocks camaraderie, and of mateship nationalism. The legend became part of the larger triumph of the Nineties. But we get a very different picture if we look at Lawson's own life and writing unimpeded by later impressions. In addition we now have available his journalism, reprinted in *Autobiographical and Other Writings 1887-1922*, edited by Colin Roderick, which throws light on what he actually thought. Lawson was representative, but more representative of the collapses than the successes in Australian life.

His father set up a small selection in poor goldfields country in the Mudgee-Gulong district to the north-west of Sydney. There Henry Lawson was born in a tent, and as a young boy he experienced the struggles of the small selectors as their farms and lives disintegrated. His parents eventually separated, and Lawson and his mother joined the drift to the cities. In a piece of journalism 'Straight Talk' published in 1890, he recognised this as a general social shift.

It was in his very earliest stories that Lawson comes closer than anyone to recreating this situation. 'The Union Buries Its Dead' shows how impoverished the routines of daily living become for those in the bush. Though it purports to be about the man who is being buried, the story really focuses on the dead souls of the living. The characters have to do two opposite things. They have to go along to the funeral as they crave companionship, but they also have to suppress the meaning of the funeral. A certain psychological adroitness is necessary to manage both. The mourners are going through elaborate devices to stop themselves having any feelings about the death of the young man. They are adept at anaesthetizing their emotions, which is how they survive in the bush. One device they use is to undercut any possible meaning which may arise: 'The departed was a 'Roman', and the majority of the town were otherwise – but unionism is strong than creed. Drink, however, is stronger than unionism.' Mateship here is the camaraderie of those who are past caring. The pretences have to be kept up, but feelings and understanding have long since gone. Burlesque behaviour diverts them from the emptiness of it all, as well as perpetuating that emptiness. Lawson's great triumph as a writer is that he can show how demoralizing this is.

In both 'The Union Buries Its Dead' and 'The Bush Undertaker' the main characters act simply for something to do. They have to find some way of passing the time in the dreadful vacuous stillness they inhabit. Bush life provided no natural patterns of communal activity, like folk festivals in peasant societies, so artificial highlights had to be created to satisfy a longing for sociability and ceremony. The characters have to do things, but at the same time to empty them of meaning, which is quite a feat. The 'mourners' go to the funeral out of curiosity: it is a rare event, a happening which makes this day special. It marks out their life, like a milepost on a lonely road. Similarly the bush undertaker has his Christmas day made when he finds a dead mate: it gives him some novel way of occupying the time. When he comes across the body he says: 'Me luck's in for the day and no mistake!' And then he reflects: 'I ain't a-spendin' sech a dull Christmas arter all'. In both cases they use incidents, not for their meaning and content, but for their excitement. It keeps them going. Hence the inverted humour of death being lucky.

In a *Bulletin* article 'Crime in the Bush', Lawson wrote of the effect of loneliness and monotony on bush people, and described how, after years together, a man will sometimes murder his mate for no explicable reason. Trying to explain this and other equally strange occurrences, Lawson wrote:

> Such crimes as those just instanced, and worse, might be described as the ultimate result of a craving for variety – for something better or brighter, perhaps, but, anyway, something *different* – the protest of the outraged nature of the black or white savage against the – to him – unnatural conditions.

Lawson's bush characters live in isolation: the bush undertaker, the drover's wife. They live without a society: this is the essential element that is missing and it drives many to eccentricity. The bush undertaker is an extreme version of the totally self-sufficient farmer gradually becoming a mad hatter. He creates an artificial society around him by talking to his dog, his sheep, his dead friend and to the goannas, as though engaging in dialogue.

In the bush the main society-substitute is the small family of the father (if present), mother and children. They form a unit which has to satisfy all human needs. But a family can't perform the functions of a society. Lawson's stories are often about the sadness of the family break-up. The family is meant to be a possible relief from a society-less country. But in fact it becomes the occasion of more sadness as it disintegrates. Andy's gone to cattle. Mrs. Baker has to be deceived. The drover's wife is being destroyed by the absence of her husband – her children aren't enough to keep her going. Her moving and pathetic habits, such as gazing at the fashion plates of the *Young Ladies' Journal* and dressing up to go for a walk through the lonely bush on Sundays, are memories of a companionable society which she plainly needs but which is no longer available. In the bush the family collapses because it lacks sustenance from sources outside itself.

The feeling in these stories comes from the agonies of young love and courtship, from members of the family leaving home or being absent, and from death. The characters often find these feelings unbearable in their naked form, and they are covered up in various ways, as in the Jack Cornstalk series:

> He 'sheds no tears on leaving home' – if he can help it; but, perhaps, something comes over father suddenly, as he goes through the novel ceremony of shaking hands with his boy – he turns away abruptly, and, in short, 'acts queer'; and mother's drawn, sunburnt face pales a shade, and her haggard eyes fill involuntarily – for the first time in years, perhaps. These things move young Jack to hammer more vigorously with a stick on the gable end of the old horse, and to fling his heels wildly against the sides in his hurry to get a start in the rusty machinery inside. Maybe his instinct tells him that what's out of sight in happily out of the minds of both parties (to a great extent) in the bush.

In his early stories Lawson shows how the habit of not showing your feelings increases the absence and loss; in the later stories Lawson himself indulges in the same sentimental evasion.

In Lawson's stories people like Jack Cornstalk, who leave farms in the settled districts, usually head further outback to take up jobs such as droving. In some of the best known Mitchell stories, such as 'On the Edge of the Plain', 'Some Day' and 'Another of Mitchell's Plans', the narrator rationalizes his present situation with the belief that settling down is somehow limiting. But at the same time he regretfully reminisces about lost opportunities of getting married or of returning home. In a crucial passage Mitchell senses he has missed out on something – the man he might have been, but wasn't – and that freedom the wallaby isn't all that it's cracked up to be:

> 'I suppose', said Mitchell's mate, as they drank their tea, 'I suppose you'll go back and marry her some day?' 'Some day! That's it; it looks like it, doesn't it? We all say, 'Some day'. I used to say it ten years ago, and look at me now. I've been knocking round for five

years, and the last two years constant on the track, and no show of getting off it unless I go for good, and what have I got for it? I look like going home and getting married, without a penny in my pocket or rag to my back scarcely, and no show of getting them. I swore I'd never go back home without a cheque, and, what's more, I never will; but the cheque days are past. Look at that boot! If we were down among the settled districts we'd be called tramps and beggars; and what's the difference? I've been a fool, I know, but I've paid for it; and now there's nothing for it but to tramp, tramp, tramp for your tucker, and keep tramping till you get old and careless and dirty, and older, and more careless and dirtier, and you get used to the dust and sand, and heat, and flies, and mosquitoes, same as a bullock does, and lose ambition and hope, and get contented with this animal life, like a dog, and till your swag seems part of yourself, and you'd be lost and uneasy and light-shouldered without it; and you don't care a damn if you'll ever get work again, or live like a Christian; and you go on like this till the spirit of a bullock takes the place of the heart of a man. Who cares?

Mitchell felt compelled to take up the roving life, but in this rare moment of insight and frankness, he knows he has made the wrong choice. Life on the track is heroicized in bush lore, but awful in reality. Leading this life means you lose your human qualities, you 'lose ambition and hope, and get contented with this animal life'. This is one form of deprivation, the deadening of normal feelings. The other form of deprivation is suppressing the realization of it. As his magnificent diatribe against the wretchedness of his condition mounts to its climax, Mitchell attempts to deny his own instant of self-knowledge by the standard demolishing shrug 'Who cares?'. The answer to this question is that Mitchell does, but only on the rare occasions when he can momentarily acknowledge it. Such remorseful reflections are always abruptly terminated – they can't be entertained for too long.

The Joe Wilson series was an attempt by Lawson, as his own life became more unsatisfactory and remorse was beginning to set in, to imaginatively create the ideal small-farm life of a character who is a surrogate for Lawson-without-his-faults. But even here he can't sustain the idyll and the familiar human weaknesses creep in as the story progresses. The latter part of the series is important for its portraits of two women, Brighten's sister-in-law and Mrs. Spicer, who have got 'past carin'. Through drudgery and isolation, they are in a much more advanced state of exhaustion than the drover's wife. Lawson gives very different psychological profiles to his men and women characters. The men are personally weak and often have a past they are escaping from. They are withdrawn, uncomfortable in family life and attracted to the life of wandering around. A certain unreality of character enables them to preserve an attractive external bravado. The women, stronger and more resilient, try to control events, or at least endure them. The trying conditions of outback life cause them to become weather-beaten and worn-out, with a tough masculine appearance. In the short term, women survive better than men, but eventually both collapse, the men because of inherent weaknesses, the women because of the strain and solitude of bush life. They have to fill all roles, including that of the father, without support, which proves impossible.

In Lawson's early journalist pieces we find statements that are quite the opposite of those identified with him in the public mind. In 'The City and the Bush' Lawson inveighs against the intolerance and narrowness that shearers display to anything outside their own domain. As he says 'A shearing shed and a pound a hundred is not the end of all things'. Lawson describes in some detail how a young man from the city is mocked daily in the shed to make him conform to the shearers' ways. Lawson vehemently opposes such initiation rituals, since:

> when they get hardened, (they) mostly treat others as they themselves have been treated. This is a cowardly custom, because the victim is generally unable to defend himself. It does no good; it only brutalises men. I can see nothing in it but ignorant brutality. It might be said that such a course of treatment is necessary to 'make a man' of a green-

hand – or, as bushmen say, to take the 'trimmings off of him'. But, judging by results, God help such 'manliness'! I'd prefer a man with the 'trimmings' left on.

The 'trimmings' were the normal feelings and sensitivities of people. When these were brutally removed, people became 'hardened' and it was this 'manliness' or exaggerated masculinity which was so admired in the bush. Manliness meant the deadening of feelings: 'The spirit of a bullock takes the place of the heart of a man'. The young Lawson was a sensitive, 'feminine' personality in a rough society which boosted such manliness. The Lawson who wrote 'God help such 'manliness'!' is the opposite of the Lawson-as-mateship-promoter legend. In another article 'The Bush and the Ideal' Lawson showed he was aware of the over-optimism of the much-vaunted bush nationalist literature.

How was it that Lawson, who so clearly saw the deficiencies of mateship nationalism, was later to be regarded as its exemplar and champion? This strange turn-about was due firstly to Lawson himself becoming 'past carin'' and turning for comfort to the mateship he had earlier been critical of. And secondly it was due to his followers projecting the sentiments of this later Lawson back on to his earlier stories. From a comparatively early age Lawson felt the pressure of facing the horror of the bush and recreating it in fiction as intolerable, and he came to adopt evasions analogous to those of the outback inhabitants he describes in his stories. This is first seen in the paragraph which is the climax of 'The Union Buries Its Dead'. Here Lawson describes the thoughts that run through the narrator's mind as the unknown man is buried:

Our grave-digger was not altogether bowelless, and, out of respect for the human quality described as 'feelin's', he scraped up some light and dusty soil and threw it down to deaden the fall of the clay lumps on the coffin. He also tried to steer the first few shovelfuls gently down against the end of the grave with the back of the shovel turned outwards, but the hard, dry Darling River clods rebounded and knocked all the same.

It didn't matter much – nothing does. The fall of lumps of clay on a stranger's coffin doesn't sound any different from the fall of the same things on an ordinary wooden box – at least I didn't notice anything awesome or unusual in the sound; but, perhaps, one of us – the most sensitive – might have been impressed by being reminded of a burial of long ago, when the thump of every sod jolted his heart.

The narrator (closely identified with Lawson himself) takes the same attitude as the characters in the story. He does things 'out of respect for that human quality described as 'feelin's'', but he has long ago lost feelings himself. Like the new chum in the shearing shed, he's had the trimmings knocked off him. Once, he remembers, he had feelings at funerals, but not now. He too has been hardened; he too is now one of the dead souls watching the funeral. When the question of meaning arises he undercuts it too, just as his characters, like Mitchell, do: 'It didn't matter much – nothing does.' He accepts the deadening of his soul; he is 'past carin''. Lawson is now a victim, an example of this attitude as well as its recorder. This was his own way of surviving.

Lawson's youthful experiences on the farm and in Sydney were gloomy, and his one trip to the outback increased this. When one adds to this his naturally melancholic temperament, his addiction to alcohol, the failure of his trip to London and the breakdown of his marriage, the tragic collapse of his later years comes to seem inevitable. His experiences and his personality reinforced each other, so that it all became too much for him. His acute understanding of the terrible things that were happening to people in Australia made him more depressed, and that depression deepened the gloom, so that in the end the two elements became inextricably mixed.

After the early stories Lawson never again wrote with the same intense focus on the horror of the bush. Unfortunately he adopted certain comforting devices against a naked exposure to it. He admitted as much in an unpublished article in 1913:

Mark the beginning of self-conceit, or self-pity, or degeneration – or my decadence! I had lost the thunder – both far and near – the mighty

142

sympathy, the splendid crudity, and the sledge-hammer force of
simplicity of that lonely boy's song, both in prose and verse. I had
found drink and comradeship and comparative happiness – I found
Mateship later on.

In Lawson's case the normal progression from hope to
disillusionment is reversed. In his early work he knew how harsh and
destructive life in the bush was. Later on he turned to the consolations
of nationalism to cover up this early sadness and to pretend that there
were great hopes for Australia still. He took up mateship, which he
had discounted earlier, as a comforter. This gave his later work and
his poetry a facile optimism. He turned to the past as a golden age,
the days of the goldfields, Ballarat, Eureka, the days when the world
was wide. The old themes were reworked with different emphases
and with diminishing results, as Brian Matthews shows in his book on
Lawson *The Receding Wave*. The atmosphere became saturated with
sentimentality and remorse, states in which he lost the ability to have
specific emotions, and just felt vaguely emotional about everything.
The narrator, or Lawson-surrogate, increasingly succumbed to
nostalgia and self-pity.

It was this later and lesser Lawson who became the subject of the
legend, and a source of self-congratulation to successive generations
of Australians. The public took up a Lawson who was convenient to
them, the comforting and relatively pressureless Lawson who praised
bush mateship. The sentiments of the later writings were transferred
back to his earlier stories which they did not fit. As a result Australians
for many decades misread the early stories in such a way that the
stark horror was evaded. 'The Union Buries Its Dead' was seen as
a celebration of bush and union solidarity, and the anthology piece
'The Drover's Wife' was read as praise of the heroic efforts of the
outback wife. Brian Matthews is much closer to the truth when he
describes the latter story as one not of pioneering steadfastness, but
of slow human disintegration. People saw the more optimistic side of
Lawson, because that is what they wanted to see; those parts which

fitted in with the Australian legend were emphasized and coloured all the stories, and the more melancholy and depressed parts were ignored. In this way the most priceless legacy of Lawson, his portrayal of reality in the bush, was diminished in the Australian consciousness.

Lawson disliked the present, believing things got worse all the time as you grew up: 'Make the most of your courting days, you young chaps, and keep them clean, for they're about the only days when there's a chance of poetry and beauty coming into this life'. A feeling of not wanting to advance or investigate things obtrudes – any adult experience is a form of despoliation which pollutes the personality. To grow up was to get oneself involved in that wearying and inevitably disappointing struggle with greed, strife and the other complexities of adult life. Like Mitchell, people in Lawson are often frozen in a posture of adolescent restlessness, which they increasingly regret but cannot break away from. This emphasis on innocence and against experience meant that Lawson reworked his original themes rather than successfully developing new ones. Like the bush families, he was cut off – he had no outlets and no new sources of life. In some of his poems he softened the suffering of the past, in contrast to his early stories:

> They carry in their swags, perhaps,
>   A portrait and a letter –
> And, maybe, deep down in their hearts,
>   The hope of 'something better'.
> Where lonely miles are long to ride,
>   And all days seem recurrent,
> There's lots of time to think of men
>   They might have been – but weren't.

This is pressureless mythmaking: the facile mateship, the sentimental letters, the vague hope of 'something better', the hurtless remorse of the 'men they might have been – but weren't'.

These escape routes were temporary and never solved Lawson's problems. Furphy was able to lose himself in contemplating the balmy strangeness of the Riverina plains. No such way was possible for Lawson. All he could do was to sentimentalize the horrors he had once rendered so starkly:

> Now up and down the siding brown
>   The great black crows are flyin',
> And down below the spur, I know,
>   Another 'milker's' dyin';
> The crops have withered from the ground,
>   The tank's clay bed is glaring,
> But from my heart no tear nor sound,
>   For I have gone past carin' –
>   Past worryin' or carin',
>   Past feelin' aught or carin';
>   But from my heart no tear nor sound,
>   For I have gone past carin'.

In this vignette of the small farm collapse – the cows dying and the children also, the husband gone shearing – the exemplary Lawson story is retold but without the earlier atmospheric directness. The emotions are glazed over with self-pity, and a giving-up has long since been accommodated.

The idea that you could anaesthetize yourself and believe that nothing matters was given a spurious legitimacy in Australia by reference to Lawson. His later writings were such a jumble of vague attitudes that almost anything could be justified in his name. And as his actual presence receded in time, he was regarded as a distant saint, who went through it on behalf of us all. His early prose writing is a priceless legacy of a crucial experience which nobody else was able to capture. Now we see it as it was, and this has increased his reputation. The fact that he couldn't keep it up for long can be explained by the tension between the hopes he had and the horror he felt, a tension which eventually tore him apart. Nobody wants to blame him for this. But by giving his work a legendary status, both a national giving-up and a spurious national success story were legitimized.

Quadrant, November, 2007

AUSTRALIA'S IRISH PROTESTANT NOVELISTS

(2003)

A neglected aspect of Irish Australian literature.

The eight most prominent Australian novelists from the 1880s to the 1940s were Rolf Boldrewood, Joseph Furphy, Norman Lindsay, Henry Handel Richardson, Mary Grant Bruce, Katharine Susannah Prichard, Vance Palmer and Martin Boyd. A remarkable thing is that all eight novelists came from Irish Protestant backgrounds, a minority tradition in Ireland, and even more so in Australia. They were Irish Protestant on the paternal side, except for Prichard and Palmer. In Furphy's case both parents were from that background. In addition, Vance Palmer and Mary Grant Bruce married into Irish Protestant families, and both their spouses, Nettie Palmer and Major George Bruce, became accomplished writers.

Thomas Browne (1826-1915), alias 'Rolf Boldrewood', came from a Protestant Galway family who arrived in Australian in 1831. Here they changed their name from Brown to Browne because the latter was more aristocratic in Ireland. But in his recent biography of Boldrewood, Paul de Serville has revealed the family, including Boldrewood himself, concealed the fact that they were illegitimately descended from William O'Flaherty, a Galway doctor whose religious affiliation is unclear. Boldrewood's mother was English.

The parents of Joseph Furphy (1843-1912), Samuel and Jane Furphy, came to Australia in 1841 from county Armagh as bounty emigrants. The Furphy family was perhaps originally Scots, and had longstanding connections with the Orange cause. They were farmers and weavers, poor and struggling. His mother, Jane Hare, also came from tenant farming stock. The parents were married in a Scots church in Armagh.

Henry Handel Richardson (1870-1946) was a daughter of Walter Richardson, born in Dublin and trained in medicine at the University of Edinburgh. The Richardsons were part of the Protestant ascendancy; members of the family had in past generations been landed gentry, clergy and military officers from the Ulster counties, particularly Tyrone. Walter Richardson came to Australia as a physician in 1852 and here married Mary Bailey, who was English.

Norman Lindsay (1879-1969) had a similar background, being a son of Robert Lindsay, an Irish-born surgeon from Londonderry, trained at the University of Glasgow. The Lindsay family, who were originally Scots from Ayrshire, had migrated to Tyrone and were prominent in the linen trade. Dr Lindsay emigrated to Melbourne in 1864 and moved to Creswick. His wife Elizabeth was a daughter of Rev. Thomas Williams, a Wesleyan missionary of Welsh descent who spent some time in Fiji.

Lewis Eyre Bruce, the father of Mary Grant Bruce (1878-1958), was an Irish Protestant surveyor who arrived in Australia in 1859. The family, of distant Scots background, were gentry in Cork with some clergy connections. Mary married her second cousin, Major George Bruce; they had a common great grandfather, Rev. Jonathon Bruce of Miltown Castle, County Cork. Major Bruce wrote four books for adolescents as well as other works. Mary Grant Bruce's mother was from the Whittakers' squatting family, who were of Welsh stock.

Katharine Susannah Prichard (1883-1969) was born in Fiji, where her father, Thomas Prichard, was a newspaper editor. He had arrived with his family in Port Phillip in 1852. His wife was Edith Isabel Fraser, whose father was Simon Lovat Fraser. This family was originally Scots, but Simon Lovat Fraser was raised in County Clare, Ireland, the son of a doctor. He also came to the Port Phillip district in 1852. Katharine Susannah Prichard wrote of him: 'Grandfather Fraser talked with an Irish brogue, the melody of which I've never forgotten. And he liked to call himself an Irishman'. He was buried as a member of the Church of England.

Vance Palmer (1885-1959) was born at Bundaberg. His father, Henry Burnet Palmer, was an Australian-born schoolmaster in Queensland country towns. His mother was Jessie Carson, the daughter of a Dublin bookseller. Palmer described his maternal grandmother telling stories of 'tiny, green-coated people who came out by moonlight to play tricks on farmers. I did not believe there were any fairies in the world about me, but I was firmly convinced they lurked behind every clump of bushes in this Ireland grandmother had left behind'. Vance married Nettie Higgins (1885-1964), daughter of the Irishman John Higgins, a Baptist, and Catherine McDonald. Her grandfather was Rev John Higgins, a Church of Ireland minister from County Down, and father of Justice Henry Bournes Higgins of the Harvester case fame.

Martin Boyd (1893-1972) came from a family of Scots background who had settled in County Mayo in the 18th century. In 1843 his grandfather, Lt John Theodore Boyd, came to Van Diemen's Land with his regiment. Boyd was stationed in Melbourne in 1854 as Assistant Military Secretary to the Acting Governor. After an interlude in New Zealand, he returned to live in Melbourne. Martin Boyd's father was Arthur Merric Boyd and his mother Emma Minnie á Beckett of the prominent Melbourne family

All eight novelists were born in Australia except Boldrewood, who was only five when he arrived, and Prichard, born in Fiji while her father was a newspaper editor there. All lived long lives, averaging over 80, with Norman Lindsay reaching 90. Seven of the eight were Victorians, Vance Palmer being the exception, coming from Queensland. The Protestant Irish were particularly strong in early Victoria, where they formed close-knit cousinage groups, of which Boldrewood was a part. In spite of this, there is no evidence that any of the eight families knew each other in Ireland or here at the level of the parents' generation.

With the exception of the Furphys, who were Presbyterian tenant farmers, these families came from the educated professional classes. Medicine is present in four (Boldrewood, Richardson, Lindsay and Prichard); clergy, army and rural gentry are other common occupations in earlier generations. A remote Scots background (Prichard, Boyd, Bruce, Furphy, Lindsay) exists in five of them, but only two (Furphy and Lindsay) come directly from Ulster. Of the others, two each derive from the Munster, Connaught and Leinster (Dublin) provinces.

A surprising thing is how little interest the eight novelists took in Ireland, and how little they wrote on it. Boldrewood and Mary Grant Bruce made trips to Ireland, and the main Irish references in their works are partly autobiographical. Boldrewood was conscious of being part of the Irish cousinage in Victoria and sometimes refers to it in his essays, but his novels reveal that England became his point of reference and influence. His novel *My Run Home* (1897), a lightly fictionalized account of his trip of 1860, is set in England and Ireland, but the main character, Boldrewood, presents himself as from an ancient Hampshire family. A third of the novel is set in Galway, but he describes it as an outsider and never reveals this is his ancestral countryside. Mary Grant Bruce's novel *Jim and Wally* (1916) is set in Ireland in world war one, following her own sojourn in Ireland at that time. In some of her novels, Irish Australians appear as minor characters favourably depicted.

The Fortunes of Richard Mahony follows biographical lines in regard to Richardson's father, but does not dwell on Ireland. Furphy has two or three pages in chapter two of *Such is Life* recounting Catholic-Protestant animosities in Ireland, derived from his reading of the historian W.E.H. Lecky's book *A History of Ireland in the Eighteenth Century*. Martin Boyd has an oblique reference to Irish ancestry in *Outbreak of Love* where a character believes 'the Teutonic English...are dreadful unless modified by Celtic or Latin blood'. I know of nothing on Ireland by Lindsay, Prichard or Palmer.

Perhaps the lack of interest in Ireland was because they came from a minority tradition, which although strong in the generations of their parents and grandparents didn't take in Australia. Australian writers of Irish Catholic descent have written prolifically on Ireland, from 'Frank the Poet' McNamara through to Vincent Buckley and Thomas Keneally. For Anglo-Australians like Boldrewood and Bruce, both Australia and England became their source countries. For Boyd, Lindsay and Richardson, Europe was a great influence. For Furphy, Prichard and Palmer, it was Australia which basically fulfilled that role.

Táin, Feb-March, 2003

THE OTHER MARY GRANT BRUCE

(2010)

As with Lawson, a closer inspection of Mary Grant Bruce reveals aspects of her writing and personality which don't entirely fit with her public reputation.

Mary Grant Bruce is firmly settled in the public mind as the author of children's novels about the Linton family of Billabong, set in an idyllic Riverina-like setting. The little bush maid Norah grows up on the wide expanses of a prosperous grazing property. Though there are necessary villains and escapades in the stories, the respectable and hard-working Lintons, exemplars of the British-Australian values admired at the time, triumph in the inevitable happy endings. The novels are written in a determinedly matter-of-fact style – no tragedies or doubts or speculation on the larger meaning of things are allowed to intrude. This was the persona the author herself presented to the public. Mary Grant Bruce was a strong, assertive woman, with her husband unknown to the public. She was one of the very few Australian writers able to support her family on book royalties between the wars.

All this is true, but masks another side of her personality obscured by the exigencies of the publishing trade at the time. She wanted to write serious adult novels reflecting the hardships she saw around her in central Gippsland as she grew up during the 1890s depression. These novels would describe the world more as it was, rather than as a wish-fulfilment version of reality, but she was trapped by the great success of the Billabong novels. The public response to *A Little Bush Maid* and the early Billabong novels was overwhelming and led her publisher, Ward Lock of London, to encourage her to continue the Billabong series. For three decades, from 1910 to 1942, she turned out on an average one book a year – Billabong novels alternated with non-Billabong ones. Some of the non-Billabong novels are stories of the tragic struggles of small farmers; her own family life was marred by a dual tragedy. But the non-Billabong novels did not sell well, so she was forced to continue the Billabong series (fifteen novels in all) to satisfy public demand and keep the family finances afloat.

Five of her novels have Gippsland locations, but are not as well known as her Billabong series: *Glen Eyre* (1912), *'Possum* (1917), *Robin* (1926), *Anderson's Jo* (1927), and *Golden Fiddles* (1928). *Karalta* (1941), based on a locality similar to Philip Island where she holidayed, may be counted as a sixth. She also wrote a collection of Aboriginal legends called *The Stone Axe of Burkamukk* (1922), which includes some Gippsland tales. Her small farm novels are opposite in most respects to her Billabong ones; they have tragic not happy endings, they are serious adult not adolescent stories, they are set on isolated dairying hill farms, not on open flat grazing country, and the approach is more realistic than idealized.

Glen Eyre, probably her best work, is a study of the life of a father running a failing family dairy farm in the south Gippsland hills. Angus Ogilvie, a hard Scot, loses his first wife after their son Martin is born, and then loses his second wife after further children, Nancy and Rob, are born. Living on an isolated hill farm, he is gruff and taciturn, bottling things up so that he becomes withdrawn and silent. The daily grind has wearied him and he finds it hard to continue. The novel may be to some extent a transposed portrait of Mary's father, whose second name was Eyre (the novel is dedicated to him), and whose life had not been as successful as the squatting family into which he had married.

Possum was partly written at Metung where the author holidayed. A Melbourne family with a sickly boy move to recuperate on a farm on the Gippsland lakes near Lakes Entrance. The central figure, the girl next door nicknamed 'Possum, is a wild but engaging tomboy figure who has great bushcraft skills and leads the town boy (and the reader) on a series of adventures around the lakes: fishing, boating trips, a regatta, visiting a black's camp, and horse rides through the bush. The Melbourne family improve their block until it conforms to the self-sufficient small farm ideal. The city-bush tension works both ways, the boy recovers his health through outdoor living, and 'Possum becomes more refined under the civilizing influence of the middle-class Melbourne family.

In *Robin*, the eponymous girl hero of the novel helps her mother run the family hill farm after her father and uncle die. Robin is a typical Mary Grant Bruce tomboy, boyish, mischievous but straight and lively, an expert in the bush, high-spirited, reckless and daring. By living on rabbits, fish, vegetables, and the produce of cows and pigs, the self-sufficient small farm ideal is once again achieved. Robin teaches a Melbourne boy Barry and his family about bush ways à la 'Possum. In *Anderson's Jo* a widower, John Anderson, is left alone on a Gippsland hill farm with an orphan girl, Jo, whose mother has died. Jo cheers him up and lifts him out of his unsociability by her nature. Delightful, wilful, full of life, independent, quicksilver, she is the hero and central character of the novel.

In *Golden Fiddles* an impoverished family on a Gippsland selection block is relieved of its misery by being left a fortune in an uncle's will. They go to Melbourne, but make the mistake of wasting their money in the flapper society of the 1920s – Mary Grant Bruce thought city life artificial and decadent. The family is not accepted by Melbourne society, even though they have money. Finally they make the sensible decision to buy a large sheep station in the Western District, a Billabong-like property. In her novels isolated small farms and cities are to be avoided in favour of the more expansive and sociable grazing life of the Western District or the Riverina. These five Gippsland books did not sell anywhere near as well as the Billabong series, with its iconic title, and so are not familiar to many readers.

The two different kinds of novels derive partly from the social situation of the Bruce family. Mary, christened Minnie Bruce, was descended on her mother's side from a pioneering squatting family, the Whittakers of Tubbut, a remote property in east Gippsland on the NSW-Victorian border. Her father, an Irish surveyor named Lewis Eyre Bruce, met and married Mary's mother, improving his station in life. The Whittakers family moved down to a property near Traralgon; one Whittakers uncle managed the legendary 'Hungry' Tyson's wealthy property at Heyfield nearby; another branch of the Whittakers moved to Deniliquin in the Riverina. Mary's family lived first at Sale, then later at Traralgon. The Bruce family were badly affected by the financial crash of the 1890s, as her father lost his surveying position and had to work as a lawyers' clerk. Her family was slipping out of the squatting life to which it had been accustomed, and it may have been nostalgia for this that stimulated Mary to imagine the idealized pastoral life of Billabong. During her childhood holidays she visited her uncles at Traralgon and at Heyfield; it was at Heyfield that she began writing. Her uncle Edward Whittakers is probably one model for the father, Mr Linton, in the Billabong books, as we recognize from this description of him in Harry Peck's *Memoirs of a Stockman*:

> Edward, lean of flesh and straight in posture, word and business, was the first citizen of the Traralgon district for many years…He was generally revered throughout Gippsland for, although of a retiring disposition, he was most emphatic in his opinions, his word was his bond and all acknowledged it…Of all the pastoralists of my knowledge he was the first to be out of the blankets and at work in all seasons and in all weathers. As a horseman his seat was a model, as upright as his straight-going life.

Mary was aware of the plight of the ordinary selectors around her and that of her own family. The Billabong novels are therefore counter-autobiographical; they are a species of wish-fulfilment of the ideal squatting life, which was not possible for her and her family as it dropped out of the squatting circle.

The family in a Mary Grant Bruce novel has a number of unusual and interconnected structural features. One parent is often missing, the mother in the Billabong series and in *Anderson's Jo*, the father in *Robin,* and the failing and psychologically absent father in *Glen Eyre*. The absence of a parent means that one of the children, always a daughter, steps up a generation to prematurely act out the role of adult, as Norah does, and as the assured and responsible Robin does in helping her mother to run their dairy farm. Anderson's daughter Jo likewise becomes a surrogate wife to her step-father. The daughter foregoes adolescence and becomes precociously adult. On the level of the children, the girl usually takes the lead over her brothers, often becoming a tomboy, like 'Possum and Robin, or at least adopting a somewhat male role – Robin and Jo have masculine names. This double changeover – sibling exchanges in gender roles and over generations – may reflect circumstances in Mary's own family. Her elder brother Patrick, two years older than Mary, was killed in a tragic shooting accident when she was seven, and she most likely felt she had to fill his role in the family, and to compensate for her father's reduced circumstances. In the novels women are the movers and shakers. This also reflects Mary's family circumstances, where the forceful Whittakers women were more assertive than the milder Bruce men. Mary devoted an article to praising them: 'The Women Who Made Us', and included her baptismal name Grant, her Whittakers grandmother's maiden name, as part of her author's name.

After a promising school career, Mary moved to Melbourne around the turn of the twentieth century. She became an independent woman, unusual at the time, developing a career as a journalist in Melbourne. She wrote both for adults and for children, and both fiction and reportage. One serialized story, 'A Little Bush Maid', became so popular that it was published in book form, and began the Billabong series. Following the early success of her Billabong books, Mary went to work as a journalist in London in 1913. On a trip to Ireland she met her father's brothers Richard and Charles, the latter being the Protestant Dean of Cork. Here she was introduced to Major George Bruce, a second cousin eleven years older than herself. They soon became engaged. The Bruce family were Anglo-Irish gentry of distant Scots background who had been living in County Cork since the 1650s. The family seat was Miltown Castle, where George had been brought up. He and Mary had a great grandfather, Rev Jonathon Bruce of Miltown Castle, in common.

Mary's husband was not a dependent old duffer, as was sometimes imagined, but an accomplished journalist as well as a military officer. Both were writers of adventure stories for adolescents, though Mary's are much better known than his. George Bruce published four novels based on his experiences with the British Army in India. Born in 1867, he revelled in shooting and fishing in the Irish countryside. After joining the British army at Sandhurst, he served in the British Army in India in the 1890s. This included taking part in forays into the wilder country to the north, the North West Frontier Province and Afghanistan, these experiences forming the basis of three of his novels. He then volunteered for service in the Andaman Islands, which housed a prison for thousands of long-term convicts from India and Burma. This experience also led to a novel.

George Bruce kept up his shooting and fishing activities in India. While on leave in London in 1900 he wrote an article on Tibet for the *Times*, which launched him on a writing career. Thereafter he produced a series of articles on natural history, specializing on new species of fish, and on military topics. From 1905 to 1910 Major Bruce served in Africa, retiring from the army in 1914, after which he and Mary travelled to Australia to be married in Melbourne. But on the outbreak of the first world war later that year they returned to

Ireland, as Major Bruce was called up to train troops. After the war the Bruces returned to Australia with their two sons and settled in Traralgon for most of the 1920s.

George's first novel *The Lion's Son* was published by Cornstalk Publishing of Sydney in 1928. Its hero is Lt. Donald Gordon, an officer at a British outpost on the Afghan border trying to keep the mountain Pathan tribes from conducting raids on the lowlands. A tribal leader calls for a *jihad* against the British and Indian troops, steals rifles, ambushes a convoy and begins a large-scale insurrection. The British and Indian troops advance into the unmapped territory of the rebellious tribes, and after many skirmishes, succeed in subduing them. 1928 also saw the appearance of a second novel by Major Bruce, *The Rainbow of Saba* published by Thomas Nelson of London, an historical novel set in the 13th century.

The Bruce family returned to Ireland in 1927 to live at Omagh, but their younger son Patrick died tragically in a shooting accident in 1929, an eerie repeat of Mary's brother Patrick's similar accidental death many years before. This tragedy turned her to spiritualism and a belief in reincarnation, a contrast to the matter-of-fact demeanour she presented to the world through her novels. When tragedy came, the easy solutions of the Billabong novels did not suffice. After a period in Europe the Bruces lived in the south of England during the 1930s. Major Bruce's third novel, *Tom in the Andamans,* was published by Whitcombe & Tombs, part of its series for children and adolescents. Tom Vereker is a 14 year old English boy who, because of poor health, is sent to recuperate on the Andaman Islands at the home of his cousin, Sir Hugh Standish, the Chief Commissioner there. The style of the book is similar to that of Mary Grant Bruce.

The Bruces returned to Victoria in 1939 with another world war threatening. In the next year George's fourth and last novel, *Red Devil*, appeared, published by Angus & Robertson. As in *The Lion's Den*, it begins in a remote town on the Afghan border. Here an Irishman, Captain Ulick Burke, in charge of Border militia, hunts raiders from an outlaw tribe who have devastated a lowland village. Burke sees a similarity between the Afghan tribes and his own Scots forebears who themselves carried out raiding parties against the English in centuries gone by. In this book Major Bruce is more sympathetic to the Pathans than in previous ones. The red-headed outlaw leader, Sher Dil, known as the 'Red Devil', is sentenced to 15 years imprisonment on the Andaman Islands. After some time he escapes to Achin (now known as Aceh) on the northern tip of Sumatra, and stirs up a successful revolt against Dutch rule there, the central event of the novel. Bruce seems to support the rebels against their imperial overlords in this case, in contrast to his earlier novels on India. Sher Dil eventually finds his way home to the frontier, and becomes reconciled with the British rulers of his land. George Bruce's novels reveal him as an intelligent, well-read man, curious about local customs, and able to describe in clear prose the texture of life in exotic places.

We think of Mary Grant Bruce as part of the Anglo-Australian tradition, which is true. She admired Britain and emphasized our connection with it. But like Rolf Boldrewood she was in her own way an Australian nationalist, believing that the Australian type was an improved version of its British original. Like Boldrewood and Henry Handel Richardson, who also had Anglo-Irish backgrounds, her allegiances were more complex; another loyalty was to Ireland, which was easily reconciled with Britain. Throughout their married life the Bruces moved constantly, almost restlessly, between these three locations. One Billabong novel, *Jim and Wally* is set in Ireland, where she lived during the first world war. Irish characters in her novels are depicted sympathetically; they are not the feckless semi-criminals of the crude derogatory stereotype of the time. Mary Grant Bruce was not like the *Bulletin* nationalists, who saw England as the foe. The publication of her book of Aboriginal legends, *The Stone Axe of Burkamukk*, goes against the view that she was an exemplar of narrow white values.

Mary Grant Bruce had an attractive demeanour – she was thin and neat with deep blue eyes. The centre of attention of any group, she had a commanding personality and was a woman of great focus and discipline. After breakfast every day she cleared away all other tasks and sat herself down to write. Later in life she became a public figure, speaking on ABC broadcasts, and encouraging the war effort in the 1940s. She was a feminist of a conservative bent, and helped found a Gippsland Womens League, and a Melbourne women's writing club, the forerunner of the Lyceum Club.

The immense success of the Billabong series is well known. They were the best read books in Australia in the first half of last century – over three millions copies were sold. Her Billabong novels caught the mood of assimilation and lack of conflict which the public yearned for at the time. They were read by boys as well as girls. The bulky Ward Lock early editions with thick pages, and illustrations by J. Macfarlane, are now collector's items. The Billabong titles had multiple reprints, but the non-Billabong books did not sell well, often having only one edition. Many copies of her books have inscriptions indicating they were birthday or Christmas presents, or presented as school prizes.

Readers treated the Billabong books as a kind a serial, eagerly awaiting the next instalment. Mary Grant Bruce conducted an immense correspondence with her readers, who wrote to her in great numbers, often treating the Lintons as a real family, and they put pressure on her, to, for example, have Norah married off to her brother's friend Wally, against Mary's own instincts. Gradually she resorted to automatic writing; even the non-Billabong novels moved towards the Billabong style, the formula was milked dry, to such an extent that her last second last novel, *Karalta*, has a similar plot to the much earlier *Jim and Wally*.

From *Foothill Farmers: The Literature of Gippsland*, 2010

Australian Society

GETTING AWAY FROM IT ALL

(1983)

Australia was not a society set up to be an improved replica of the Old World.

Australian folklore is very different from the triumphalist 'Advance Australia Fair' kind of nationalism. If we look at collections of folklore like Bill Wannan's *The Australian,* we are struck by all the defeat and desperation, with people making the best of a bad lot, and with sad cow cockies and various bush oddballs struggling to survive. One joke is typical:

> An old bagman was tramping across a station property, when the station owner appeared in his utility truck, travelling in the same direction.
> 'Like a lift?' the owner called out.
> 'No flamin' fear!' said the bagman. 'You open yer own gates.'

We notice here the wariness behind the deflating humour: both literally and metaphorically, the swaggie isn't going to be taken for a ride. This attitude isn't really negative; 'defensive' or 'minimalist' would better describe it, but it is not at all like the positive, confident temper of earlier beliefs. The two attitudes don't come from the same stable. Where do they originate?

Settlers in new societies have, broadly speaking, two different impulses. One is the positive task of creating a New World which is better than the old one. The second impulse draws the opposite lesson: because the old world has failed, the emigrant is too world-weary to go through the struggle over again. The reason for emigration is to remove yourself from all society, not only in the old world, but from society in the new country as well. He wants to get it out of his hair once and for all. At the first sign of pressure, an instinctive tendency to withdraw, to shrink back into privacy and non-caring comes into play. Paradise consists in letting nothing start up. This is one way of describing 'getting away from it all'. Perhaps the best description is found in D.H. Lawrence's *Kangaroo*:

> Richard found he never wanted to talk to anybody, never wanted to be with anybody. He had fallen apart out of the human association. And the rest of the people either were the same, or they herded together in a promiscuous fashion. But this speechless, aimless solitariness was in the air. It was natural to the country. The people left you alone. They didn't follow you with their curiosity and their inquisitiveness and their human fellowship. You passed, and they forgot you. You came again, and they hardly saw you. You spoke, and they were friendly. But they never asked any questions, and they never encroached. They didn't care. The profound Australian indifference, which still is not really apathy. The disintegration of the social mankind back to its elements.

Both impulses – to start afresh and to retire from strife – have been strong in Australia, and we oscillate between them. But their representation has not been in proportion to their strength: the impulse to withdraw has been more profound, but less prominent. The first impulse is recorded in history and in literature: the sons of the south will banish the old world errors and wrongs and lies, and create a paradise here. But the optimistic temper of such beliefs can never provide a full explanation of the Australian experience. Dad and Dave hardly exemplify it. Australia has been a harsh and disillusioning country as well as an enticing one, and over the decades a shoulder-shrugging, failure-absorbing temperament has been developed to meet these conditions. Phrases like 'she'll be apples' and 'no worries' cannot be elevated into patriotic slogans. The battler and the survivor are just as important as the Australia-promoter.

The United States was founded with a purpose, and its constitutional documents enshrine certain basic beliefs, 'We hold these truths....' and so on. Being a convict dump, no similar sense of purpose accompanied our foundation. Convicts hardly regarded Australia under its utopian aspect. We see among them the beginning of several traits common in Australia life and folklore: contempt for authority, indifference to the common good, improvisation at best and bludging at worst, a mortal fear of being taken for a ride, and a general scepticism and suspicion. In America, an immigrant moving across the continent always knew he was heading somewhere. But on an island, however large, there is only one way to go – inwards – and there was little or nothing in the middle. Once off the thin, fertile coastal rim, things thinned out. The traveller was always going away from something, but never to anything. The vastness of the continent dissipated energies rather than concentrated them. The population was too thinly spread to counter these centrifugal pressures.

The land, whether balmy or harsh, induced retreat and withdrawal; living on the great flat plains country made people unwind and forget their cares. You could easily lose yourself in it. The land exhausted you and evacuated your emotions. Only enough energy to keep yourself going was needed as you imperceptibly slowed down to its pace. Vance Palmer wrote of 'the dreamy indolence of the day'. You retained a certain innocence by rejecting experiences outside your context. Retreat into a timeless present, with neither hope nor nostalgia, and amnesia about the rest, made life at worst bearable and at best quite pleasant. Furphy described the inland plains as 'grave, self-centred, subdued', qualities which describe not only the country but also those who inhabited it.

What were the characteristics of people who were 'grave, self-centred, subdued'? One was the retreat back to the individual. Originally the whole country was to be independent, then this shrank back to the family farm, a cosy little world with the same qualities, then after this failed, it shrank back further to individual, who was to contain within himself those virtues which were elsewhere being denied. But this retreat to the individual should not be confused with today's search for self-identity; it was not a bid to understand yourself, but a wish to discard the burden of consciousness itself. You were withdrawing into yourself, but at the same time you were getting away from yourself. You dissolved the firm outlines of your personality by merging with the background and so losing yourself. Lawrence has many images for this shedding of the self, 'the strange falling away of everything', the obliteration of consciousness.

A second characteristic follows on from the first. The desire for release is not a carefully worked out view of the world nor a set of propositions. It is not a point of view, but the absence of a point of view and, even more importantly, the prevention of a point of view. Lawrence once again: 'They've got no will except to stop anybody else having any'. To be past carin', to say, as Lawson does, 'It doesn't matter much – nothing does', and in general the attitudes of shoulder-shrugging resignation are a form of blotting out everything. In its ultimate state, it is a constant, applied amnesia which prevents questions arising.

Various commentators have tried to fit such peculiar Australian attitudes into some ideology, such as romanticism, existentialism, nihilism or modernism. But, however much elements of these may be present, withdrawal is not an intellectual position at all. Our writers were not antipodean cousins of Dostoevsky and Kafka. They faced a situation marked by the absence of the power generated by social and political forces; European writers became existentialists or nihilists because they were overwhelmed by an excess of such power. Not to experience something is quite different from rejecting something you have experienced. The whole tenor of Camus' life and writings was to keep trying to find meaning in a world which persistently refused to reveal a coherent answers. This has nothing in common with basking in the absence of answers. Using the vocabulary of the extremities of the European psyche over the past century imports an inappropriate *angst* into local attitudes, and may give them a spurious grandeur.

In normal times, 'getting away from it all' subverts overt expressions of patriotism and exists subterraneously, as a kind of *nationalism sans doctrines*. However the two do have some things in common. In times of crisis, the two combine: the silent individual now needs to express himself, and relies on nationalistic sentiments to do this. For example, in the Second World War everyone noticed the unanimity of the Australian people under the threat of invasion, but there was little visible patriotism, and little of the adventurist rallying cries of previous wars. Vance Palmer in his article 'Battle' made a direct connection between the two:

> If Australia had no more character than could be seen on its surface, it would be annihilated as surely and swiftly as those colonial outposts white men built for their commercial profit in the East – pretentious facades of stucco that looked imposing as long as the wind kept from blowing. But there is an Australia of the spirit, submerged and not very articulate, that is quite different from these bubbles of old-world imperialism. Born of the lean loins of the country itself, of the dreams of men who came here to form a new society, of hard conflicts in many fields, it has developed a toughness all of its own. Sardonic, idealist, tongue-tied perhaps, it is the Australia of all who truly belong here. (*Meanjin*, 1942)

Palmer calls this an 'Australia of the spirit', and it coheres in a more-than-individual form only when the perimeter of the paradise has to be defended.

Ultimately the desire to withdraw relies on a protector to keep others out. Some outside agency is needed to ensure that the hermetically sealed capsule of self-protection is not punctured. Ordinary Australians, being private and apolitical, have to shelter under some else's activities. This leads to an anomaly: Australians leave bureaucrats free to do the running of the country for them, which increases the government's power enormously. Thus Australia is at once a highly bureaucratized and highly privatized country. It is anti-government in attitude, which allows it to be over-governed in reality.

Withdrawal has two sides: indifference, but also a wary defence of that condition. How this is achieved at a personal level is seen in Russell Drysdale's familiar painting 'Moody's Pub'. One's immediate impression is that the figures in the painting are beaten, resigned survivors, with the stuffing knocked out of them by adversity – and so they are. But there is something else present in their demeanour: they stand there watching the tourists or the painter or us, who are intruding on them, with a show of quiet, truculent defiance. They are warning outsiders to keep their distance, and to keep out of their hair. Though living in a reduced state, they have their pride; their last comfort is freedom from interference, and that is not going to be easily taken away from them.

One form of insulation was words. In the cities you cannot be silent, but words can be used as a barrage to ward off others and keep yourself intact, to enclose rather than disclose. Often speech has no meaning in itself, it just babbles along on the surface forming a barrier to communication. Edna Everage spurts out her strings of clichés like this. Such talk is disconcerting to immigrants, who take time to realize that the content may not matter very much. As Mary Rose Liverani's family learnt in *The Winter Sparrows*:

> It was difficult to differentiate one from the other, for their speeches were all formulaic, and the set phrases were punctuated with niggling little irruptions of laughter that made you drop your eyes. It took time to work out that words should be discarded as identity markers.

Speech could be just verbal insulation, which allowed you to disguise what you really felt, or to disguise the fact that you felt nothing at all.

Withdrawal has limitations in both time and space. It can work over one generation, but a person in this condition has little to bequeath to his or her children, and even less ability to communicate it. Retreat in the country can be rewarding, but once removed from this source, it withers from lack of replenishment. In the cities, there is plenty to retire from, but little to retire into. 'Getting away from it all' does make Australia a pleasant place, especially in an age when the private realm is diminishing. It can too easily cross the fine line separating it from merely giving up, and become a balm which legitimizes defeat.

The happy man (*beatus ille*) in Europe retired from active life to contemplate nature and to see in it analogies to the whole of creation, to rest and restore his energies so that he might once again participate in the world of affairs. The Australian version is so loose and defensive that it can lack new sources of sustenance, and peter out into nothingness. 'Getting away from it all' produces a society which is resilient and adaptive. It absorbs threats. The US poet Kenneth Rexroth said when he visited Australia:

> Of course, in Australia you have a homogeneous society, with a largely classless and very dense structure, so you don't get the literature of alienation. What is there to alienate from? If some Paris intellectual came to chop into your structure it would just close behind the sword. It is a low-pressure utopia here.

This makes Australia a much more complex country than it seems on the surface, hard to interpret and baffling to outsiders. Things can't always be taken at their face value. Content and meaning are not always connected in a straight-forward way. Anomalies abound. The attempt to undermine things make analysis difficult. 'Getting away from it all' constitutes a kind of anti-tradition running through Australian history. These attitudes are stronger than the more publicized beliefs of triumphalist optimism, of which they are not really a part. They have been more persistent and influential, and they explain the country better.

Kunapipi, May, 1983

KEEPING IT IN THE FAMILY

(1974)

The Australian family structure between the wars.

> There is for all of us a twilight zone of time, stretching back for a generation or two before we were born, which never quite belongs to the rest of history. Our elders have talked their memories into our memories until we have come to possess some sense of a continuity exceeding and traversing our own individual being. The degree to which we possess that continuity and the form it takes – national, religious, racial and social – depend on our own imagination and on the personality, opinions and talkativeness of our elder relatives. Children of small and vocal communities are likely to possess it to a high degree, and, if they are imaginative, have the power of incorporating into their own lives a significant span of time before their individual births.

This is Conor Cruise O'Brien describing how a growing child normally gathers together and absorbs the immediate memory of his race. O'Brien is talking about the Ireland of James Joyce's childhood here. But when we turn to the Australian experience, 'the degree in which we possess that continuity' seems a very limited one. Memories of the two World Wars and the Great Depression of the 1930s have come through to the present, but not the memory of the ordinary patterns of life in that society which these three world catastrophes interrupted. There has been a strange silence about the first fifty years of the 20th century in Australia. The generations who lived through these years don't recollect or talk about them very much. The period, especially the years between the wars, has become a forgotten, or at least a suppressed time, a no-man's-land which shuts off history from the present.

Looking forward through the 19th century, the traditional interpretation has been that by the 1890s the Australian people were a vigorous, restlessly initiating race, with unique characteristics, on the verge of a great nationalist take-off. But all this energy seems to run into the sand in that mysterious period between Federation and the First World War. Some disillusioning force, some unexplained exhaustion of dynamism occurs, nationalism gives way to colonial imitation of Britain, and the traditional interpretation increasingly parts company with reality as the 20th century progresses. What happened to all those supposedly typical Australian characteristics of last century? By the 1950s they had been transformed into their opposites: the society was composed of quiet, largely suburbanized, largely middle-class and relatively undistinguished people. When Barry Humphries began to assemble his portrait gallery of Australian stereotypes in the 1950s, we wondered how we'd been blind for so long to all the Mrs. Everages and Sandy Stones we now noticed around (and in) us. What transformation had taken place to alter Australian society so much?

Shame and disappointment that the country wasn't living up to its exciting 19th century hopes would also have contributed to the silence. So the present experience was suppressed, or at least passed over as a time without worth. Nobody wanted to admit that a society inimical to all their hopes was being established. Further, those who were oriented towards Britain and saw Australia simply as a dependency of the British Empire, shared with local cultural alienates a disdain for Australian activities *per se*; deferential provincials, they didn't believe that anything significant could happen here, much less be worth writing about.

In the mid 60s, four autobiographical works appeared which provide much of the material needed for filling in the period: Hal

Porter's *The Watcher on the Cast-Iron Balcony* (1963), George Johnston's *My Brother Jack* (1964), Graham McInnes' *The Road to Gundagai* (1965) and Donald Horne's *The Education of Young Donald* (1967). The four authors provide a source from which our memories, so long deprived of oral evidence, can nourish themselves. The similarities between these four books are much more remarkable than the individual differences, and suggest that there may be something representative about the early lives of their authors. The original element which these four books have in common is stated by Donald Horne in his Foreword: 'Since the central character is presented as a social animal, his adolescent revolt shaped and coloured by social circumstance, I would use the word 'sociography' rather than 'autobiography''. Horne also describes his book as an 'attempt to show what social history can look like when told through people'.

Reminiscences of childhood in literature usually concentrate on the developing personality of the sensitive artist-author. As he becomes more aware of the pressure of family, environment and society, he tends to reject them as philistine and stultifying to his personal growth, which matters most to him in life. James Joyce's *A Portrait of the Artist as a Young Man* and Henry Handel Richardson's *The Getting of Wisdom* are books of this kind. There are elements of the self-sustaining individual's rejection of family and society in these four books, but the interesting thing is that the attempt gradually peters out, and certain unusual features emerge. The object of the books comes to be a portrait of the society as well as the author-hero, who is the passive, not the initiating element here, and is important more as a reflector of society than as its rejector.

In these books there is no struggle to free oneself from some powerful, already existing force, as in Joyce. There is very little to react against, Australian society in this period being hollow rather than cohesive. The authors come to see the society not as hostile, but as both uncomprehending and incomprehensible. They come to

170

see that their task is to try to understand the society rather than to struggle against it. Instead of moving away from his family (as Joyce does), the hero in these books becomes increasingly enmeshed in it. The authors gradually see the futility of making the standard revolt; Horne and Porter are subtly self-deprecating when they recount many of their youthful enthusiasms. If their family turned out to be somewhat pathetic, it was to be understood, not rejected, on that account.

My Brother Jack, unlike the other books, has two main characters. Jack is not really successful as a literary creation. He is interesting primarily as a social type, the stereotyped mateship personality who, while still admired, was steadily becoming redundant as the century progressed; in contrast, the skinny, out-of-things young artist David Meredith/George Johnston is a success in the world's eyes. This piece of social comparison is excellently handled. But David's success is less socially significant than Jack's failure. In all four books, it is failure that is interesting. The sociographical orientation of the books can be more clearly seen by comparing them with Henry Handel Richardson's attempt at non-fictional autobiography *Myself When Young* (1946). The milieu is similar: a respectable middle-class family, once living in a genteel fashion, now desperately keeping up its fading charms and staving off collapse. Henry Handel Richardson describes her mother scratching to make ends meet after the father's death. The family is very conscious of having 'come down in the world', but they try not to admit it, and keep up appearances in the world's eyes: being sent to a private girls' school in Melbourne, PLC, is part of this. The family see their position as exceptional, and shameful to their pride. The young HHR triumphs over this situation by developing her talents until she feels superior to that 'society' out of which her family is gradually slipping.

The four recent books also describe families in a state of collapsing gentility who keep to themselves. But the authors, looking back from the 1960s, now see that their families' defensive point of view at the time was largely mistaken: their circumstances weren't as exceptional and unusual as they then imagined. The authors retrospectively realise that their families and their own youthful experiences were typical of a large section of society. No equivalent revaluation of the past occurs in HHR's *Myself When Young*; her attitude when she was writing in the 1940s was the same as when she was young. In each of the four books the family's loss of social status and self-esteem is exactly reproduced – they don't seem to be mere isolated cases. Each family is of respectable middle-class background and imbued with British imperial sentiments. They have all come from England a couple of generations previously; they were once relatively wealthy and comfortable (particularly on the mother's side), but have been sinking down the social scale ever since. The decline in fortunes is most marked in the Johnston family. Of his mother's family, Johnston says:

> From the wealthy, sheltered, and respectable life into which they were born, all three children for the rest of their lives steadily and conscientiously descended on the social, economic and perhaps even on the moral scale.

McInnes describes his grandmother Meo in similar terms:

> Listening to the endless stories of country balls, picnic parties, horseback riding, vast dinners with tables groaning under the spread, candlelight romance and, by implication, deferential servants always at a discreet distance, one could not but believe that Meo had come down in the world.

Hal Porter, living in Kensington, remembers his grandfather as 'a Fine Old Gentleman', and Donald Horne compares the Camden property and the great house 'Fernside' with suburban 'Denbigh' and a rented house at Muswellbrook.

A spiritual collapse accompanies the material one. Each book describes the depressing decline of purpose in the family as it struggles on in a round of spurious respectability and fading dreams. The principal agents of the decline are male – the author's grandfather and father. The waywardness of the grandfather begins the dissipation of family energy. He never fully accepts his present reduced circumstances and retreats into a world of harmless fantasy and daydreaming about the great days of the past (Porter's grandfather paints scenes of his military past, Horne's remembers when he wandered around Australia). Stubbornly individual and refusing to settle down, he clings to his old ways and becomes an eccentric. McInnes' Pere is a shambling, furtive idler around the streets of Hobart. By living in the great past and disdaining the present, the grandfather retains his independence and verve, as well as a pride which will not be surrendered. He is, at least, a 'character'. Horne's Pa retains these qualities even when shining people's shoes as a train conductor. The grandmother, forced to be more realistic, has the burden of managing her family thrust upon her, and she desperately strives to retain the external appearances of the decent living of a more leisurely age. In Australian houses at the time, the shrine of the once-respectable was the front parlour, the 'best' room in the house, hardly ever used and cluttered up with all the old family furniture which was too big for it.

The split in personality seen in the grandfather is exactly re-enacted in the father, but in a more extreme way. The father becomes withdrawn, and with less of the compensating belief in the heroic past which the grandfather has. He restlessly potters at hobbies, and displays only fitful vestiges of lively activity, but underneath it all there is a terrible numbness. Vocationally frustrated and unable to cope with the dull normalcy of life between the wars, he gets a certain bitter, quiet, defeated air about him. A lethargy of body and spirit overcomes him as his connections with reality become attenuated. Four quotations tell the story:

> But what I realise now, although I never did at the time, is that my father, too, was oppressed by the intimidating factors of fear and change. By disillusionment and ill-health too. As is often the case

with big, strong, athletic men, he was an extreme hypochondriac. Moreover, he was frustrated by his failure to have made anything of his life – he could see no possible advancement in his trade beyond the position of depot foreman, which involved very little more pay but a great deal more responsibility – and this had made him morose, intolerant, bitter, and violently bad tempered. (Johnston)

Five-eighths of an inch of whisky, usually in the middle of a wet Sunday afternoon when he was poring over his wonderful stamp collection, I shall take as the essence, psyche or anima of my stepfather, Think, Dad. There you have – in one nip, as it were – his engineering training, his happy-go-lucky geniality, and yet again his lethargy. (McInnes)

The danger in Father's simplicity is that years later, step by hidden ruthless step, it has transmitted itself to stubbornness, thence to simon-pure indifference, the final and most killing of self-treacheries. His ultimate destruction of himself and others by unfortified simplicity is something not foreseeable. (Porter)

He told jokes and recounted long anecdotes again; he was devoted to Janet; he went swimming and fishing in Botany Bay; he played golf occasionally; we took up bridge and mah-jongg again: although instead of going to school he now filled out much of his day in the basketwork they had taught him as occupational therapy. But it did not take us long to realize that he seemed to have become like one of his own baskets, sturdy enough to look at, but empty inside. He went on much as usual, repeating old habits, but with nothing new happening to him. (Horne)

The problem begins with the grandfathers: 'settling down' in suburbia is the opposite to all they had imagined Australia to be. Optimistic mateship behaviour becomes more and more an extrovert veneer; behind this smokescreen disillusionment becomes embedded in the core of their personalities. But for the fathers the hope filled past is only a family memory, and the effort to be both a larrikin and a quiet suburbanite exhausts them. In the next generation the problem is acutely present in George

Johnston's portrayal of his brother Jack's failure to find a role for himself in society. In Barry Humphries' creation Sandy Stone the defeat is final: the extrovert bravado has completely disappeared.

The family pattern in the four books fits in very well with the perceptive account of the Australian family in Ronald Conway's *The Great Australian Stupor* (1971):

> Fathers, as links between sons and 'other-directed' cultural roles sons were expected to occupy, all too often coughed, swore and fell tipsily into the shadows, leaving youth to make its own botched adjustments. What [D.H.] Lawrence encountered with such poignancy in the twenties was a set of generous but shallow personality characteristics groping vainly toward an integrated identity. Here all too often, was a man subconsciously in search of a personal centre, a ramshackle ego without contact with the Self.

The four authors notice the same contrast between father and mother:

> With Mother everything was sharp and tight and on schedule. Bells rang, cannons boomed, gongs clanged, flags were run up and the form was more important than the substance. With Dad it was more a world of laisser faire, sudden impulses, tuneless whistling, odd tasks begun and never finished. (McInnes)

> Although there was sometimes a certain reserve in my Father's manner, a thud of silence as if he were suddenly contemplating something within himself, my mother's personality invariably flowed out into her surroundings. (Horne)

> Most of his displeasure and resentment he focused upon Mother. He had altogether lost patience with her role of Florence Nightingale to the halt and the lame, even though two of the three who were in our house at this time were his own sisters. (Johnston)

> Unlike Father, who has nothing of himself to give, or only the shadows of virtues, and weaknesses not fit for children tough as children, Mother is perpetually generous with herself. This is either

because she can freshly remake herself, good and bad, and therefore inexhaustible, or because she is by nature indestructible. (Porter)

The enormous importance of the First World War on the circumstances and attitudes of these families emerges from these books. The Great War created a style of life; everything seemed to originate from it. The Depression, by contrast, didn't so much change life as make it much worse, deepening the frustrations already existing in ordinary life. All four families supported the Australian effort in the Great War (both of Johnston's parents served), and were ideologically caught up in the world of British imperial sentiments, their main belief system. The continuing influence of the First World War was ultimately a dangerously diverting one. It seemed to restore that sense of the heroic in life which had been lost since the 1890s, but its heroics were far away and not connected with Australia. The experience of the war provided a convenient compensation for 'going down in the world' at home. As the soldiers returned, the memory of its valour contrasted sharply with the predictability of daily life. The First World War caused a fusion of two elements that had been pretty antagonistic to each other in 19th century Australia: Australian nationalism and the British connection. As McInnes notes, it was a fusion of contradictory elements: 'The ironic thing is that although this terrible baptism of fire helped, as perhaps nothing else did, to create the Australian spirit, it was to England that the young looked as they enlisted. England was still Home; it was the 'there' where Australia was to be in *Australia Will Be There*.'

Two processes of creation are simultaneously at work in these books. For the first time, the past is described exactly as it was; the feeling that it wasn't worthwhile and should be passed over has gone. But at the same time, the past is revalued by looking at it from today's vantage point. It is seen not only from the point of view of a middle-aged man looking back on his childhood, but also from today's Australia looking back and asking how we got this way. When they were living through the period, people thought it a dull and unimportant period, a sort of lapsed, unusual, time. Something had gone radically wrong, this wasn't the Australia they expected, but a transitional, impermanent time which they hoped would soon be over and completely forgotten, a kind of 'time out of life'. True to the provincial mentality, the people believed that the important events happened elsewhere in the great outside world. McInnes says his mother had 'taken the view that, broadly speaking, nothing worthwhile ever happened in Melbourne anyway.'

The authors record this attitude, but they now see, looking backwards, that this period has perpetuated itself, in that it is the origin of today's society. Between 1900 and 1950 a permanent culture – in the broadest sense and however impoverished – was being set up in Australia. Hence the compulsion to establish a continuity through to the present. The events of the past are relived so that there is more excitement in their recreation than there was in the actual living of them. At the time each family saw itself as isolated and exceptional; they are now being put at the centre of the stage. By recreating the places of their childhood – Muswellbrook and Malvern, Bairnsdale and Brighton, Westmead and Williamstown – the authors give them a proper sense of their particular and unique atmosphere. Australia is subtly making its presence felt, and has a history of its own. Australians aren't searching for an identity, restlessly torn, like Martin Boyd's characters, between England and Australia. That problem is over. They have an identity. The problem is to recognize it against the wishes of the time.

The child-hero, whether egoistical like Horne and Porter, or quieter like Johnston and McInnes, watches the sad family drama enacted before his eyes. At the time he identifies with the mother and can never get close to the father. But the decades that have elapsed have allowed a certain detachment to intervene. It is all over now. The father is created with some affection and his terrible situation is treated with sympathy. The act of writing the autobiography is a kind of homage to the family, especially the parents. It endows their frustrations and boredoms with a meaning that wasn't apparent at the time, and makes their struggles seem more worthwhile. The son has arrested the family decline by his success in the world; he is now redeeming it by his art. He also benefits himself, for he now has a past which is valuable to him in understanding himself and the society of today.

All for authors eventually make a move out of the milieu of family and suburbia, Horne and McInnes to university, and Porter and Johnston to the bohemian life of Melbourne's art colonies of the 1930s. Initially there is a great sense of relief in this move – it is seen as an escape into a world of vitality from the debilitating suburbs. Although they all become successful by using these talents and so reverse the families' fortunes, the four authors gradually become disillusioned with the artistic and intellectual groups they mix in and come to realize, looking back, that these groups are in their own way just as remote from life as the denizens of the suburbs and country towns which they have left.

Also important is the formation of the great Australian middle class from the gradual levelling out process since 1900 among the groups which composed Australian society. The middle-class families of English background described in the autobiographies were certainly not representative of the whole society, but they have been largely ignored by social commentators. To put it very generally, they were settling down to the lower middle-class suburban level to which the ordinary working Australians were aspiring. We have heard a lot about 'upward social mobility' recently, but the prevalence of 'going down in the world' and the accompanying sense of failure is surprising in a relatively new country like this one. It goes against the commonly held belief that people here are always improving themselves, on the analogy of the American success story 'from log cabin to White House'.

Quadrant, May-June, 1974

FORGOTTEN IN THE FERTILE CRESCENT

(1983)

*A talk given at a conference on regional identity at Toowoomba,
September, 1983.*

Two different types of countryside exist in Australia. The first is
the fertile crescent running down the east coast from Queensland to
Adelaide, as well as Tasmania and the southwest corner of Western
Australia. This is the wet, fertile, green, wooded region of the small
farms, stretching back to the Great Dividing Range. Over the range
is quite different country, the open plains turning into the outback.
Different types inhabited these different areas. The closer areas had
settled, law-abiding families, with the men staying on the family
farm. The outback type was usually a single male, gregarious and
footloose, and often iconoclastic. Most of Australia's distinctive
regions are in fertile areas near the coast. Gippsland is not outback.
It fits the first pattern, a pattern not as widely recognised as the
second. As Hal Porter has put it:

> Fashionable painters would have the world of mugs believe, it seems,
> that Australia is a beige waste littered with dehydrated tree-roots,
> blanched heifer skulls, and larrikin Kellys. That, maybe, is one truth.
> It does not work for South Gippsland, Victoria, where, for example,
> in November, ditches and drains and soggier depressions are clogged
> to overbrimming with lacquered buttercups; hawthorn hedges are
> clotted with curds of blossom; here are dandelions and brier roses
> and gorse – Pre-Raphaelite stuff, dewdrops and all.

My interest in Gippsland is personal in origin. I moved to Gippsland a decade ago, having previously lived in Melbourne all my life. We are all familiar with the cultural clashes these moves caused in the early 1970s: city people were moving out and trying to buy small, country weatherboard cottages just at the time the farmer, slightly ashamed of his, was using it as a hayshed, and building a brick veneer home instead. Each group had opposite ideas about the good life. The farmer wanted to catch up on the gradations of affluence the cities had experienced since the Second World War. For the newcomer, it was precisely the country's escaping these developments that attracted him. This nice balancing of opposites has best been expressed by Ronald Blythe in his classic study of an English country village *Akenfield:*

> The first thing a newcomer does when arriving in a village is to begin to claim it. He doesn't state or stake his claim, he simply starts to feel his way towards the village's identity, recognise it for what it is and shape himself to fit it. He will often envy the old indigenous stock – but in effect his life will be far freer than theirs. The sometimes crushing, limiting power which the village exerts on families which have never escaped will be unknown to him...The nearer native and newcomer come together, the more obvious their difference. [The newcomer] will obey district rules and take immense care not to offend against the least of its little foibles. But he never becomes joined to the place. Whilst the atavistic thread, whether he likes it or not, remains unbroken for the native. It is both his advantage and his fetter.

This is typical of many areas, but we found Gippsland very different in atmosphere from other Australian country districts, like the Riverina, with which we had some familiarity. It seemed tighter, warier, less open. Going into the reasons why this was so led to an interest in the history of the region. So I'm trying here to describe the characteristic features of Gippsland, exaggerating them a bit, perhaps, for purposes of emphasis. I am distinguishing them from the general view we have of Australian and Victorian history, though other regions may, of course, share some of them.

Gippsland is a more distinctive region geographically than most other regions in Australia. It is surrounded by natural barriers on all sides: by the Alps to the north, Bass Strait with its wild weather and lack of harbours to the south, and swamps and mountains separating it from the Melbourne area. These boundaries also acted as barriers to getting in – it was opened up (very late) in the 1840s. And once people got in, there were internal barriers (water, forests and mountains) which made settlement difficult. It wasn't easy to penetrate, and it wasn't easy to establish yourself once you had penetrated. You didn't just make roads, you had to keep re-making them. This struggle continued for decades; it didn't encourage notions of progress. Perseverance was the prime Gippsland virtue. Much of this remains true this century. It's not a region that flows naturally and imperceptibly into adjacent regions. Its geographic boundaries have remained barriers against integration. Apart from the highway corridor to Melbourne, Gippsland remains relatively isolated from the rest of Victoria.

Because of the difficulties of penetration, Gippsland was entered only in the late 1830s, fifty years after 1788; already a quarter of our European history had gone. South and west Gippsland were settled even later, in the 1870s and 1880s. The town I live in, Boolarra, is celebrating its centenary next year. Such towns, only 60-100 miles from Melbourne, have existed for only half our brief history. From another perspective, this means that all history is within living memory over two generations: an 80 year-old Gippslander today would have spoken in his youth to the district's first settlers. This late foundation meant that Gippsland lacked many of the formative and heroic events of Australia's early years: it had no pre-squatting era, no convicts, no early towns, no [early] free settlers. Its pre-gold era was very short; the squatters didn't have time to establish themselves as a 'squattocracy'; you don't get 'old families' distanced from the rest as in some other areas. As a consequence, Gippsland had no aristocracy, and no proletariat; in social terms, everything was moving towards the centre.

Gippsland's most unusual feature was its founders: they were Gaelic-speaking Scots from the highlands and islands of remote north-west Scotland, coming here after the highland clearances. These 'children of the mist' came from a culture very different from the mainstream of the British Isles and Europe. They were exceptional in our history too. The founder of Gippsland, Angus McMillan, called it 'Caledonia Australis' ('Scotland in the South'), as its contours and inland waters reminded him of home. In an allusion to the highland clearances, he wrote: 'Here was a country lying dormant, capable of supporting all my starving countrymen'. Who stood in the way? The Aborigines, the local tribe of which were called the Kurnai. In the colonies, one normally had a dominant, imperially confident race wreaking havoc on bewildered indigenes. But in Gippsland, two suppressed races were coming into conflict, the Scots themselves the victims of imperial expansion and released from that suppression by leaving Scotland, and the other race about to be suppressed. The highland Scots harried the Aborigines out of their ancestral lands, just as they had been driven off the lands that fed them in Scotland. But the Scots did not notice the parallel. When one of the young Macalisters was killed, Angus McMillan led the 'Highland Brigade' (an unofficial, armed posse), and many Aborigines were slaughtered at Warrigal Creek and elsewhere. Don Watson has a book on this subject, *Caledonia Australis*.

In the upshot, both suppressed races were dispersed. The highland Scots were restless and unsettled. In his local history *Bairnsdale*, Hal Porter points out that they left no solid stone edifices as permanent monuments to their presence and status, as the other kind of Scots were doing in Victoria's Western District. Their Gaelic culture didn't transplant here, as it did in parts of Nova Scotia. It wasn't Caledonia Australis, it was Anglo-Saxon Gippsland. But there was one legacy: the Calvinism of these Scots remained, to be reinforced by the evangelical Puritanism of the selectors some decades later.

The Central Gippsland plain was developed by the squatters from the centre outwards, and towards known boundaries, which is unusual in Australia. There was no pushing out into the unknown, beyond the known, beyond the Black Stump. So you really had no frontier, and no frontier mentality. The late founding, the quick infilling and the short distance from Melbourne, meant Gippsland had hardly any uncivilised or wild period. Within a couple of years of founding, most places had a church, post office, police magistrate, courts, schools, bank and so on, the symbols of order and civilisation.

There is an interesting qualification to the idea that Gippsland is not like the outback. Gippsland has its own outback, as Peter Kerr has pointed out. Gippslanders consider the east (the untouched forest) and the north (the mountains) as their outback. A sort of frontier life still exists among timber workers and cattlemen in the mountain valleys. They are unreconstructed nineteenth century mateship types, drinking themselves to death and having road accidents in high style. Because their life is so remote and different they are romanticised and heroicised in the same way as urban Australians have divinised the outback type. The east and north of Gippsland are full of forests and mountains and so are, in terms of nature, opposite to the outback; but psychologically they perform the same function as an endless, untamed, free, sparsely inhabited region. It's been an area of folk heroes since the days of Bogong Jack and the Man from Snowy River. Since the film, we may be witnessing an interesting change: the cattlemen of the high plains are being elevated into legendary heroes, replacing the former outback ones. The film explicitly promoted the Man from Snowy River triumphing over the old hero, Jack Thompson's Clancy from the 'broad sunlit plains unending'.

The very late founding of Gippsland produced a telescoped chronology, which distorted the normal relations between eras, particularly the relations between squatting, mining and selection. The squatting period was late and squashed into a short time, so the squatters weren't so firmly established when the gold rushes came. The gold rushes came later, in the 1860s and 1870s, than in many other areas, and they occurred in remote, almost inaccessible mountain valleys well north of today's Princes Highway. Selection acts and mining coincided in Gippsland history; you don't get the usual pattern of miners wanting to unlock the land when alluvial gold ran out. Because mining was in remote mountain areas, miners couldn't farm nearby, so they moved away, leaving deserted gold towns, unlike Ballarat and Bendigo, which remained relatively heavily populated. Most selection came much later (in the 1870s and 1880s) and wasn't predominantly by miners or by locals, but by outsiders. Gippsland history is not marked by the famous selector-squatter squabble over the Selection Acts (dummying, peacocking, etc). This was partly because the squatters were less strong than elsewhere and the selectors were more middle class, so there was less rivalry and more blurring between the two groups. Also, most selection was in forest country previously unoccupied, so there were no resident squatters whose wiles had to be coped with.

West and South Gippsland were settled from the 1870s and 1880s onwards, when all the good, easy land in the rest of Victoria had run out. Many selectors came from the Ballarat district. The struggle wasn't acquiring a block from grasping squatters, but clearing it once you had secured a selection. The tasks of felling, burning and clearing giant mountain ash in dense fern gullies, and then preventing the forest growing, exhausted a settler, consumed his whole life just getting started, and even then it wasn't complete. Mud, rain and poor transport systems meant a lifetime of back-breaking tasks. Pioneering continued up till the 1940s.

This produced the typical Gippsland farmer, the poor struggling small dairy farmer without much capital or machinery. 1890-1940 was a low period in Australian life, both economically and psychologically, and it was the formative period in Gippsland history. These dairy farmers had unreliable markets and poor returns, as well as the difficulty of getting their milk, butter and cheese to consumers. There wasn't much money around – 'making ends meet' was the commonly heard phrase. They never made fortunes, like their wool and wheat cousins on the plains in other districts of the continent, nor did they have much social visibility. They remained a forgotten group, mentioned, if mentioned at all, only derisively as 'poor cow cockies'. They reciprocated by retreating into silence; Gippsland witnessed no overt demands like a New State movement. Ronald Blythe's assessment in *Akenfield* can be applied here:

> On the whole the villagers don't volunteer much about themselves. They are not loquacious people. The old ones have emerged from indignities and sufferings which taught a man how to hold his tongue and a guarded note marks much of their conversation. On the whole, they will admit certain information about their lives during the 'bad days' and will courteously rake up a few old customs as makeweight, but they remain intrinsically private folk and their characters cannot be termed open.

John Hirst's description of the pioneer legend (in *Historical Studies*, October, 1978) fits Gippsland very closely. Hirst sets up a model which differs a lot from Ward's mateship one, though it does overlap in certain respects. Hirst believes that a common unifying thread is respect for the pioneers. There is filial deference to them, and a belief that their legacy should be passed down to future generations untampered with. A recent golden age in the past is created, when there were no divisions:

> The pioneers are depicted in a world limited by the boundaries of their properties, subduing the land, and battling the elements. Their enemies are drought, flood, fire, sometimes Aborigines; never low prices, middle men, lack of capital or other pioneers.

There is no class bitterness, selector and squatter being merged. The more conservative implications of the pioneer legend in comparison to Ward's fit Gippsland well, as do the respectable, British-Australian attitudes and the deification of endless hard work. A Gippslander gave imaginative expression to the values of the pioneer legend in its most popular form: Mary Grant Bruce's Billabong series.

Gippsland (with Tasmania) looks most like the British Isles of all parts of Australia. The Rev. Login wrote in his diary of his first impressions of the district: 'It was all, too, in such striking contrast to my previously formed ideas of Australia as a dry, waterless waste, that it seemed, indeed, even then, a land flowing with milk and honey.' Goldmining in Gippsland was in the hills, and so the gold fever didn't affect the plains areas with its restlessness. Even the miners of Walhalla were respectable family men, who dressed up to go to balls and concerts, to promenade on the streets on Saturday nights and to have nice flower and vegetable plots around their cottages. The selectors who came from the 1870s onwards were in general an equally respectable lot, some being Melbourne people with a small business background, and some of the artisan-craftsman type. Photographs of the time and Hal Porter's book on Bairnsdale reinforce this impression of sturdy, proper lower-middle-class propriety and diligence. Because the mass of people came to Gippsland so late, it missed the mateship-producing epics (convicts, outback, gold), and it was settled in the later period when the move back to a British-Australian position became more pronounced in Australian life. Geoffrey Serle comments generally on Victoria:

> In his respectability and pride in his property he [the Victorian farmer] was the antithesis of the classical Australian bushworker, who indeed played only a peripheral role in Victoria.

Although Gippsland is geographically compact, with short distances and densely populated for an Australian rural area, one is struck by the social isolation of the farmers and by the lack of community life. The farmers rarely left their farms, as people did in more open areas like the Riverina. Such an enormous effort went into clearing that there was little time for anything else. Milking twice a day and long, rainy winters meant you had to batten down for much of the year.

The life that developed in Gippsland was self-sufficient, independent and ungregarious. The best description of this is by M. Hansen in *The Land of the Lyre Bird*, a compilation of the memoirs of South Gippsland's pioneers:

> One of the first incentives to take up land was to get a home, also to enable me to work for myself and not for anyone else, and thus enjoy the glorious privilege of being independent. A home is surely, and ought to be, a place where one feels there is rest when weary, and peace from the world's strife, and to one's self a spot like none other on earth, even though it be ever so humble. My first abode was indeed humble enough for anyone: it measured about 18 x 14 feet, built of logs and thatched with bark – still it was a home. It was where I could go when I had nowhere else to go; it was where my ideas were centred, where I could work and do as I liked, provided my action did not directly or indirectly bring harm to myself or others. Looking into the future, I confidently hoped to build a better house in later years, which was started in the early part of 1887.

Hansen had repeated setbacks but kept at it. First, his house was burnt down. He had to go to Melbourne to pay off his debts, which took six years. He started to work the land again and built another house, and adds: 'Then there was fencing and yards and sheds to build, enough to keep me in constant employment and out of mischief, and I did not get many holidays.' Then the great fires of 1898 burnt him out and he had to start again.

The selectors of Gippsland were low-church and evangelical in demeanour. We notice in Gippsland history how soon the clergymen arrived, on the heels of the explorers. These men were welcomed into the homes of the squatters. And this tradition continued: in books like *The Land of the Lyre Bird* people hold services in their own houses and in trees with hollow trunks, and religions of all types are soon present, like the Salvation Army in Walhalla. It's not just a question of church attendance; these men describe themselves as pious and God-fearing in all their endeavours, and their strong puritan beliefs are evident in their accounts of perseverance in tasks like clearing the enormous forests. They believe they have a God-given vocation, and hard work and success are seen as morally wholesome and spiritually rewarding.

The settlers, with their combination of isolation and religious vocation, are like Robinson Crusoes, each hacking out his tiny, independent principality. Their little corner of the bush is their own empire; they look no further than it. They devote themselves to carving their own domain out of the virgin bush, and they become completely absorbed in this. They are filial and pious: they work as their forefathers told them to, and they pass the message on to their sons, who will complete the task and who will in turn act in deference to the father. It is only their own generational line, stretching fore and aft, that they see; they are blind to any wider social dimension.

This is all very like the Weber-Tawney thesis of religion and the rise of capitalism, of which Robinson Crusoe is an exemplary case. The God-fearing puritan felt called by God, but was unsure of his real vocation. This caused ceaseless tension and striving to prove he was one of the elect. Success would prove his life worthwhile and be a sign that he was saved. So he went into the wilderness to create something and to build it up with a single, self-righteous purpose. He was extremely hard-working and frugal. When he succeeded, he never went and luxuriated in the world's fleshpots and relaxed, but ploughed it all back into his enterprise. He was unable to stop. He was tight, closed, devoted to one single thing with religious fervour to prove himself worthy. This Weber calls intra-mundane asceticism. Much of the writing, especially about South Gippsland, seems to fit this thesis. The elect took the place of the absent aristocracy.

Contrasting with this isolation was the fact that Gippsland is one of Australia's most densely populated rural areas. The towns are very close together by Australian standards. The Latrobe Valley is the only case in Australia of a heavily populated industrial area situated in a heavily populated rural area. Gippsland has remained relatively isolated and socially invisible, compared with the other side of Victoria. The Western District is prominent and influential, and aware of its influence. In all the consecutive Liberal state Ministries from 1955 to 1982, I can't think of a Gippsland Cabinet Minister, though many – such as Bolte, Dickie, Austin, Smith, Crozier and McDonald – have come from the Western District. (In the Federal sphere, Mr. Nixon was a typical Gippslander.) Melbourne people's ignorance of Gippsland's geography is legendary.

Being a world of its own, Gippsland hasn't been so affected by the changes in ideas, education and wealth that have transformed Australia since the Second World War. It is still close to its own history. Without old families, it has lacked historical consciousness of itself, but it is now becoming more influential and in the news. It has most of Victoria's energy – brown coal, oil and natural gas– and there are enormous developments in these areas. It also has a prosperous dairy industry and huge timber reserves. South Gippsland was shown to be drought-proof during the recent drought, which increases its attractiveness. So one now has an anomalous mixture: present importance unmatched by a similar historical awareness of what Gippsland is.

Quadrant, November, 1983

This article became the basis for my regional history The Settling of Gippsland.

MELBOURNE'S NORTH-WEST SUBURBS

(2007)

Our family lived on the outskirts of Melbourne just beyond North Essendon.

The north-west of Melbourne developed separately from the rest of the city – Moonee Ponds Creek is the dividing line. These suburbs became a sort of world of their own, as people did not usually move out of them. If you made money in Essendon you moved to Strathmore, not to the south-eastern suburbs. So the rest of Melbourne doesn't know much about of these suburbs – they have lower social visibility and mobility.

Maps of Irish Catholics in Melbourne show them settling first in the inner suburbs, but when they moved out, it was mainly to the north-west. These suburbs had the highest Catholic proportion in Melbourne, and this was reinforced after the second world war with Catholics from Italy and Malta, and from Poland, Ukraine and the Baltic states. By this stage the federal electorate of Maribyrnong, which included Essendon and surrounding suburbs, had the highest proportion of Catholics in Australia. Essendon Council figures in the 1970s demonstrate this: it was 40% Catholic (very high), the Church of England was 17% (low), and other Christians 23% (high). The Catholic national average at the time was about 24% and the Church of England 28%.

We know Irish immigrants to Melbourne usually boarded first

at Emerald Hill (South Melbourne), but the place of employment for many was the North Melbourne area, also known as Hotham and West Melbourne. Here there were a number of important employment centres, all connected with transport: Spencer Street railway station, the market in Victoria St, the Newmarket stockyards, the Metropolitan Meat Market in North Melbourne, and the Flemington racecourse. Connected to these were associated industries, like tanneries, abattoirs for the meat industry, and allied trades. Horses were important for transport and racing stock, and for drays transporting building materials for roads, sewerage and houses as Melbourne grew. The north-west suburbs were characterized by these trades, rather than, say, manufacturing industries, which were in the inner east and later the south-east.

People in the transport and livestock trades moved out northwest as they successively set up homes in Flemington, Ascot Vale, Moonee Ponds, Essendon, North Essendon and Glenroy, as the stock and station agent Harry Peck's book *Memoirs of a Stockman* shows. Kirk's Horse Bazaar moved out from the city to North Essendon. The Irish, being poor immigrants, often with rural backgrounds, naturally gravitated to these trades. Our family and our Ascot Vale cousins, the Spillanes, were typical Irish Catholic families starting in the later 19th century at the labourer, not proprietary, level, but gradually rising in the social scale. There were other trades in the north-west suburbs, but these were the most noticeable.

There is a further, earlier dimension to this story. It's a story of moving in to Melbourne as well as moving out. In transport terms Melbourne is accessible only to the north and west. There are three great roads to the hinterland, the Ballarat road to the west, the Sydney road to the north, and the Castlemaine-Bendigo road, called Mt Alexander Rd, to the north-west bisecting the other two. The rest of Melbourne is blocked by hills and forests to the north east and east, and by the bay. The north-west area therefore became the hub for transport to and from the hinterland and interstate. Livestock brought to Melbourne to be sold came in by walking, by train or by truck through this northwest salient. Just outside the suburbs, properties were used for agistment, the last chance to feed up the animals before the final walk into Newmarket.

As the Irish Catholics moved out to Essendon and beyond, they eventually met up with an original, much earlier Irish Catholic settlement of farmers around Keilor, such as the Dodds, Foxes and Hogans, all old Keilor families. When my grandfather Patrick Morgan bought the 'Niddrie' property (now the Essendon airport) in 1900, he first went to Mass at St Augustine's Church, Keilor, the nearest Catholic Church. The natural link and orientation was to Keilor, rather than to the suburbs of Melbourne. Later St Monica's, Moonee Ponds became the family's parish church, then later on St Teresa's, Essendon.

As the Irish moved out beyond Essendon past the suburbs they also met Protestant Irish, Scots and English landlords and their great houses. There were mansions in the suburbs e.g. Travancore at Ascot Vale (which got its name from the family selling horses to the British army in India), and McCracken's at Strathmore, but further out there existed a ring of comfortable farms with great houses (at Bulla, Tullamarine, Keilor, Sunbury, Broadmeadows, Cragieburn, and so on), where those who had money and social pretensions set themselves up as landed gentlemen on comfortable properties outside a large city, as they had seen wealthy people do at home in the British Isles. Brewster and Foster were early Protestant Irish, as was William Pomeroy Greene at 'Woodlands', Oaklands Junction. Other large houses included Taylor's 'Overnewton', McDougall's 'Arundel' and Big Clarke at 'Rupertswood' at Sunbury. The Catholic foundling home at Broadmeadows had originally been one of these grand houses. The property 'Niddrie', begun in the early 1860s, was a minor example of this type.

The McCrackens ran hunts starting at the Lincolnshire Arms

Hotel in North Essendon, and in the 1890s the Melbourne Hunt Club operated from Oaklands Junction. It's hard to realize it today, but this was a snob area of Melbourne then, because other areas didn't have these broad acres, or broadmeadows. Ultimately these properties didn't succeed as farms because the fields are dry and full of stones, scotch thistles and tussocks. The Aborigines called the area *dutigalla* (Doutta Galla), which means treeless plains. The famous Australian writer Rolf Bolrewood was a relative of the Greenes of Woodlands and in *Old Melbourne Memories* he remembers an early steeplechase there with his Protestant Irish relatives and friends. Then he adds: 'In this connection came Tom Brannigan, an active, resolute, humorous young Irishman. He was stud groom, and a model retainer during the first years of the settlement of Woodlands'. So there were Irish Catholic workers on these farms, and Irish small farmers at Donnybrook, Ballan, and the Romsey area.

Patrick Morgan came to Melbourne as an uneducated Irish farm worker from County Louth with nothing. He worked as a navvy on construction sites, then brought drays, moved into transport and small construction, building laneways, streets, and finally sewers, some under the Yarra, under contract to the Melbourne Metropolitan Board of Works (MMBW), and became moderately wealthy. For the first two decades of his life in Australia he lived as a bachelor in various North Melbourne boarding houses, mixing with his fellow Irish immigrants. His business partner Patrick McGrath came from West Meath, only 10 miles away from his home in Ireland. My grandfather educated himself at evening classes, had a love of learning, and in 1900, after two decades of hard work and at 45, married his partner's daughter, Catherine McGrath, aged 20, and brought the 'Niddrie' property as a family home, but also as a vertically integrated investment, as horses and oats were raised there for his business. He knew Archbishop Mannix but was not entirely a supporter. Coming from a part of Ireland with strong English influence, he admired the British Empire for its progress and organising abilities, and so didn't fit the anti-British Irish stereotype.

Our Spillane cousins were an Irish Australian North Melbourne family who started at the Melbourne Meat Market, and graduated to being wholesale butchers over three generations. My uncle John Spillane went to North Melbourne Christian Brothers College (CBC), and eventually bought a large house with extensive grounds, 'St Ives', in Ascot Vale. The Morgan and Spillane families had enough money to visit Irish relatives and kept up contact by letters. They sang 'The Mountains of Mourne', 'Cockles and Mussels', and 'It's a long way to Tipperary', and were conscious of Ireland not as a place of persecution, but as an amiable country, but with lesser prospects than Australia. My grandfather subsidized his family back in Ireland, and bought out sisters and cousins and settled them here.

My wife's family were also from North Melbourne, but they got there by a different route. Irish Catholics with the family names of Hearn, Hehir, O'Donnell and Livingston (a converted Scot), they moved from Maldon after gold and their small farm failed, and arrived at North Melbourne during the 1890s depression, a typical move at the time. They were closely connected with Dr William Maloney, the local Federal member, in Labor politics, himself the illegitimate son of Big Clarke of Rupertswood, and an Irish Catholic North Melbourne lass. My wife's father graduated through the Catholic Young Men's Society (CYMS) to be an ALP branch secretary and union official, and then after the split to be a DLP branch secretary. One part of the family moved to Kensington while working in the railways.

The Irish Catholic families of the north-west suburbs were dutiful, respectable and hard working, by no means Brendan Behan types. Senator Frank McManus was a typical example in personality, formerly a school teacher, direct, basic, without frills. The north-west suburbs had a large number of influential Evangelical churches, puritan, low church, wowserish, and the Catholics in some ways assimilated to the Methodist image. Many rarely went to a pub or the races, in spite of proximity of the horse racing industry; there was no wild behaviour, no singlets at the table, there were a large number of unmarried aunts and uncles at family gatherings, women wore fox furs like Dame Nellie Melba, respectable even if lower middle class.

Before you tried anything, you were taught to ask in your mind: What would people say? What would people think? It was not a Catholic ghetto, but though we mixed with others, Catholics also kept tightly together, wholly caught up in a spiritual and moral world deriving from Catholicism of a traditional kind, an endless round of novenas, retreats, emphasis on the final things, worry about sin, personal prayers, embracing a collective mind of some considerable antiquity. Tribal habits of mind persisted, though we were not living a tribal life.

I went to school at St Bernard's CBC Moonee Ponds with the Tobin family, who told me their family laid out the bodies of their fellow Irish in North Melbourne who were too poor to pay for funerals during the great depression of the 1930s, and so they got into the funeral business. Uncle Phonse Tobin was president of the North Melbourne Football Club as it, like Collingwood, was a predominately Catholic club, so Catholic its club history was written by a priest, Fr Gerry Dowling. In contrast the Essendon team, dominated by Essendon Baptists-St Johns, with John Birt, a lay preacher, Ken Fraser and Ken Fletcher, had surprisingly, given the demographics, few Catholics in it in the 1950s, though later contemporaries of mine at St Bernard's made the firsts. The brothers told us in the 1950s that the Essendon City Council was allegedly Mason controlled and perhaps anti-Catholic, and wouldn't allow CBC Moonee Ponds to use the Essendon Football Ground for weekly sports days. But sectarianism was generally mild.

In the mid 1960s three out of the four Labor Federal parliamentary leaders, Senators Pat Keneally and Nick McKenna, and Arthur Caldwell, were all Catholics from this part of Melbourne; the other one was Gough Whitlam. Senator McManus and Bob Santamaria were also prominent. They were all from the same stable, CBC North Melbourne, except for Keneally. My father and his brothers went to CBC North Melbourne and knew these politicians as acquaintances, rather than as political friends or enemies. CBC North Melbourne was founded after 1900, and St Bernard's CBC Moonee Ponds in 1941 for the same group of Irish Australian Catholics who had moved further out. St Aloysius North Melbourne and St Columba's Essendon were equivalent Catholic girls schools. The brothers were mildly anti-British: we were told not to admire Churchill who had sold out Australians in both world wars. Australian nationalism was stronger than Irish nationalism, though the penal law injustices in Ireland that led to hedge schooling (and to the Christian Brothers) were frequently mentioned. Catholicism, of the moral and anti-Communist variety, was the dominant influence, not Irishness.

Tinteán, August-December, 2007

THE 1974 FEDERAL ELECTION

(1974)

Developments which were new in the 1974 Federal election campaign have become more prominent in succeeding decades: the rising influence of the universities and the media, group think in the Canberra parliamentary press gallery, and partisan commentary and spin.

Most political correspondents [of the Canberra parliamentary press gallery] spend a lot of time in each other's company. They work in the same small area of Parliament House, they have access to the same parliamentary bar, they mostly drink at the same hotel, and they often will spend a reasonable amount of their social time at weekends with other journalists.

David Solomon *Australian Politics: A Third Reader*

The more one reads the newspapers and the magazines of the recent past, the more one realizes how little they know of the society which they affect to report, and how they understand even less. They seem to pass around each other's information and intimations, until their voice becomes one, and they succeed in creating a wholly artificial national mood.

Henry Fairlie *The Kennedy Promise*

It's surprising how much public opinion has changed recently when one reflects that Hugo Wolfsohn's influential *Dissent* article 'The Ideology Makers' was first published only a decade ago. Wolfsohn identified the old, WASP, legal-clerical Government House elite

('Fear God and honour the King') as the opinion-making circle who wielded influence (as distinct from direct power) in the community. How quickly and how completely have they faded from grace! 'This Day Tonight's' Geoffrey Watson last year interviewed some hard-faced old ladies from one of those innumerable Commonwealth societies which still abound, if not exactly flourish, here in Australia. These ladies saw quite clearly that they had been pushed from the centre of the stage, and they took up an anguished and rather bitter sniping position from the sidelines. Society was no longer theirs.

To the question: 'Who are the new opinion formers in the community?' the answer isn't hard to find. You just have to go to the old guard's champion to find out. When Sir Robert Menzies retired in 1966, he publicly prided himself on the two great achievements of his long term in power: the growth of Canberra and the growth of the universities. What terrible achievements to bequeath to his own party! The terminal result of this process unwittingly encouraged by Menzies is now becoming evident in the ballot box. The number of petitions from academics falling over each other to go into bat for Gough during the recent Federal election was truly staggering. Canberra itself has now expanded into two seats, both solidly Labor, and there may be a couple of senators on the way. And in the last two election campaigns, the parliamentary press gallery and associated journalists covering the campaign were solidly and openly behind Mr Whitlam, as Mungo MacCallum writing in *Nation Review* and Solomon and Oakes in *The Making of an Australian Prime Minister* make no attempt to hide.

As is well known, one of the significant factors in the 1972 election was the movement of the media, particularly the newspapers, into the Whitlam, if not the Labor, camp. Under the editorship of Graham Perkin, the Melbourne *Age* came out strongly for Whitlam who responded in kind by referring to it as 'one of the great Australian dailies' (he didn't name the others). Even the new owners, the Fairfax family, couldn't change its stance. Murdoch's *Australian* and *Mirror* were also patently Whitlam supporters, and the group's purchase of Packer's *Telegraph* removed the most stalwart, not to say bare-faced, supporter of the incumbent LCP administration. The advent of *Nation Review* only added to this swing.

Moreover, one big change in the press is that ownership is no longer synonymous with control. There are three kinds of newspapers, roughly speaking, when it comes to the question of control: owner-controlled, editor-controlled or journalist-controlled. By controlled here I mean who determines what goes into the paper, and the ideas and emphases it reflects. During the last few decades, effective control has in many cases shifted to the editor and his immediate colleagues who meet him in conference every day, and in some cases this process has gone further and the journalists themselves greatly influence the policy of the paper.

Australian metropolitan dailies represent all of these types of influence. The late Sir Frank Packer, until he sold the *Telegraph* in 1972, ran the paper directly on crucial issues in the old tycoon style perfected by Hearst and Beaverbrook. Fairfax Pty. Ltd. has a strong direct influence on the *Sydney Morning Herald*. When Murdoch bought the *Telegraph*, it was still owner-dominated, except its line was completely opposite to Packer's, so much so that McMahon described it as 'rancid' during the 1972 election campaign. The Melbourne *Age* is a good example of a paper which is controlled by its editor, Mr Graham Perkin, who personally dictates the editorial policy after the daily news and editorial conference. During the 1972 election Solomon and Oakes report that the owners were not able to make Perkin change his strongly pro-Labor line. In the recent election *Nation Review* claimed that Fairfax Ltd had been more successful in changing the *Age* back to an even-handed stance.

In many ways the flavour and opinions of *The Australian* come from its working journalists, columnists, reviewers and cartoonists, as much as from the editor or owner. This was shown a few years back when John Gorton objected to the way that people like Philip Adams, Bruce Petty, Ray Taylor etc. were always having a go at him. (*The Australian,* however, sometimes reverts sharply to owner domination when Rupert Murdoch is in the country or otherwise shows an interest in his paper). The ABC is another example of a mass media organization which is run by its working staff as far as its opinions and general flavour go.

These reflections on who controls the media were immediately occasioned by a rather curious and to my mind disingenuous statement signed by over 100 writers and journalists which appeared in the *SMH* on (guess when?) May 18th, which just happened to be the election day, although no mention of the election was explicitly alluded to in the ad. The copy went:

> We the undersigned writers and journalists voice our independence. Conscious of the overwhelming concentration of media ownership in Australia in so few hands we, the undersigned, wish to dissociate ourselves from the conservative bias expressed by the majority of proprietors. We support all efforts to make the Press truly impartial.

At the end of the ad. the following little note appeared: 'A group of journalists on the *Age* wish to make it clear that by signing this statement they feel they are endorsing the present impartial policy of their paper.'

I call this ad curious and disingenuous because it conceals much more than it discloses, and on the other hand implies many things without actually committing itself to them. For the ad implies, coming out on election morning that most papers were strongly supporting Snedden and the LCP ('conservative bias') and that the undersigned were dissociating themselves from this. Now this is a truly fantasy-ridden picture when practically all the reporting and comment on the election (which is the influential part, not the editorials) was favourable to Whitlam; this was quite openly admitted by Mungo MacCallum (one of the signatories of the ad incidentally) in *Nation*

Review. He doesn't hide how all the journalists were thoroughly cheesed off with Snedden before and during the campaign. If such an ad had come out a decade ago, when the mass media was owner-dominated and (with rare exceptions like the *SMH* in 1961) always automatically supported Menzies and the LCP coalition, then there would have been a lot of truth in it. But the situation is not at all as simple today. The ad performs its sleight-of-hand trick by presuming that ownership is synonymous with control and influence as it was in the past, but it's much too facile a judgement for the present time.

I thought it was assumed that the media was pro-Whitlam in the last two Federal election campaigns. The following four statements don't seem to leave much doubt:

> My guess is that, in early 1972, there was a strong preference for Labor (in the press gallery).   David Solomon *Australian Politics: A Third Reader*

> Most of the best and highest paid journalists in Australia vote Labor. Several of them vote Communist; but they're still happily employed in the capitalist press.   Mungo MacCallum, op. cit.

> In the area of the arts and the media, people there were again saying that they like the sound of what Labor are saying, but waited to see. Now, I think they are much more on our side.   Bob Hawke, *Farrago*, 16 May 1974.

> On one occasion, Murdoch even had a hand in the issuing of a Labor Party press release. He phoned [Eric] Walsh and said: 'What do you think of this idea – a press statement saying national service will end within a week of the election of a Labor government?' Walsh thought the idea was not bad, drafted the release, and phoned the news editor of the *Sydney Mirror*, Mark Day, to give him the story. Day listened as Walsh read out the statement, then asked somewhat unenthusiastically: 'What's news about that? Walsh replied: 'As far as you're concerned, mate, what's news is that it's Rupert's idea.' Solomon and Oakes *The Making of an Australian Prime Minister*

This last quotation is a particularly instructive one. Here is an example of all that journalists have cried out against for decades: owners of papers directly interfering in politics, journalists being forced to include material against their will because it comes from the proprietor. Yet we notice here a strange absence of horror and outrage on the part of Solomon and Oakes as they recount the story. In fact, the tone seems to admire Eric Walsh as he brings out his big gun in the last line. Why this strange double standard? Why no sympathy for their colleague Mark Day?

I'm pleased but rather puzzled to see that the signatories of the ad also want an impartial press. It's rather surprising because I'd thought that writers in *Nation Review*, the *New Journalist*, and the student press had, all for slightly different reasons, come out in favour of subjective and opinionated journalism recently and believed that 'objective' and 'impartial' reporting was, á la Marcuse, a myth. I don't remember any *Age* journalists complaining publicly about the pro-Labor partiality of their paper in 1972, or any Murdoch journalists for that matter. Indeed an article in *Nation Review* by C.M. Evans *complained* that the *Age* this time was being forced into an impartial stand by its owners. Do *Nation Review* journalists who signed the ad believe they are thereby criticizing their journal and Gordon Barton for allowing it to be such a biased and partial paper? Not very likely. Doubtless the signatories have some complex meaning for the word 'impartial' which eludes ordinary definition and explains the matter away. It seems to me a case of wanting to have the best of both worlds. Either you support the right of all proprietors (The Herald and Weekly Times, Fairfax and the late Frank Packer as well as Rupert Murdoch and Gordon Barton) to let their biases show, or you support the proposition that the press should be truly impartial. Here we have journalists condemning proprietors because they are partial, yet in other places justifying the anti-Establishment press because it is partial. This is an untenable position, for it can only be justified by such ludicrous propositions as: when Sir Warwick

Fairfax speaks he is evincing bias, but when Gordon Barton speaks he is stating impartial facts, or that: proprietors must be impartial, but journalists needn't be.

The position of the *Age* in all this is a peculiar one. It is a sort of schizoid paper. Part of it retains the old solid Scots conservatism of its origins and fits in with the establishment rhetoric of Wolfsohn's deposed ideology makers. When a new Governor of Victoria is appointed, its editorials still quiver with vice-regal delight. On Northern Ireland it betrays its old world background. Yet on other issues it is modern and progressive, even though it expresses itself in an absurdly pompous and superior way, as though it is announcing its liberalism from on high. It can't help affecting a mandarin tone even on the most trivial of matters. The two main commentators on the *Age,* Allan Barnes and John Jost, were openly pro-Labor during the recent election. On election morning Jost had an article very favourable to Whitlam and Labor. During the campaign the *Age* journalists like most others concentrated rather damagingly on Snedden's economic programme and on its alleged contradictions. This they were entitled to do, but they weren't entitled to keep quiet about Whitlam's economic programme, which they did. It was astounding to read articles by Jost and Kenneth Davidson in the *Age, after* the election, mentioning that contradictions had shown up in Whitlam's economics during the campaign and that there were dark days ahead. A crucial element in Mr. Snedden being brought back to the field in the last two weeks of the election was the attempted demolition of his economic policies by the financial journalists. The *Age* could hardly be called impartial in not analysing Whitlam's.

The Canberra press gallery does view the rest of Australia as the people 'out there' and wonder what they think. But that does not mean that there are not many out there who think the same way as they do. Where have all the new ideas come from which have displaced Wolfsohn's old 'ideology makers', and which the journalists agree with so readily? The short answer is, I think, from the academics.

Many of the journalists were former student editors (MacCallum, Solomon, Oakes, Richard Walsh). Moreover journalists as a rule have an admiration for academics in so far as the latter do seem to have ideas and can think about things and research them, whereas the average journalist feels pretty rushed with deadlines and having to spend a lot of time on ephemera. Academics themselves like to have their views heard by a wide public, naturally, so it's a nice cosy relationship. Listen any night to the ABC's 'Lateline' and you will see what I mean.

Wolfsohn in his article saw no decisive influence of universities on Australian life, only a fragmentary one. I think it is now a formidable and cohesive one. This change can be dated from about 1966 and 1967. President Johnson's adviser Clark Clifford said in a retrospective article that the crucial decision in the US withdrawal from Vietnam and Asia was the visit he made when he found that the South East Asian countries like Australia would not take up any more of the burden themselves. Holt told him that domestic pressures wouldn't allow him to commit more Australian troops. Now this pressure came mainly and initially from the academic left in Australia, and ever since this major political achievement their influence on the community has been growing. I am not saying that most people vote for the ALP because they believe the arguments of Marcuse as mediated through his Australian imitators, but an increasing number do.

Education (particularly tertiary) is tremendously important in our society as the focus for hopes of social improvement and advancement, and I don't think it is an exaggeration to say that in political terms the institutes of higher learning in Australia are a source for turning out Marcuse-believing ALP-voting products. It is instructive to note that the Victorian electorate of Henty, the only one won decisively by the ALP in the recent election, has Monash University within its boundaries. Teachers' federations and university SRCs contributed fair amounts of their members' funds to the ALP in recent campaigns. The conformity of ideological opinion in universities is quite staggering, and often bears no relation to the world outside. For example, the universal hatred of ex-Victorian Premier Bolte, not a particularly vicious or tyrannical man, I would have thought, was very noticeable, even though he was very popular in the community at large.

On all these matters the Liberal Party seems to know little and do less. There seems to me to be two main reasons for this. The first is that Menzies set up the federal Liberal Party primarily to put and keep himself in office. (The State Liberal parties do have some semblances of belief and grass root support and rapport.) Like the Gaullist Party after de Gaulle, the Liberal Party since Menzies has been without a *raison d'etre,* and a long collapse has set in. The total intellectual nullity of the Federal Liberal outfit is best seen in the Tanner drawing of ex-PM John Gorton in *Quadrant* November-December 1968. And in his first 18 months as Opposition leader Mr. Snedden thought he could get away with meeting the press without policies: they were always in the pipeline, he kept explaining, some committee somewhere was working on them at that very moment, etc. etc. You can't expect to get away with this sort of bankruptcy.

The other reason is that the university and media worlds (and their inter-connection) are completely foreign to most Liberals, who haven't a clue how they work and who treat them with awe when the old disdainful bluff has ceased to work any longer. The Liberals haven't started to understand the social change which has pushed the academies and ideas much closer to the centre of the stage, and displaced business and money in the process. Even eight years ago, it was striking how the Young Liberals, apart from the socialites, consisted 95% of misfits led by 5% of Young Lawyers all desperately trying to do an Andrew Peacock and get their pre-selection. The Liberals haven't yet realized that the hegemony of ideas in university/media circles is inimical to them in every way. 'Trendiness' means a blind accommodation to what one vaguely fears but doesn't understand, and it is dignified under the guise of 'pragmatism'.

A tell-tale sign was the way the media suddenly became nice to Messrs. Gorton, McMahon and Snedden as soon as they were defeated, while giving them a terrible hammering while they were trying to win election campaigns. The way the Liberal party stood by and watched Mr. McMahon crucified during his 18 months as Prime Minister was a suicidal act, because it was directed not at Mr. McMahon (the best Liberal Minister since Menzies) but at the Liberal Party itself, as was shown by the way the press eased up on McMahon after 1972 and transferred their venom to Snedden. Mungo MacCallum has said: 'It's almost unheard of for a press campaign on any political subject to change public opinion in a short time. Obviously, though, if every paper in Australia talked like the *Review* about McMahon for a year, there would be a very definite influence on public opinion.' (*Australian Politics*). Well, every paper in Australia practically did talk like the *Review* about McMahon for 1½ years, and the result was seen in the ballot box.

With Labor the case is much more complex. One notices about the phenomenon of [Federal ALP secretary] Mr. Mick Young that it is the press who keep telling us how phenomenally successful he was in selling the Labor Party to the press in 1972. There's something very strange and incestuous in all this; we are continually being told by the victims of Mr. Young's wiles what a great guy he is. With clients like these, he wouldn't have to work too hard for his bread and butter. Labor's natural honeymoon with the media would probably have gone on for about six months except for Senator Murphy's raid on ASIO early in the piece, which broke the spell; the polls started to go against the Labor government, and the pieces could never be put together again. At this point a certain sense of unreality came over the Labor Government. While Labor Ministers launched into their pet hobbies, the Government developed the curious mid-term mythology that Labor 'wasn't getting its ideas across' to the people.

This was in spite of all the favourable publicity they were getting. As I saw it, they were getting across what they wanted to do very well, and the people didn't like it.

Since the election, a new set of conditions has developed in which the Whitlam Government has to operate. The old vote-defying unrealism of Ministerial individuality has gone now with cold draughts of the election, the shock of Snedden's bid on inflation, and the post-election programme of austerity and restraint. On the other hand the far left of the Labor Party, who felt a certain restraint during the first Labor Government, are beginning to flex their muscles now that their government is relatively secure electorally. During the Vietnam period and Labor's long absence from office, many of them saw their chance in extra-Parliamentary politics. They now seem to have their chance from within.

The 1972 election showed, and the recent one confirmed the trend, that the electorate was moving in two opposite directions. The closer you got to the Canberra-Sydney-Melbourne and big cities complex, the more solid the vote for Labor; the more you moved to the country areas and the outer states, the more solid the vote for the LCP coalition. It was a rather heartening irony that the computer arrived on the scene to compute a national swing at the very two elections when the idea of a roughly uniform national swing ceased to have any meaning. Many interpretations have been placed on this dual movement of allegiance, and one which is worth considering is that those who had been most frequently exposed to the media and education in all its forms voted more for Labor, and those who were less affected voted more for the LCP. It's not just a matter of the country vote going against Labor. It's that the people feel generally disenfranchised. They feel less and less able to affect the centres of power and influence controlled by education, promoted by the media, and now endorsed by the government.

Quadrant, July-August 1974

THE PROGRESSIVE LIBERAL STRAND IN VICTORIAN POLITICS

(2000)

Victoria voted strongly ALP at the last Federal election, but this was historically unusual – the ALP has been electorally unsuccessful in Victoria, being in office for only 10 years out of 83 before John Cain Jnr's government in 1983. This is in contrast to the NSW ALP which was mostly in power. The left or labor forces in Victoria have been an uneasy amalgam of two groups: the working classes and trades unions on the one hand, and ideological progressives on the other. In the past the prominence of the latter group damaged the Labor image, but over the last few decades the trendy vote has flourished as the traditional Labor one has declined. The long tradition of moralizing in a superior tone on issues, inaugurated by Melbourne's early liberals such as George Higinbotham, Charles Pearson, David Syme, and Henry Bournes Higgins, is now paying electoral dividends.

To begin at 1850. In New South Wales authority was gradually devolved over seven decades from Governor rule through appointed members to self government; compromise and gradualism were the natural way of conducting affairs. Victoria, in contrast, had only a very short period of fifteen years from its founding before experiencing the shocks of the 1850s, when it had to cope simultaneously with four developments: separation, self government, the finding of gold, and a massive population influx. Authority did not have a chance to establish itself – the rules of the game had not been worked out. This was seen at Eureka, a relatively minor everyday grievance that was not handed well by either side, because no tradition of negotiation existed. Both sides quickly went to extremes, thus setting the Victorian pattern of heightening tension and seeking conflict. Victoria had got off to a bad start. What can be called the Melbourne mentality (and this applies to all sides of politics) converts issues into overtly political ones and ideologizes them; people hunt in packs, behave aggressively, and conduct gang warfare. Vincent Buckley once wrote that if you have an idea and want to spread it, in Sydney you throw a party, in Melbourne you found a journal.

At this early stage the clearest marker people brought with them was their religion. Power in Victoria is best analysed through four roughly equal, religiously based groups:

* Anglicans, over 30%, but not as strong as in Sydney.

* Scots Presbyterians, over 20%, influential in business, farming and politics, and with an extreme Orange wing.

* Irish Catholics, also over 20%, moving from radical to middle-of-the-road politics, and repudiating the secular liberals after State Aid was ended in the 1870s.

* Non-Conformists, including Methodists, Baptists, Congrega-tionalists, and others, 16% and rising, strong in the gold towns, and more wealthy, numerous and fashionable than in England.

These four religiously based groups were roughly equal in influence, there was no one dominant group, there was no established church, indeed no establishment to corral them, as in the old world, so they all threw their weight around. As a result visitors to Victoria were amazed by the depth of sectarian animosity.

The Victorian high liberals came from the fourth group. We have to imagine a non-conformist spectrum running from believers to non-believers, starting with the Evangelicals and moving across to the Unitarians and other vague Deists, and further on to agnostics, liberals, atheists, secularists, and so on. The non-believing end of this spectrum gained recruits and became more influential as some people suffered the loss of faith common in the later 19th century. Along this spectrum, those who remained religious argued for the 'social gospel', social justice in today's terms; those who discarded religion often used politics as a religion substitute, the kingdom of heaven on earth. Charles Pearson's biographer noted: 'Like many another reared in the Evangelical tradition Pearson found fulfilment in fighting for a cause'. Higgins' biographer wrote: 'Higgins had rejected his father's religion (though not religion entirely), but the moral zeal inherited from his father, which had been directed to personal salvation, was now being channelled, if in a confused way, towards broader social and political concerns'. In summary: the liberals came, not from those who remained religious, nor from those with no religious interests, but from those moving away from a previously strong religious belief. Very often you find a clergyman in the family background.

Five dominant liberals (Higinbotham, Pearson, Syme, Deakin and Higgins) set the tone of Victorian politics and public life. They held power by positioning themselves between the radicals and conservatives. Higinbotham, Pearson and Syme comprised the first group, coming to prominence from the 1860s, and they mentored their proteges of the next generation, Deakin, Higgins and others, who came to prominence from the 1880s onwards.

George Higinbotham was of Irish Protestant and Trinity College background. After a goldfield's stint, he became a journalist, precocious editor of the *Argus* at 30, a barrister, then a politician, Attorney-General, Chair of a Royal Commission on Education in 1866 encouraging a secular education system, then a Supreme Court Judge, and finally Chief Justice of Victoria. Like Dr Evatt, who admired him, he was a champion of civil liberties, like Justice Michael

Kirby he loved to give dissenting judgments and to grandstand. He was very subjective and self-regarding, so ideologically pure that he was ineffective in politics, and he transferred this trait – principles before votes – to the incipient Victorian ALP which he supported and of which he was a hero. He had a particular bug about an alleged conflict-of-interest in the Governor's position. This was a factor in Victoria's two constitutional crises, but he caused chaos by subsequently intruding this irrelevant obsession into many of the political and legal cases he was involved in.

Charles Pearson was a paler version of Higinbotham. His father was a clergyman of English evangelical Anglican background, the Clapham Sect. Pearson was in England an academic historian, here a headmaster, founder of Presbyterian Ladies College, an educationalist, *Age* journalist, politician, Education Minister and Chair of another Royal Commission on Education in 1877. A dry scholarly speaker and reserved in personality, he was only marginally more practical than Higinbotham.

David Syme's early interests were in religion: he studied for two years at a dissenting liberal Presbyterian theological academy in Scotland, and late in life wrote a book on the soul. With his brother he founded *The Age,* and made it famous for promoting protection, and for its political and public influence. *The Age*, the creator and carrier of the liberal tradition in Victoria, was supported by miners, radicals and urban manufacturers, and in turn supported them. Syme was dour and dry like other two, even more so. He was an impossible person – there was no give-and-take in his personality. The lawyer Sir Frederick Eggleston wrote of him: 'Syme was largely responsible for the heresy-chasing and head-hunting that are a feature of Victorian politics'. In other words, the Melbourne mentality.

Henry Bournes Higgins' father was a Church of Ireland clergyman who had moved to Methodism, not a good career move, as Methodists were thin on the ground in Ireland, so the family decamped to Victoria, where Methodists were almost flavour of the month. Higgins became a barrister, Home Ruler, state and federal politician, and eventually a High Court judge in charge of the Conciliation & Arbitration Commission, famous (or infamous) for his Harvester judgement. A contemporary, Wise, wrote of him as one 'whose preference for being in a minority, to his own disadvantage, was so pronounced'.

Alfred Deakin is well known: barrister, an *Age* journalist, politician and minister, state and federally, and finally Prime Minister. His main personal interests were literature and religion, rather than law and politics. Like the others he eschewed formal or organized Christianity, but remained a deist. In his twenties he was the head of Melbourne's spiritualists, believing in seances. All his life he wrote diary entries of self admonishment; his was a troubled puritan conscience, worried if he was fulfilling his true vocation in life.

Overall these five were a very successful group, reasonably wealthy, who became influential politicians, journalists and lawyers and received massive public attention; they largely set the tone of public life in Victoria down to the present. They were in favour of tolerance, equality and of liberation of all kinds, including women's rights, in favour of the separation of church and state, extending the franchise, freedom of individual conscience, and non-ostracism of dissenting opinions. They strove to redress inequalities and poverty. They opposed class domination and inherited privilege, and supported factory legislation, trade union rights, and the founding of universities and higher techs. In Victoria their particular liberal program included emancipation from the church and organized religions back to early simple days of Christianity. They favoured state intervention and state utilities, state control of education and urban housing. The state school system they introduced was highly centralized, and was the carrier of state-sponsored secular liberal ideas. They vigorously opposed the conservative establishment, arguing for reform of the Legislative Council, and a land tax to break squatter dominance.

Like any influential group, the liberals operated a closely interlinked network (their five biographies read almost like one). For example Pearson chaired debates at the Athenaeum which the young Higgins and Deakin participated in. As a judge Higinbotham sponsored the young Higgins' admission to the bar. Reciprocally the proteges returned the favours: Deakin in the Gillies-Victorian govemment appointed Higinbotham as Chief Justice and Pearson as a minister. Deakin in his Federal cabinet appointed Higgins to his High Court position. Pearson and Deakin wrote articles for Syme's *Age* as cabinet ministers. All were close (if you could get close) to Syme, who converted them from free trade to protectionism. Four of the five were journalists, three barristers, four politicians (but the non-politician Syme and Deakin were more politically influential than the other three), and two had clergymen fathers. They remained vaguely religious, Deakin and Higgins supporting the Unitarians and the heretical liberal breakaway Presbyterian Australian Church of the Rev. Charles Strong. Higinbotham, Pearson and Higgins were too high principled to be successful as politicians; Deakin was a sensible compromiser, and a more complex and impressive figure than the other four.

Reviewing their careers, we can draw certain conclusions which go against received opinion. They claimed to be victims and radical dissenters against the colonial and British administrations, against the squatters and the wealthy old establishment, but they formed a new establishment themselves. They invented as their target the straw man of an all-powerful establishment on British lines which did not exist in Victoria. *They* were the establishment. Positioned in the centre between conservatives and radicals, they had great influence in politics and in public opinion forming in this period. To get support and credibility they performed the trick – which left liberals still do today – of presenting themselves as courageous dissenters against the powerful.

They set up a tone of superior high mindedness, seen most noticeably in *The Age*. They spoke in favour of liberty and freedom and tolerance, yet their yearning for moral purity meant they were prone to impose their views on others in a quasi-coercive way. They lectured audiences on their failings in a parsonical tone learnt from their fathers. They never opened their own views up to scrutiny. Higinbotham and Pearson were early exponents of political correctness. They arranged to have removed from school texts certain Christian passages which they thought might offend agnostics, Jews, Hindoos and infidels. (The true motivation for this was, I think, their dislike of formal Christianity). They were dogmatic imposers as much as liberals. A contemporary, Professor H. Strong, said of them: 'I always hated all liberals, and disbelieved in their honesty. They would certainly crucify the Saviour'. This tendency to moral dictatorship increased under later pressures, and many of their successors ultimately dropped liberal values. We should note that Melbourne has produced the world's leading contemporary moralizer, Peter Singer, inventor of infanticide ethics, hardly a liberal position.

Melbourne's radicals were not scruffy marginalized outsiders who suffered for their courageous views. They were an elite, establishment dissenters playing both sides; this tradition of ruling class radicalism has continued down to the present. They did not advocate civil liberties for individuals so much as for categories of people (workers, women, the oppressed), and to achieve this they supported state intervention to solve social problems. A final contradiction: they were against British and Colonial Office rules when they interfered with their pet designs, but were pro-British empire in foreign policy – they were first to demand Britain act to secure Papua and the New Hebrides. They were not Australian nationalists. These anomalies, which arose in the formative period of Victoria's development, got into the DNA of the system and gave rise to the 'moral vanity' still bedevils public life in Melbourne – commentators taking themselves too seriously. (I leave readers to provide their own contemporary examples.)

Some years ago Ray Evans undertook a revisionist critique of arbitration and industrial relations history via Higgins's Harvester 'family wage' judgment. A similar and broader critique on the whole Melbourne progressive liberal phenomenon is needed for the following reason. The Victorian liberals carefully protected their legacy. Relatives and descendants controlled their biographies. Nettie Higgins, niece of Higgins, wrote his memoir; Edward Morris the son-in-law wrote a memoir of Higinbotham; Pearson's wife organized his memorial volume. They passed their ideology down to their disciples. The Melbourne school of history grew up learning left liberal ideas from them as their worldview, and they have returned the compliment by writing up a very favourable version of their predecessors. It's a closed circle – they are all in the same bubble. But in a new biography of Higinbothan, the legal historian J.M. Bennett shows that the *Australian Dictionary of Biography* entry on him is often inaccurate and quite biased in his favour. So the revisionist critique has begun.

Syme's promotion of protectionism is a familiar story. But Victoria was also protectionist in a more elevated sense. By the 1880s it was the economically dominant colony, with much more money and a more diversified economy than the so called 'premier' colony, NSW. Considering itself now the real premier colony it developed a superiority complex. It set itself up as better and opposite to NSW, which was considered traditionalist and set in its ways, even dowdy compared with progressive Victoria. Victoria was self-sufficient, it could go it alone (as WA contemplates today), it didn't need the other colonies, it could metaphysically quarantine itself from the rest. And not just in the Australian context. Victoria's hubris went further – it was, it believed, leading the world in social organization. The British

Liberal reformist politician Sir Charles Dilke was often quoted when he wrote in his *Problems of Great Britain*: 'Victoria has been the leader in the democratic and State-socialistic movements which render Australia a pioneer for England's good'. It was the world's exciting and innovative liberal socialist laboratory. Victoria led the world in wages' boards, old age pensions, eight hour day, factory legislation and so on. The collapse of the boom meant Victoria surrendered economic dominance, and it extinguished some but not all of this arrogance. Victoria prides itself that it has produced most political leaders and Prime Ministers since Federation; Hawke and Gillard had to come to Victoria to get to the top.

Where did the liberal lineage go to? The short answer is – it split. In the later 19th century there were two broadly contending camps, conservatives and liberals, but the increasing vote for Labor changed this. The liberals and conservatives had to merge to survive the new challenge. This split the liberals, as some like Higinbotham and Pearson and Isaac Isaacs moved to Labor rather than to the right. Deakin was crucial. In Victorian politics he had joined with Gillies in a centre-right ministry. In Federal politics he finally formed a Fusion one with conservative support; unlike the other four he was a sensible pragmatist. Deakin's liberal lineage (I think the truer liberal heritage) went through his son-in-law Herbert Brookes to Menzies' Liberal Party, whereas the Liberal Party in NSW is arguably more a conservative party.

The other part of the liberal tradition went to the left and the Labor Party. But did it remain liberal? Higinbotham and Higgins supported Labor while judges (no reprimand from their earlier biographers for this) and became Labor heroes; a portrait of Higinbotham was given pride of place at Melbourne's Trades Hall. This tradition was passed on to Higgins's niece Nettie Higgins, who married the left-wing novelist Vance Palmer. The Victorian ALP was a mixture of workers and trade unions, plus the progressive liberal tradition, (the middle-class thinkers, ideologists, lawyers, and later intellectuals and academics). This progressive group influenced the ALP via the magazine *Tocsin* and the Victorian Socialist Party (VSP), the main ginger group, the left but dominant third of the party, like the later Socialist Left.

Members of the VSP included the utopian poet Bernard O'Dowd, the politicians Dr Maloney, Frank Anstey and Maurice Blackburn, the young John Curtin then leaving religion, John Cain Snr, the Rev. Frederick Sinclaire, a radical Unitarian minister, and others. The VSP was like a small religious cult or sect; it ran Sunday Schools where it promulgated a socialist ten commandments. The VSP charged that the ALP was selling out to the capitalist system. The two groups (Laborites and liberals) did not fit well together, and the VSP influence helped keep the party out of power, as its radical agenda put off Labor voters. The Catholic *Tribune* of May 20, 1912, wrote: 'We want an annual conference [of Labor] that is a true representation of Labor, not merely the extreme section of it... The Labor Party in Victoria has for many years been on the rocks.' This was a reference to the left secularist clique, more interested in doctrinal purity than electoral success, which ran the Victorian party, as it did with Bill Hartley decades later in the 1960s.

The Victorian Labor Party was therefore very different from the NSW one. The Australian Labor Party was founded in Sydney. Cardinal Moran supported the London dock strikers and the Australian strikers in the 1890s and helped form a respectable, right wing ALP which was very successful electorally compared with its Victorian counterpart. This Labor-Catholic alliance lasted for a century, and is only now crumbling before our eyes. In Victoria the two groups, the socialist left and the Catholics, rejoined forces during the conscription campaigns and remained uneasily together until they fell out totally in 1955, but not in Sydney. Moreover Australian nationalism was stronger in Sydney, home of its main promoter *The Bulletin*, than in Melbourne, which had, strangely, both a more Anglo-Australian and a more radical atmosphere.

It's difficult to trace the precise trajectory of liberals discarding their liberal values. Obviously the first world war, which made many people disillusioned and cynical, and the Bolshevik revolution, which made many people pseudo-idealistic, had a great influence. The co-existence of cynicism and idealism is a dangerous mixture. Authoritarianism, always latent in 19th century liberalism with its superior moral tone, came to the fore. By the 1920s and 1930s left liberals involved in domestic politics favoured socialism, nationalization and state intervention, in other words widespread schemes of social engineering to impose their views on the community. Those involved in world politics often supported regimes that got to power by killing and kept in power by killing, like the Bolsheviks, hardly exponents of liberal beliefs.

Between the wars the fellow travellers Brian Fitzpatrick and Maurice Blackburn (the latter went to school at Melbourne Grammar) kept the civil liberties tradition alive, but they were radicals now on the margins of society, not at the centre like the 19th century liberals. Their bona fides as genuine liberals were severely compromised by their support of the Soviet Union. Continued emphasis on individual infringements of civil liberties in our society carried with it the implication that we were victims of a tyrannical society; there was no mention of the British civic virtues which make us basically a free society. Encouraging an individual's autonomous economic progress (the Deakin-Brookes-Menzies line) is a broader and truer form of liberalism than the civil liberties' concern with occasional victims of injustice.

For these reasons the Victorian ALP, identified in the public mind with extremists, continued to be in the wilderness. Nettie Higgins' family despaired of liberalism. Her brother Esmonde Higgins became an early Communist, and Melbourne radicals now made trips to Moscow or the Spanish Civil War as fellow travellers of Communism. In contrast in Sydney the influential philosopher John Anderson was a true libertarian turned anti-Communist, and inoculated Sydney thinkers from the Stalinist virus. In addition under his influence the liberal impulse was diverted away from the political realm into the libertarian push and its penumbra. By this stage both major [Melbourne] parties were to the left of their Sydney counterparts – a left Victorian ALP and a right wing NSW ALP, and Menzies more classically liberal than his NSW counterparts. Melbourne's long history of progressivism meant that under the pressure of events these ideas morphed into extreme, non-liberal ones. It became the home and repository of the hard left in Australia, and remains so to this day.

It is therefore no coincidence that when the antipodean Kim Philby, the Soviet agent Ian Milner, came to Australia from New Zealand he chose Melbourne where he felt quite at home. He helped set up the Melbourne University Politics Department, and arranged in 1944 a position in politics for Manning Clark, whose father was an Anglican clergyman and who swung between admiration for Christ and Lenin. When Milner left in 1945, he was replaced by the hard-line Communist Lloyd Churchward, whose family has been described as 'saturated with Methodist parsons and missionaries'. The Department was soon headed by William MacMahon Ball, whose father was an Anglican clergyman. The young MacMahon Ball contemplated joining the ministry but became a rationalist. Norman Richmond, an NZ friend of Milner and another crypto-Communist, was also appointed. Milner moved to External Affairs in Canberra, where the head under Dr Evatt had been Dr John Burton, whose father was a Methodist clergyman. James Jupp has written that there were 'many idealistic Stalinists at Melbourne University in the 1940s'. The Communist Party was founded in Sydney but the dominant Aarons family were from Melbourne, and its extreme wing, Jim Hill, a Soviet agent, and his brother Ted Hill, a Maoist agent, came from Melbourne. The Monash Maoists under Albert Langer were the most extreme of the Australian student demonstrations, thus continuing Melbourne's reputation for ideological fanaticism.

On the other side of politics only Melbourne had the ideological fervour to produce a Santamaria.

Liberation movements began in nineteenth century England as small middle-class and marginalized elites (sexual and homosexual liberation, socialists, agnostics, anarchists, bohemians, Marxists, nudists, nature lovers, vegetarians, etc), and after a long hibernation caused by two world wars and two depressions, they emerged in the 1960s onwards as the counter-culture, a mass movement, not a small elite. The bearded sandal wearers and fruit juice drinkers Orwell noticed as off-beat people at Fabian summer schools in the 1930s were now everywhere. Melbourne became the centre for political campaigns such as opposing the white Australia policy, supporting nuclear disarmament, the moratorium marches and so on. The progressive strand inherited from the 19th century grew as the traditional working class vote and trade unions diminished. *The Age* turned left liberal. Now wealthier university-educated people read it and voted Labor, and *Herald* and *Sun* readers began to look to the non-Labor parties. This first showed up in voting patterns in the 1974 elections under Whitlam: Melbourne, Canberra (known ideologically as a suburb of Melbourne), Sydney and the eastern states began to move to Labor, as did university seats. The left liberal ideological tradition began at last to have electoral success. Melbourne Labor voters don't emote when they see Simon Crean, but they do when they see Julian Burnside.

Quadrant, June, 2011

The result of these developments today is that, whereas in every other state the two party preferred vote is usually neck and neck, in Victoria Labor has a substantial lead.

Russia and East Europe

DISSIDENT MOVEMENTS IN THE SOVIET UNION

(1970)

The beginnings of a visible dissent movement in the Soviet Union and its satellites.

In the worst days of the past in the Soviet Union, opposition was not even possible. In Stalin's simple society, there were only two categories: the rulers and the ruled. Those who disagreed in any way either had to leave or become 'internal emigres', reduced to silence, to the same level as the other victims in the society. For a decade since 1956, due to the relaxation of the total nature of the terror (but not an elimination of control-by-terror itself), a new and precarious development took place: the 'internal emigres' were able to speak, only just, and not with impunity, and the most courageous did. Because of these men, we now have documents from inside the Soviet Union: underground manuscripts which have found their way to the West; the transcripts of some of the trials at which the defendants spoke; and the appeals, petitions and protests to the courts, to their rulers and to world opinion against their arrests and sentences, and against the conditions in the forced labour camps to which they have been condemned.

The opposition has arisen on three fronts, which, though separate and distinct, are remarkably similar in style and content. The best known in the West is that of the dissident writers and critics. From the trial of the young Leningrad poet Josif Brodski (1964) and the publication of the Yugoslav Mihajlo Mihajlov's *Moscow Summer* (1965) to the recent series of trials and imprisonments of Daniel and Sinyavsky (1966), Bukovsky (1967) and Ginzburg, Galanskoy and Dobrovolsky (1968), and the harassment of the leading novelist Solzhenitsyn and the leading poet Voznesensky, the world has witnessed a continuous contest between the regime and these writers, who are irrepressible and keep producing more of their kind. But they are still small in numbers, loosely grouped, un-institutionalized and without coherent political demands.

Less well known in the West, but now coming to public attention through the large number of studies on it, is the extraordinary persistence of religious belief in Russia, and the increased repression, amounting to persecution, of it. Because its adherents are so numerous and are gathered in revered bodies such as the Russian Orthodox Church, the regime, which fears above all the establishment of alternative centres of loyalty and power, has intensified its anti-religious propaganda and severely curtailed religious practice, especially among the young. New legislation to this effect was introduced in 1963 and 1966. The number of Orthodox clergy and buildings was almost halved between 1961 and 1964. Scores of Baptist clergy and hundreds of Baptist laymen have been tried and given long sentences in labour camps. A de-registration policy has been applied by the regime to atomize the congregations and prevent new structures forming. Repression of religion in the last decade has been worse than in the later years of Stalin.

Hardly at all known in the West is the most widespread and most political opposition, the ferment among the nationalities within the USSR, of which the Ukrainian is the largest, though its extent is not known. It is a movement objecting to the forcible Russification of local life, culture and administration, which reduces the 'Republics' to the status of a colony under imperialist domination. The most articulate leader of the Ukrainian movement for national autonomy and independence is the young literary critic Ivan Dzyuba, the author of *Internationalism or Russification?* (1965), who describes the Ukrainians' struggle as 'the spontaneous, multiform, widespread, self-originating processes of a nation's 'self-defence' in face of a clear prospect of disappearing from the human family'. Scores of young Ukrainian intellectuals were rounded up in the mass arrests, secret trials and imprisonments, for promoting nationalism and defending the use of their own language. The seriousness with which the Ukrainian Communist Party viewed the political implications of this development can be seen in the severe sentences imposed, often 10-15 years' hard labour; but instead of eliminating the opposition, the trials produced much more public support and discontent than ever before.

The three movements are composed of fairly young writers, intellectuals, poets, critics and religious people, both Christians and Jewish. The most sensitive people in the society cannot live with the constant everyday human deprivations which the regime causes, and they insist that areas of free moral judgment be left outside the regime's jurisdiction. The protest does not at first take a political form – all state that they are not anti-Soviet. But it is anomalous that those brought up entirely within the mind-warping Soviet atmosphere are the most strongly against it. The new opposition is the visible part of the iceberg of the underground. It has dissociated itself from official organizations. Solzhenitsyn and other writers have accused the Writers' Union of carrying out governmental censorship and of attacking persecuted writers like Pasternak. In all cases, they consider that their official organizations have, by collaborating with the regime's policy of suppressing their proper interest, abdicated any moral leadership they might have; so they appeal over the heads of these bodies directly to the State administrative and legal systems for what they want.

The first means of protest devised by the three groups have been petitions and appeals to the country's leaders or to constitutional authorities. They take up the post-Stalin leaders' professed concern for legality, constitutional correctness and fair trials, and with meticulous attention to legal detail, and confining themselves to a documentation of objective facts, they point out the discrepancy between the law and what happens in practice, e.g. the right to practise religion and the right of nationalities to secede if they want to are guaranteed by the Soviet Constitution; there is no law against publishing in the West. They state openly, at length and without rash accusations, how bad the situation is, in what way it is illegal and irregular, and ask for it to be remedied. And others keep this up when those who wrote the original petitions are arrested, illegally, for doing so.

One of the most insistent demands in all these documents is not only for freedom in the present, but for a revelation of the full truth about the past, the full truth about the purges, secret police terror, illegal arrests, forced migrations, camps and the maladministration of justice under Stalin. Daniel, Solzhenitsyn and Karavansky have for the first time publicly recited lists of the names of those who were murdered. Daniel ended his final plea by saying: 'Evidently these people must have died in their beds from a cold in the head, if we are to believe the assertion that we did not kill. To pretend that it didn't happen, that we didn't kill these people, is an insult. It is – forgive me for putting it so bluntly – like spitting at the memory of those who have perished'. In all cases, the result of these demands for truth and legality has been increased suppression. At first a semblance of legality was observed in having semi-public trials, but more recent ones have reverted to secrecy. The defendants are obviously condemned beforehand; the striking resemblances to the trials of the thirties have been pointed out inside Russia itself. The trials are used by the regime to eliminate the most forthright dissenters and to intimidate and terrorize the others into submission.

But this has not always worked. The defendants use their interrogation and trials as a platform to try to put their case once again. The transcripts reveal that their calm, rational and persevering answers show up the hectoring, Vyshinsky style methods still employed by the prosecution. So the trials themselves become a further example of inhumanity and the knowledge of their sentences becomes a further cause of protest. The trials have been marked by public demonstrations of support by showering the defendants with flowers. Since the series of illegal trials, there has been a further claim by the opposition movements: that not only was there brutality and terror in the past, but that it exists today, and that the two are continuous and similar. One Ukrainian, Mikhailo Masyutko, says in a letter to the Prosecutor of his republic: 'The unavoidable conclusion is that people are condemned for their words, for voicing their thoughts, as they used to be in the days of Yezhov and Beria, the times of terror and repression.'

There is a basic religious impulse and religious imagery in the work of those poets like Pasternak and Anna Akhmatova who kept alive the Russian literary heritage from pre-Revolutionary to post-Stalin times. A significant number of today's writers and intellectuals of the dissident kind have become religious, often Christians (e.g. Mihajlo Mihajlov, Svetlana Stalin, Valery Tarsis). Much underground literature has religious overtones: there is an interest in religious philosophy, particularly the Russian Christian humanism of the Berdayev variety. This suggests that here is some connection between religious attitudes and rejection of the regime. One glimpse of the way things may be going can be got by following the progress of Sinyavsky's religious position through the pages of *On Trial*. Sinyavsky started off as a fairly vehement anti-religious rationalist of the 19th century variety. However, during the course of trying to discover and link up with Russian cultural traditions by a study of old Russian culture, folklore and primitive art, he came to see the crucial role of religion, and in particular that of the Orthodox Church, as a bearer of that culture. By the time of his imprisonment he had come to a theist position, as shown in his *Unguarded Thoughts*.

One commentator has said that 'increasingly the Church looms as the single institutional repository of the past, of national cultural traditions and ancestral style'. This is just as relevant in the Ukraine where many of the jailed writers are also interested in their own folklore and cultural traditions, and find them inseparable from their nationalist-religious base. The Ukraine is one of the most religious areas in the USSR; many of the persecuted Baptist communities are found there and in peripheral places associated with an ethnic nationalism. The Ukrainian national movement has been expressed through literary means from the time of its founder, the poet Taras Shevchenko (1814-1861), to the symbol of the modern upsurge, the young, dead poet Vasyl Symonenko, the critic Dzyuba and many other writers.

The writings of these movements reveal attitudes exactly opposite to those of official Soviet ideology. They are characterized by pessimism, a belief in the existence of evil, and a conviction that Communism is limited to the economic-material sphere and can't of itself bring happiness or produce, in Mayakovsky's phrase, a 'spiritual revolution'. Typical of the mood of pessimism and sadness is this underground poem by V. Kovskin:

> Here everything reeks of gradual death.
> We are fishermen. Here people don't cry,
> But only drink and drink and drink,
> And sing dreadful songs,
> And pay for their songs with their lives.

The Party and Communism are seen as limited; they can produce only certain things, material comfort and economic advancement perhaps, but that is all. To claim Communism has limits is an unforgivable heresy, as it denies the chiliastic pretensions of the creed. The following stanza in a new Baptist hymn replies to the State's anti-religious propaganda that the Sputnik astronauts have proved that God doesn't exist because they found no signs of him:

What of it that you can soar above the earth.
With transient glory on your mortal brow?
You will take off into space again,
But you will still die here on earth.

Chornovil states in his petition:

The highest material saturation, without free thought and will, does
not constitute Communism. It constitutes a great prison, in which
the food rations for prisoners have been increased. Even under
Communism people will suffer – the sufferings of the ever-striving
intellect. Even under Communism there will be contradictions,
occasionally tragic ones.

Mihajlov concludes *Moscow Summer* similarly:

At root, the psychology of *homo sovieticus* is a blind trust in a
science which knows better than we do how to sleep with our own
wives, how to be friends with our friends, even what we really want
in life...Just at that point (an economically and socially just society)
the essential problems will arise – and then what? For man will never
be satisfied with the idea that he is born in this cosmos and 'that's
all', that his only aim in life is to live well.

The 'man does not live by bread alone' theme is also seen in the
way the dissidents accept habituation to deprivation.

The holocaust which Stalin and his small Party elite put Russia
through for a quarter of a century created all the conditions
for producing in a naturally religious people what has always
been regarded in the Occidental world as the classical religious
disposition, that the world is a vale of tears and that there is nothing
permanent under the sun. Robert Conquest remarks in the Editor's
Preface to *Religion in the USSR* (1968):

On Marx's view, religion will flourish in proportion to the
unpleasantness of ordinary existence...It is clear that even now
both material and spiritual conditions in the Soviet Union are not
at the required level (for religion to die out). Of the generation now

in middle age, large numbers underwent senseless bereavement, an experience notoriously tending to turn many minds to religion.

With their tone of long-suffering and their description of man as a frail and suffering human being, today's documents show their authors to be the authentic heirs of those who experienced and wrote about the great terror, such as the recently published *Into the Whirlwind* by Evgenia Ginzburg and *The Deserted House* by Lydia Chukovskaya. But the situation is different now in certain ways. At the time of the holocaust itself, the terror was so artificial, unnatural and incomprehensible that it could neither be described nor analyzed, and the reaction was often one of total and absolute rejection; millenarian sects flourished in and around the camps.

Usually these sentiments exist today not in explicit statement but in a certain calmness of tone which invades the writing – the end of Ginzburg's letter to Kosygin is an example: 'But I love my country and I do not wish to see its name sullied by the latest unchecked activities of the KCB. I love Russian literature and I do not wish to see two more writers sent off, under guard, to fell trees.' The tone arises from the fact that the present regime has been just permissive enough to enable the most sensitive people to comprehend the ordinary life and sufferings that men endure in normal times, what is in the nature of life and not artificially imposed, and to be able to distinguish this from the especial deprivations peculiar to the Soviet regime. And because they know the lot of man on earth, they can repudiate the Party's chiliastic claim to lift people above that condition.

As the dissidents' views don't appear as an explicitly stated programme, the regime's officials don't quite know what they are up against, though they sense in it a tremendous threat, ultimately subversive of the regime's intentions. They are bewildered, not in taking action – in which they have been increasingly decisive – but in understanding. Chornovil relates the case of a high-ranking KGB officer in the Ukraine who believed that 'a person whose ideological foundations are weak will immediately develop anti-Soviet feelings upon reading a book with a 'hidden text' which contains a valid criticism of our system'. He quotes other examples of the secret police looking for 'underground currents' and 'forbidden hints', as though they believed that the Ukrainian writers were secreting in their works cryptic passages for the enlightenment of the initiated.

It may be that their complaint against the regime, which is persecuted and suppressed if stated openly, is manifesting itself in literature as a way of surviving and propagating itself. Chornoril asks the question: 'Is it possible that non-Marxists have absorbed better than our leaders the Marxist-Leninist thesis that to forbid the spreading of ideas is to increase their strength and attractiveness?' In *Love Declared*, an appendage to his earlier work, Denis de Rougemont suggests that Pasternak's *Doctor Zhivago* is a modern example of the same process. A similar, though unconscious process may be taking place today in that the complaint is being expressed in literary form in a manner subliminal to the heresy-detection apparatus of the State's cultural policemen.

There has been for a decade in Soviet Union a situation precariously maintained, in which the regime was tyrannical enough to provoke opposition, but not tyrannical enough to totally silence it. When the Russians invaded Czechoslovakia, the world at large realized that this situation had come to an end. But anyone who knew how the three main opposition groups in Russia were being treated would not have been surprised (though he would still have been shocked) at the Russian decision to invade. The movement towards freedom in Czechoslovakia had the same origins, characteristics and demands as those in Russia, with one important addition: from January last year their demands (e.g. for a ventilation of the past) were actually being carried out. Moreover, combined with the economic grievances, they had become a political force. The speed at which the demands were escalating was remarkable. The Russians could hardly have missed the similarities with the movements which had been worrying and preoccupying them inside Russia.

The Soviet government had to make a choice: to allow liberalization or to suppress it. They have decided to suppress it, and the future looks grim for Soviet citizens. Mrs. Daniel, Pavel Litvinov and others have already been tried and sentenced for demonstrating against the invasion. The precarious balance has gone. That situation, during which we heard for a short while the voices of resistance and humanity, has ended. The opposition has been silenced and the society reduced again to a simple one in which there are only the rulers and the ruled. The idea that there would inevitably be a continuous, liberalizing slide towards freedom in Russia has been disproved. The tragedy is that it was the best people, the most courageous and fearless, who spoke up and it is they, in Russia and in the Ukraine and in Czechoslovakia, who are now being repressed and slowly eliminated.

Quadrant, January-February, 1970, abridged

Another stalemate with some similarities prevails today in Russia under Putin.

THE TRIUMPH OF THE PROLES

(1993)

The ramifications of the collapse of Communism.

When the Communist regimes of Eastern Europe and the Soviet Union collapsed, some people gleefully announced that those who had been publicly anti-Communist now had no *raison d'etre* in life. Others said that Communist regimes had never been a threat, so why all the fuss for seventy years? A third reaction went even further, claiming the demise of Communism in the East as a setback for world peace since no counter-balancing power now existed to inhibit the dominant power of the United States. These are peculiarly contorted reactions. Anti-Communists should have been praised for being proved correct; instead in these cases they were spoken of as the losers, if not indeed the culprits.

Anti-Communism was not primarily negative. As its name implies, the Congress for Cultural Freedom and like-minded groups were devoted to expanding the realm of freedom in our societies. As James McAuley put it in *Quadrant* in October 1971:

> The principle of a healthy society and culture is that different institutions and activities have a considerable degree of autonomy. Science has its own way of working, its own canons of value. So do literature and the arts, each in its own way. So do economic activities, or the family, or education. So does politics itself have its proper activity. Each of these things has a principle of health and integrity.

This was the positive aim. When a community stimulates its

members into a variety of independent functions, civilization is possible. We are fortunate to have evolved a political system (based on the classical Greek notion of democracy, the Judaeo-Christian emphasis on the individual, the British parliamentary system of representative government and the Enlightenment belief in tolerance) which gives us the ability to do this. Cultural freedoms already in existence must be preserved from encroachment, a point McAuley also understood:

> The politicisation of culture occurs when any institution or activity is subjected to control or manipulation in such a way that its proper nature and canons of value are no longer the chief consideration. Instead, the controllers and manipulators have as their overriding criterion how much political advantage can be squeezed out of any institution or activity. It seems to me that the need to resist and overcome the totalitarian tendencies working openly or under masks for the politicisation of our culture is greater now than fifteen years ago.

That was written in 1971 – it is at least equally true today.

It so happened that over the last six decades the dominant threat to the workings of free societies came from totalitarianisms of the right and left; then after the Allies' military defeat of Nazism in 1945, Communism remained for four decades the principal threat. It is a great relief that Communism seems to be disappearing, but the tasks of encouraging structures which allow vibrant activity, and of preventing incursions on them, remain. To do this we have to recognize the totalitarian tendencies in both Eastern cultures and in our own.

Though it had virtues, the Enlightenment also had weaknesses which have shown up over time. In its view the individual was an all-powerful, all-encompassing agent of self-transcendence. Once we had sloughed off the obscurantist cloak of religious superstition holding us back, we could emerge resplendent as controlling deities, remaking the world in our own image. No obeisance to a higher wisdom, no deference to the past or tradition, no recognition that we don't understand everything would impede our progress towards a more exalted state. Coupled with various monomanias, like scientism and materialism, this Enlightenment arrogance has over the centuries paradoxically eroded the human freedoms that the Enlightenment itself proclaimed (this is one of the motifs of Paul Johnson's *History of the Modern World*). In its communal strain, this engorging hubris led to the totalitarian state, which appropriated to itself all rights, achievements and control. It allowed no inputs, being sufficient unto itself; in a gross parody of religion, it claimed to provide citizens with meaning and transcendence.

In a much less virulent, though still debilitating form, these same beliefs have permeated Western cultures and remained influential, but more in the personal than in the political sphere. This has led to our current obsessions: overemphasis on rights, on narcissism, on the here and now, on envy, on dominance and on the struggle for power for its own sake. Modern liberated individuals believe they live under no thrall, countenance no taboos, and acknowledge no domain outside their own resources. 'Doing your own thing' leads by logical extension to the belief that we have dominion over the conditions of our own life and death.

Many encroachments on freedom in both East and West derive therefore from the same source. It is, as a consequence, not true to state that the collapse of Communism means that we now have nothing to strive for or against. The demise of one virulent strain, Communism, does not lay to rest the whole virus, which breeds in the danker recesses of the human psyche. We have had the good fortune to be able to watch (but not undergo) in Eastern Europe and the Soviet Union the horror story which results if these tendencies are not contained.

The extraordinary thing about recent events in Eastern Europe and Russia is that regimes looked solid and immovable, and yet they crumbled, completely discredited, at the first serious challenge. Since George Orwell wrote *Nineteen Eighty-Four*, the novel has been widely acclaimed but one thing puzzled its readers. Why did Orwell say, 'If there is hope, it lay in the Proles'? This seemed a weakness in the book; it looked a long shot that the demoralised, unorganised ordinary citizens, who were outside the power hierarchy, would eventually triumph over it. It appeared that change would more likely come from disgruntled intellectuals and apparatchiks within the system. Yet Solidarity in Poland was made up of Proles, ordinary Polish people united for communal ends. Orwell was right in foreseeing the split which would develop between the ruling elite and the masses. The structure of the regime in Poland looked solid and stable yet under it a new, civic society was slowly growing up, though we could not see it at the time. Ordinary people wanted nothing to do with the party and determined not to play its game; instead they went about setting up normal social organisations outside its orbit. They did not make a direct political challenge, but simply created an alternative society by utilising the 'power of the powerless'. This was happening throughout the 1980s. A living healthy organism had come into being under the carapace of the regime; in Moroz's phrase the cogs had become human. (One the best accounts of this process is Jeffrey Goldfarb's *Beyond Glasnost: The Post-Totalitarian Mind* (1989).)

Individual dissidents had for decades taken this position. The word 'dissident' is not a good description of their activities, implying as it does a negative disposition, like the West's adversary culture. Those who were identified as dissidents were actually creating oases of cultural freedom. The next move was for whole societies to act the way these individuals had; this happened first in Poland. In his novels Tadeusz Konwicki prophetically listed the conditions necessary for freedom-loving groups to break the regime's grip: that the movement be spontaneous (not politically organised), communal (not individual dissidents), and linked with the nation's past. When things came to a head in 1989, the regime's structures quickly disintegrated; it had the rigidity not of firm control, but of death. Its skeletal remains couldn't even hold the Party together, much less the whole country. A new type of society was revealed to those watching. This appeared to happen quickly in 1989, but the necessary groundwork had been going on unseen for a decade.

The people to be thanked for causing the collapse of Communism are those who took a stand at great personal cost over many years to remain spiritually free of the regime's mentality. Some names which spring to mind are: Solzhenitsyn, Sakharov, Sinyavsky, Bukovsky, Grigorenko, Moroz, Chornovil, Havel, Walesa, Michnik and Kuron. Solzhenitsyn worked on the principle that 'one cannot accept that the disastrous course of history is impossible to undo, that a soul with confidence in itself cannot influence the most powerful force in the world'. He was correct and the dissidents, and now whole countries, have triumphed. They believed that liberal Communism was not possible. Every attempt at liberalisation (in Poland in 1955 and 1980, in East Germany in 1953, in Czechoslovakia in 1968 and in Russia in the thaw years of the early 1960s) failed, because when the threshold of liberal Communism was reached, it couldn't be held in a stable state – further freedoms meant it would topple over into democracy, with alternative political parties and so on, and the system worked to drag it back from that. In Poland in 1989 for the first time, a liberalised system did topple over into freedom, and the game was up. It happened in the Soviet Union two years later. The old guard had lost their will to power; only Boris Pugo was faithful to the old ways in the end.

Solzhenitsyn much more than Gorbachev brought the regime down, but many Western commentators, addicted to the thirty-second sound bite rather than the thirty-year panorama of events, seemed blind to this. The Gorbachevites were swept along by events swirling out of their control. They believed in working within the system to rationalise it as much as possible, so that Communism would work more effectively. They failed in their own eyes, so it is strange that they have received so much praise in the West. That praise came from those who held a similarly unlikely position: that there was nothing inherently wrong with Communism, that Communism and pluralism could co-exist peacefully, and that there was no moral difference between the Communist and capitalist systems. The point of view with which *Quadrant* has been associated, that Communism was utterly unviable, has been vindicated, even though we made the mistake of overestimating Communism's longevity, focusing too much on its rigid, overlying political structures and missing what was going on underneath.

A civic society was one kind of development. Another possibility, more apparent in the Soviet Union than in Eastern Europe, was that the system had normalised itself over the decades. So many compromising elements existed in daily life that a *modus vivendi*, a kind of perverse social contract between citizen and state, had become internalised. The dissident's desire to be spiritually free had not taken hold. The regime's designs had been imprinted in the minds of its citizens, but without obvious physical coercion. People had come adept at terrorising themselves from within. This is called 'totalitarianism from below', control by mutual complicity. Havel has explained many times how it operates:

> Almost every day I am struck by the ambiguity of this social quiescence...The killing and war merely assume a different form: they have been shifted from the sphere of observable social events to the twilight of an unobservable inner destruction...the slow, secretive. bloodless, never quite absolute yet horrifying ever-present death of 'non- action, 'non-story', 'non-life', and 'non-time'; the strange collective deadening – or more precisely anaesthetising – of social and historical nihilization.

Modernity arose early this century, around the time of the First World War. The Russian Revolution took place at the same time. Totalitarian regimes ushered in the uncertainties of our century while at the same time claiming to have a solution to them. They postponed the plunge into modernity by offering coherence, meaning and transcendence. Opposing these regimes also gave to some of their citizens a certain meaning to life. Communism was therefore profoundly reactionary. People in the East are now being lowered into the cauldron of modernity after many decades in a state of suspended animation. So when party and state crumbled in Russia, we saw not a civic society underneath, but a black hole, an implosion, with many of the old tensions, envies and anxieties given new rein under different auspices. We see now in some states of the former Soviet Union little ability to retrieve the situation, because long-existing webs of complicity can't easily be untangled. In this way some strains of the totalitarian virus may survive the demise of Communism – Bolshevik tactics without Bolshevism itself, as Adam Michnik described it during his visit to Australia last year. This present condition is one for which we as yet have no name.

Incapacity for clear-cut action cripples any society. Top heavy command bureaucracies are an illustration. A productive base of 80 per cent of an economy can support a superstructure of 20 per cent of mendicant enclaves, but if the superstructure begins to outstrip the base and dictate to it (as happened in Communist countries), then the enterprising areas of the economy wilt and stagnate. Even worse, gradually the productive sectors become infected by the prevailing malaise; they come to envy the cosy rackets of the 'sheltered workshop' sector, which society's powerbrokers reward. What's the point of striving? They eventually join what they cannot beat. Almost the entire economy, diverted by sloppiness, becomes attenuated from reality and collapses. Whole generations may lose the very idea of entrepreneurial drive, even after liberation, and become used to slackness and inertia. In this situation it becomes very hard to restart. The heroic actions by Yeltsin and his allies at the time of the August coup did however show signs of a different style emerging. In both Eastern Europe and the old Soviet empire the 'civic culture' and the 'black hole' scenarios contend for dominance, and we don't know what will eventuate.

Faced with this dilemma, the people of the East are naturally reacting against modernity's large, impersonal agglomerations, back to earlier and smaller groupings. Their basic point of identification is with their race not with their country. From Yugoslavia to Azerbaijan, ethnic origin is the determining factor. Marx was wrong – class doesn't matter half as much as clan. Sick of the future-oriented fantasies of the former Communist states people are fleeing to the past to give meaning to their lives. The Ukrainian Valentin Moroz has defined what is objectionable in progressive ideologies:

> In America as in Russia, a person without roots is not regarded as inferior, but, on the contrary, boasts of his break with tradition and [of his] 'open-mindedness'. A person attached to definite traditions is regarded as 'backward' both here and there...If you wish to prove you are 'progressive', forget your ancestry, and become a 'universal man' (which actually means a Russian).

At the same time as people are moving to smaller social groupings in search of meaning, economic circumstances demand larger units to survive in today's world of multinational corporations and trading blocs. We are at present witnessing the unbearable strain on these emergent peoples as they are being pulled in two contrary directions simultaneously.

In less drastic form we see some of these problems in our own societies. Many East European thinkers (such as Kundera, Brandys, Zinoviev and Konwicki) believe that a species of 'normalised' totalitarianism is coming to the west as the form of societal organisation which naturally fits modern life. The characteristics include control of information sources, large single-employer monopolies, artificially generated crises which disorient ordinary people, attacks on the possibility of objectivity, the rearranging of reality to suit ideology, and the use of language games for control.

By these means independent activities are made difficult, and complicity the norm. The East is now forced to face the dispiriting experience of modernity while the totalitarian temptations in our society increase. There may be some convergence between the two types of society, though each has had a different trajectory. From opposite perspectives novelists like Milan Kundera (in *The Unbearable Lightness of Being*) and Saul Bellow (in *The Dean's December*) write on this theme.

In the East a rigid pattern was imposed on society, though a civic culture was able to flourish in places. Our situation is the reverse: we have political freedom, but some of our cultural myths are so ingrained that they could erode it. A significant part of public opinion is formed by a media-academic nexus based on lack of faith in ourselves. This mindset holds that the capitalist, consumerist West is the root of all evil; that thinkers should engage in critique of our society to reveal the hidden sources of our iniquity; that other societies, including socialist ones, unlike us at least have good intentions; that all problems, including international ones, can be solved by caring; that the environment should be privileged at the expense of commerce; and that we should look primarily to the state to solve problems.

Recent events should have demolished this world view. Among the biggest changes have been the collapse of Communism, the economic move away from big government and pump-priming, and international policies against delinquent regimes, as in the Gulf War. Surprisingly the old mindset persists among some Western intellectuals while ordinary people turn away from it. One now notices a yawning gulf between the actual state of the world and interpretations of it. This means that the dangerous split between elite and masses, so noticeable in Eastern Europe and Russia, is embryonically present here.

To defend a mindset that doesn't accord with reality, ever

more opaque, paradoxical and mystifying concepts are invented. Deconstructionist theory is an example. After the death of Paul de Man, it was disclosed that as a young man during the Nazi occupation of his country Belgium, he had written articles in favour of Hitler and the deportation of Jews. Most of de Man's defenders argued that his later critical work denied and atoned for his earlier indiscretions. But in the *Times Literary Supplement* of 17-24th June 1988, Tzvetan Todorov pointed out a continuity between the two phases of de Man's life – in both cases de Man believed there was no connection between literature and truth; in both cases he placed the claims of myth above rational thought. Many totalitarian tendencies are apparent in deconstructionist theory. It has no priorities or values, is endlessly self-referring and denies objectivity. Like Marxism it interrogates everything else with great suspicion to bring out hidden insincerity, but refuses to apply the same techniques to itself. It exemplifies the modern spirit of narcissistic totalism, the critic as god. Being overcritical, haughty and intolerant, it caught on like wildfire in the academies of the West. Communism has faded, but the *forma mentis* originally established by Marxist ideology persists.

The phenomenon of thinkers who are suspicious of ordinary life is not new. The Romantic rebellion last century produced self-sufficient thinkers, who adopted an adversarial stance. But these cultural dissidents retreated into the world of nature; they did not take action to carry out their beliefs. When the designs of similar people this century were thwarted, they turned to the will to power to enforce their ideas. Figures like Lenin, Lukacs, Hitler and Brecht all exhibit this pattern. Scratch a radical and you will often find an autocrat. It is the paradoxical combination of negative, destructive beliefs with a passionate desire to change things by eradicating existing structures which causes the problem. In conditions of extreme societal breakdown, this combination has produced many of the horrors of this century.

As Robert Nisbet pointed out in the Spring 1992 issue of the

National Interest, one way of defining totalitarianism is as the invasion by the state of its own civic culture. It is a form of internal imperialism, by which the political organs freeze autonomous cultural activity. One way this is achieved is by quasi-governmental tribunals which act as cultural policemen with coercive powers. These replace the independent, intermediate bodies which a normal society needs as a cushioning device between citizen and state. In our societies this danger arises when the adversary culture gets itself into positions of power as a New Class. The danger to freedom today comes from those who use the language of 'liberation', a characteristic inversion, like 'war is peace'. Some individuals and groups claim victim status to in effect act with impunity. In the *New York Review of Books*, 15th August 1991, Professor Peter Singer, who provides arguments in favour of euthanasia and infanticide, complained that German audiences shouted 'Singer raus!' at his lectures, saying this was like the Nazis shouting 'Juden raus!'. In fact the Germans have learned their lesson. It was Singer who was the offender; the similarity was between him and the Nazis, as the audience recognised, not between him and the Jews.

People now do not by and large believe in individual immortality. We inhabit cultures which operate horizontally, having lost their capacity for transcendence; they spawn endless webs of functions on the same level, but are incapable of a clean break, of lifting themselves above the mire of circling make-work. Our societies have little agreement about national goals, objectives and deeply held beliefs. This causes constant uncertainty and anguish. Camus wrote of this essentially modern situation in *The Myth of Sisyphus*:

> I don't know whether this world has a meaning that transcends it... what I touch, what resists me – that is what I understand. And these two certainties – my appetite for the absolute and for unity, and the impossibility of reducing this world to a rational and reasonable principle – I also know that I cannot reconcile them.

The danger in our societies is to bask in the refuge of scepticism and uncertainty. The danger in Eastern ones was an excess of 'certainty'. The best writers from the East have experienced both totalitarianism and modernity and can distinguish between them. They know what to accept and what to reject, nor do they use one as an escape from the other.

Quadrant, March, 1993

It now increasingly looks as though 'civic culture' is the future in East Europe, and the 'black hole' in Russia.

END OF EMPIRE

(1998)

Joseph Roth's novels The Radetsky March *and* The String of Pearls.

The countries of central and east Europe are now in 1998 seeking collective security within the European Union. They have learnt from the past, and from observing ethnic cleansing in the Balkans. The origin of these problems is traced in Joseph Roth's great novel of central Europe, *The Radetsky March* (1932), which reveals how the Austro-Hungarian Empire functioned and how it finally faltered. *The Radetsky March* is structured around contrasting geographical locations. At the centre is Vienna, with the Emperor, Franz Joseph, bringing a working order to his vast, disparate domains. In the provinces at the edge of the empire, the lives of his struggling subjects have less cohesion. Both spheres eventually threaten the empire with dissolution.

The wars between Maria Theresa of Austria and Frederick the Great of Prussia in the 18th century precluded a unified German-speaking state in central Europe. The Austrians were forced to seek their empire in the east, in the lands of the Slavs, Hungarians, Jews and Romanians. Like the British Empire, the Austrian one had to encompass a mixture of races, tongues and religions. The novel takes us to provinces where the Trotta family serve in military and civilian posts: Slovenia, Moravia, Ruthenia and Galicia. Roth's novel deals only with the Austrian realm, not the Hungarian one, of the dual monarchy. The remotest provinces, Galicia and Bukovina, were under Austrian suzerainty, though closer to Budapest than Vienna.

Roth experienced life both on the periphery and at the centre. His family of Jewish traders came from Brody, a town at the eastern edge of Galicia on the border with Russia. The province of Galicia (which today forms part of south-west Poland and north-east Ukraine) had a teeming population of poor peasants and townsfolk, a high proportion of whom were Jewish. Brody, the most prosperous trading town in Galicia last century, is one of the great forgotten Jewish cities of the east. It appears lightly disguised in many of Roth's works, such as his novella *Hotel Savoy*. In *The Radetsky March* the name Hotel Brodnitzer is a hint that Brody is being described. Like many East European Jews in the 19th century, Roth moved west. He interrupted his education in Vienna to join the Austrian army as an officer during the first world war. By moving Roth had lost his original homeland, the world of his fathers; he would soon lose his adopted homeland, greater Austria, which collapsed at the end of the war. Writing in the 1930s, he recreated both with mixed affection.

However the apparent polarity between disadvantaged Jewish east and sophisticated Vienna is not as clearcut it looks at first sight. Jews were among the Empire's most loyal subjects, as they often felt at home in its supranational climate. Assimilation rates were high. In his book *A History of the Habsburg Jews 1670-1918*, William McCagg writes that in the later 19th century 'the enlightened Jews of Galicia had clung to the German language and to a Viennese political allegiance because they distrusted the flickering Jew-hatred of the Poles'. Moreover some of the higher ranks of the Austrian army, unlike the German ones, were open to Jews like Joseph Roth. In *Beyond Nationalism*, a study of the Habsburg Officer Corps, Istvàn Deàk shows that 18% of reserve officers were Jews in 1900, when Jews composed less than 5% of the empire's population. Though Jews were under-represented as career officers, the army was nonetheless a vocation open to talents. In all this, Roth's career, involving a transition from one world to the other, was typical. The army, whose signature tune in the novel is the Radetzky March, was the cement which held the empire together. In its barracks, messes, clubs, bars and brothels, its officers, like the British in India, enjoyed social life in exotic locales.

In *The Radetsky March* Roth, who died as an impoverished journalist and under-recognized novelist from the effects of alcoholism in 1939, provides a number of partial portraits of himself. The hero of the novel, the young Trotta, is an outsider who wants to leave the army, but yearns for order to assuage his fundamental unhappiness. The alcoholic, bohemian artist Moser is emotionally effusive but a failure in the world's eyes. The medical officer Max Demant, who like Roth comes from a Galician Jewish family, joins the army, has an unhappy marriage and is moving inexorably towards an untimely death.

The action of the novel is generated by one significant [fictional] act in the past. At the battle of Solferino in 1859, a junior Slovenian officer, Captain Joseph Trotta, bravely saves the life of the young Emperor Franz Joseph by pulling him out of the line of enemy fire. The officer is promoted, known forever after as 'the Hero of Solferino', and eventually ennobled as Baron Joseph von Trotta und Sipolje. So in one generation the family moves from being subjects to rulers. The son of the hero, a provincial governor in the Austrian civil service, writes to his own son: 'Fate has turned our family of frontier peasants into an Austrian dynasty. That is what we shall remain'. For some the empire was a vehicle for rapid advancement.

The phrase 'the Hero of Solferino' echoes like a chorus through the novel, a talisman which opens many doors for the Trotta family, but it also operates as a chorus of doom, since it aligns the fortunes of the family with that of Emperor and Empire. To save the Emperor in 1859 was to save the Empire, since, as in ancient myths, the semi-divine king is married to the land like a fertility god. When he withers the country becomes a waste land, as happened after 1916, when Franz Joseph died. The Trottas have given the empire a half-century reprieve.

The Emperor Franz Joseph is a brooding presence who dominates the public life of the novel, not so much on the few occasions when he appears, but as a magic icon, his portrait presiding over every official gathering, his stiff bewiskered features, powerful yet remote, inducing an almost religious awe in beholders. The whole empire works because of him, down to the minutest details, as when he cancels the debts of the young Trotta with a stroke of his pen. Authority is not devolved. Roth deftly manages to merge the Habsburg and Trotta dynasties: the Trotta's Christian names are variations of the imperial ones, Joseph, Franz and Carl Joseph. On the provincial and family level, the portrait of 'the Hero of Solferino', also bewiskered and rigidifying into an icon, dominates the generations of the Trotta family. In the Demant family, the old Jewish grandfather's long white beard is the equivalent of the Emperor's whiskers. Each paterfamilias is worshipped like a god but is without creativity.

The grandfathers – formal, detached, addicted to responsibility, and unable to convey emotion – induce deference and subservience in sons and citizens, but at a cost. Like the father in James McAuley's poem 'Because', they have 'stiffened into stone and creaking wood'. *The Radetzky March* is a novel of lost fathers. Roth never knew his own father. Later he lost his newly found fatherland, Austria, and his life became, in the title of one of his novels, a *Flight Without End* He wrote in 1930: 'My fatherland is where I am unhappy. Happiness for me exists only outside it'.

The descendants live off their grandfathers, but are emotionally disabled by them. They feel the need to escape their bondage – the young Trotta does this by having affairs with older women. Ordinary citizens begin to dissent; the empire begins to fray at the edges. In the novel a strike in the Galician town where the hero is stationed is a sign of things to come. The empire, like Franz Joseph himself, is slowly dying of lethargy. Only the Polish Count Chojnicki realizes the empire is already dead, even though the wheels keep turning. The Empress Elizabeth was assassinated in 1898. Just before the first world war Trotta hears the locals singing a haunting song about the Emperor and Empress, and the narrator comments: 'The Empress had died long ago. But the Ruthenian peasants believed she was still alive'. Roth reveals an empire too scared to reform for fear of the forces it might unleash. At the first sign of trouble it freezes itself into an utterly defensive posture. The little fighting the army does is against the locals, not against external enemies. Too many groups have been excluded, the gap between rulers and ruled has become too great. The young Trotta, pulled in contrary directions, orders his troops to fire on Galician strikers out of confusion. We, as part of the British dispensation, realize that in the 19th century, the British monarchy and imperial system, for all their shortcomings, were able to adapt much more effectively than their Austrian, German and Russian counterparts.

Count Chojnicki explains. 'This era wants to create independent nation states. People no longer believe in God. The new religion is nationalism. Nations no longer go to church. They go to national associations'. We have tended to see the favourable side of this development, as long-suppressed races threw off the shackles of their unwanted Austro-Hungarian overlords. But Roth shows the downside. Near the end of the novel, when the officers hear reports of the assassination of the Archduke Franz Fredinand at Sarajevo, they immediately jettison their imperial identities and foment quarrels based on race and nationality. This is the beginning of the drive towards racial purity, the horrors of which we know today as ethnic cleansing.

Having left the army at the end of the first world war, Roth saw himself as a 'superfluous man', floating round Europe without home or homeland. But he soon noticed that Europe was full of superfluous men whose intentions were not as benign as his. Roth had acute antennae for social developments. In his first novel, published in 1923, he mentions Hitler by name; in a later novel, *Flight Without End*, he shows his disillusion with the Communist Red Guard activity he experienced on the eastern front. With the coming to power of the Nazis he fled from Berlin to Paris. Roth was one of the first in inter-war Europe to see through both left and right. The former nations of the Austrian-Hungarian empire, now on their own, were vulnerable, and were soon picked off by the dictators. Two primitive nationalists who moved whole peoples round in the name of national purity were Hitler and Stalin. We don't fully know what Roth thought of the Austrian empire while he was part of it, but when Europe between the wars was taken over by superfluous men, he became sympathetic to the old order: 'That was how things were back then. Anything that grew took its time growing, and anything that perished took a long time to be forgotten...people lived on memories just as they now live on the ability to forget quickly and emphatically'.

In this sympathy for the past Roth was once again representative. Claudio Magris in his book *Danube* describes today's retrospective admiration for the Habsburgs: 'Central Europe, nowadays idealized as a harmony between different people, was without doubt a very real thing in the latter days of the Habsburg Empire, a tolerant association of peoples understandably lamented when it was all over, not least when compared with the totalitarian barbarism that replaced it in the lands of the Danube between the two World Wars'. In these regions the solid edifices of the Habsburgs are still functioning, whereas the panel buildings of the Communists are already falling into disuse. In certain parts of north and east Africa today the silver Maria Theresa thaler is still used as a stable form of currency.

A lavish film version of his masterpiece *The Radetsky March*, was shown recently on SBS. The television adaption of the novel is faithful to the original, and captures its atmosphere. But it can't reproduce Roth's wonderful prose style where in long but easy sentences he combines observation, social satire, comedy of manners, tragedy and a detached perspective in a graceful unity. The novel is neither morbid nor merely nostalgic – Roth can recompose a whole society's way of life without sentiment or scorn.

In Roth's later novel *The String of Pearls* Vienna itself is in decline. Once again things reveal themselves passing away. Here imperial Vienna is memorialised in all its overblown glory. Between the wars Roth was an influential journalist; his fifteen novels, slowly acknowledged as a major achievement, are now being translated. *The String of Pearls*, written in 1936-7, after Roth fled Berlin for Paris, is one of the most remarkable. Mid-19th century Vienna was a great civilised city teetering on the brink of decadence. Like Martin Boyd, Roth exploits for comic ends the gap that exists in all highly mannered societies between approved and actual behaviour. He understands this is not hypocrisy, but worldly duplicity. Society has three layers: the beau monde, represented here by the cavalry captain Baron Taittinger; the demi-monde of young call girls 'at once vulnerable and ready', including Taittinger's mistress, the courtesan Mitzi Schinagl; and the 'plain old underworld' of police spies, con men and scribblers from the gutter press.

Originally called *The Story of the 1002nd Night*, the novel begins as an elaborate joke based on the Arabian Nights. The Shah of Persia believes Vienna to be the most exotic place on earth – a form of reverse Orientalism – and arranges to visit it. Tired of his harem of 365 women, he pines for the western ideal of romantic love, of being besotted by 'the one and only': 'To think that every one of these (Viennese) women belonged, or would belong, to one single man!

Each of them a closely guarded jewel!' At a ball, his eye lights on an exquisite young married countess, whom, he lets it be known, he wants to sleep with. A diplomatic impasse between the contending claims of hospitality and decency ensues, until Taittinger, acting as high-class tout, informs the authorities that his Mitzi is a double of the countess, and a substitution is arranged. The Shah unknowingly has his night of western erotic bliss in a well-known Viennese brothel. Next morning, he wakes: 'From the dark green canopy over the bed hung a tasselled rope. It had seen considerable wear. He gave it a tug...it was in fact a bell. Many other men had used it before him.' The delighted Shah gives Mitzi an expensive string of pearls in gratitude.

The scandal these events cause drives the rest of the novel. The repercussions take on a momentum of their own. Mitzi, suddenly elevated in wealth but not in status, is pursued by various racketeers. Crime reporters repackage the original elevated fable as a criminal scandal, and the waxworks stages it as a tawdry farce. The story slips along quickly as one character after another, caught in the whirlpool, briefly appears centre stage and then bows out, each a victim 'like a quarry seeking its own hunters.' Only the louche Taittinger remains forever in the foreground. Unmalicious but self-centered, oscillating between comfort and self-disgust, he affects a fashionable *longueur* while remaining deeply unsatisfied. Other Viennese, who have 'the sure instinct that alerts them to the presence of danger, food, pleasure or prey', are in a constant state of arousal, but nothing pierces the Baron's ennui. He doesn't bother to open his letters, is fleeced on all sides, evades reality and like Roth himself, is in terminal decline. Here, a major moment in history, the collapse of imperial Austria, is captured in the fate of one man.

Dog-eat-dog attitudes replace aristocratic largess. But the novel is not gloomy. This is a metropolitan society with plenty of variety in its coffee houses, state departments, *trafik* shops, clubs, bars, and bordellos. Underneath the bright surface glitter, however, is the sadder realization that life is basically evanescent and ungraspable. The novel is more serious than the operettas we associate with *fin de siècle* Vienna. In recomposing a society, Roth's silky, elastic style can one minute create a tableau, like Lippizaner horses at the Spanish Riding School, then next a swirl of movement. Amazingly Roth wrote *The String of Pearls* during the 'slow self-annihilation' (Stefan Zweig's phrase) which led to his death in 1939. Despite his despair at the Nazi takeover, his writing is serene, witty and on top of things, a supreme example of grace under pressure. What Tom Wolfe did for contemporary New York in *The Bonfire of the Vanities,* Roth has done for the former society of central Europe, but at a quarter of the length. A minor masterpiece to set alongside *The Radetsky March.*

Quadrant, November, 1998, and *The Australian,* September 7, 1998

I wish to thank Mr Peter Farago, a friend and academic colleague with a central European Jewish background, for assistance in preparing this article.

TO THE KYSAK STATION

(2001)

Travelling in eastern Slovakia in 1994.

People in Prague told us the canteen ladies of Kysak were one the great sights of Eastern Europe. Kysak is a small Slovakian railway junction town near the Ukrainian border. Night and day, trains pull in from the major cities of Central Europe. On the platform is an immense barn-like building noisy with the hubbub of travellers twenty-four hours a day. The crowds and movement are continuous, the hall is full of beery, urinous fumes, smoke haze dims the bare-bulb light glare as people read papers, chat, take a nap, drink, smoke, snore, loll in corners, or wander outside for a leak. It could be a scene in Les Halles, the Parisian provision market of Zola's *Le Ventre de Paris*.

Large women of indeterminate age in shapeless blue uniforms and plastic shower-caps, with huge arms, wide cheeks and cheery countenances, serve customers in canteen-style queues. Jovial, they slop beer, take change, fry eggs and bacon, pour tea, wipe the counters, swap banter, all seemingly in the same motion. The queues never end. The 1950s-style food is fried US diner fare, fat globules swim in the white coffee, concern over cholesterol is unknown here – there are greater worries, like getting through the day. Truck drivers, locals, passengers, railway crew, vagabonds, refugees from the east, gypsies, shift workers, the well dressed and the shabby mingle together. The noise, energy, anxiety and good-hearted confusion never stop. This is one side of East European life – an unreconstructed, natural existence in which people have learnt how to survive at a very basic level. At least, that's how it looks to outsiders like ourselves. But for the indigenes life is tough and unromantic.

Kysak lies between the provincial cities of Presov and Kosice at the eastern end of Slovakia. Nearby are borders with Poland, Ukraine, Romania and Hungary. This is a region seemingly at the edge of everything, hard to locate in relation to other landmarks. But Nicholas Crane in *Clear Waters Rising* introduces another perspective: the nearby city of Uzhgorod in Ukraine is 'Europe's pole of Continentality. It is the town in Europe most distant from the sea. As the crow flies, Uzhgorod is 670 kilometres from the Baltic, the Adriatic and the Black Sea'. So this unknown region where five countries meet it is actually the geographic heart of Europe, the centre as well as the borderlands.

Paul Magocsi in his *Historical Atlas of East Central Europe* divides Europe into three east-west zones. To the north is the broad sweep of lowland stretching from Russia to Holland, much of it along the Baltic Sea. In the middle is the mountainous region stretching from the Carpathians of Romania to the Pyrenees. To the south is the Mediterranean coastal region from Greece to Spain. Far eastern Slovakia, the region in which Kysak is located, lies halfway between north and south in the mountainous zone, and halfway also between east and west. The Carpathian mountains have historically acted as a barrier protecting Europe from being overrun by nomads from the steppes.

In medieval times Kysak lay on major trade routes connecting Vienna with Krakow, and Breslau with Lvov. Today it is in an area defined not by connection but by division. Many of what Norman Davies in *Europe: A History* calls the fault lines of Europe go through this region. The people to the west are Catholic, to the east Orthodox, with Uniates in between. Nineteenth-century industrialisation reached as far as the Czech lands, but not as far east as here. Europe's vineyard line is a little to the south, as were the Roman *limes*, the northern frontiers of the Roman Empire's provinces. Similarly the Ottomans never quite reached here, but they came close. At a small wooden Ruthenian Uniate church nearby, we were surprised to find that the local saint is St John of Suceava, a town in north-eastern Romania. His sacred relics had been brought here for safe keeping when the Turks pushed to their furthest limits of expansion in the 1530s. The bones were returned after the Ottoman retreat, but the local cult still flourishes.

Though at the heart of Europe, this region is the opposite of an imperial centre from which lines of force radiate. It is a black hole, an implosion remote from real centres of political and cultural influence. Up till a decade ago the inhabitants have almost never ruled their own lives. Eastern Europe has been a battleground for the imperial ambitions of outsiders: Germans from the north-west, the Habsburgs from the south-west, Russians from the north-east, and the Ottomans from the south-east, all dominated these areas. The designation 'borderlands', which today features in the titles of many books, is the arc stretching from Belarus in the north, through western Ukraine and the provinces known as Galicia, Bukovina and Bessarabia, down through Romania, Moldova and Bulgaria to the Black Sea. These realms have a shadowy existence even to most Europeans. In them few peoples were able to establish a permanent identity as nation states with clear and recognised boundaries, since they were unable to control their own destiny. Belarus was never until now a state.

The centre of power, from the point of view of the conquerors, was somewhere else. People in Eastern Europe often have two names: what they call themselves, and what they are slightingly called by others. It is often the latter name that sticks. In English Romanies are called 'Gypsies' from the mistaken belief they came from Egypt; in Eastern Europe they are called 'Zigane' from the mistaken belief they came from an heretical Greek sect called the Atzinganoi. Many people think the *Rom* derives from Romania, where the largest concentration them exists, whereas it comes from a Sanskrit word meaning familiar tribes. Locals are marginalised by having their identity thrust on them by others. One Slavic word for land is *krainy* – 'Ukraine' means at the edge of the land, or borderland, a place not existing in its own right. In *Between East and West* Anne Applebaum explains that the word 'Belarus' means not 'White Russian', as many think, but 'White Ruthenian'. Some people respond to this uncertainty by identifying themselves by the word '*tutejszy*' or '*tuteshni*', meaning simply 'people from here', that is, people without a nation. When races reached their further limits of expansion, they were named by their new neighbours. Thus the Celts were named Galatians (that is, Celts) by their non-Celtic neighbours at their furthest expansion in north-western Spain, southern Poland and in the Middle East. Borderland Slavic domains were by a similar process named Slovakia, Slovenia and Slavonia by non-Slavs.

Western European regions became nations relatively early. Britain took over Ireland, Scotland and Wales and formed a 'united kingdom' in late medieval times. Similarly with France some time later. Inheriting this tradition, we think of a nation as having a reasonably stable mix of cultural, religious, ethnic and political factors. But in Eastern Europe nation did not signify identity in the same way. 'A traveller,' writes Applebaum, 'can meet a man born in Poland, brought up in the Soviet Union, who now lives in Belarus – and he has never left his village'. She tells the wonderful tale of the 'four Mickiewiczs'. Mickiewicz is regarded by Poles as their national poet par excellence. Poland, however, was joined to Lithuania over many centuries, and scholars in Vilnius call him Mickievicius, giving him a Lithuanian genealogy, and pointing out that his epic poem 'Pan Tadeusz' opens with the invocation:

'Lithuania, my fatherland!' But now Belarusians in Minsk query the conventional story, saying Adam Mickievic (as they call him) was a Polonised Belarusian, as the place he came from is in today's Belarus. And academics in Israel have shown that his mother's family were Frankists, a sect of converted Jews, so the fourth Miskiewicz is the Jewish Miskiewicz.

Mickiewicz is an example of how one person can have multiple national identities. Another case is of a group of people whose culture, religion, ethnicity and politics are naturally interconnected, but who have no stable homeland. A distinctive group in eastern Slovakia is the Ruthenians or Rysyns, a Ukrainian-speaking people living in the Carpathian foothills. They are contiguous with Ruthenian communities in Poland, Ukraine, Romania and Hungary, spread, like the Kurds, over five countries but without one of their own. Uniate in religion, they give allegiance to Rome in the west, but culturally they are Slavic, facing east towards Russia. Yet as anti-Communists, they endured persecution from that quarter during most of this century. They have faced opposition from all directions, and do not now feel at home in Slovakia.

Because of similar disparities, many people now identify with regions formed in pre-modern times which are smaller than nations, for example with Galicia, Ruthenia, Volhynia, Silesia, or Bukovina, since each constitutes a recognisable entity, though it may have shifted between different countries. Even smaller sub-regions, like Polesia on the border of Poland and Belarus, are claiming a distinct identity. In Eastern Europe people identify with race more with place. The desire for purity – to align political, ethnic, religious and cultural allegiances as an entity – can lead to ethnic cleansing, which Hitler and Stalin and more recently the Serbs, attempted in this region. Lithuanians tell Anne Applebaum they want to be Lithuanian Lithuanians, not Polish ones, but this is impossible after the close ties the two countries have had. The notion that identity can come about as an amalgam, always in the process of subtle change, of conflicting races and heritage, that our personalities are built on submerged but active layers of heterogeneous deposits, seems scarcely to have taken root here.

In eastern Slovakia there were traditionally six races arranged hierarchically: Hungarians the rulers, Germans and Jews the traders, Slovaks and Rysyns the rural workers, and Gypsies the urban peasants. In Presov, Slovakia, we were surprised to find a street just off the town centre called Slovak Street. Last century this was the place where Slovak peasants came to live in poor conditions when their country was part of Hungary. They were outsiders in their own country (just as there were suburbs called Irishtown and Poortown in Dublin in the eighteenth century). The Jews were murdered and the Germans left after the Second World War. The new pecking order among the four remaining races is clearly visible: the Slovaks are politically dominant, the Hungarians are now the urban traders, Ruthenians are the rural poor and the Gypsies the urban poor. Racial tensions are high, kept in check mainly in the knowledge that Western money and help would dry up if the locals began to behave like the Yugoslavs. Ex-communist demagogues who have become 'reform' nationalists, like the former Prime Minister Meciar, gained electoral support by playing on the Slovak desire to rule the roost and subjugate other races. The latest fault-line is the divide between those nations (Hungary, Czech Republic and Poland) which face west and want free trade and democratic institutions, and those (Slovakia, Serbia, Romania, Belarus, Bulgaria) which face east and retain command economies and demagogic rulers à la Milosevic.

Some movements towards racial purity have been involuntary. The Czech lands between the wars had many peoples: Czechs, Slovaks, Jews, Germans, Gypsies, Ruthenians and Hungarians. The population today is much more homogenous, but not by design. Czech Jews were murdered by Nazis during the war, and the Sudeten Germans were expelled to Germany in 1946, for which the Czechs have recently apologised. With the split in their country in 1994, the Slovaks, Ruthenians and Hungarians are largely gone, so the Czech Republic is almost pure Czech, with only Gypsies and Vietnamese (Eastern bloc guest workers) left as conspicuous minority groups. Up to 40 per cent of the population of the Polish Republic between the wars were non-Poles, mainly Jews, Volksdeutsch, Ukrainians, Ruthenians and Byelorussians. Today its population is almost all ethnically Polish.

The mountains of the European landmass slope down from east to west. But, as Norman Davies points out, an alleged cultural gradient slopes the other way. The west of Europe has always considered itself more civilised, and believes order diminishes as one moves east. This is to a large extent a cultural prejudice. Europeans still have in their consciousness the immemorial fear of Tartar and Ottoman invasions. The 'East' to them means barbarism, serfs and oriental despotism. This demonising of 'Easterners' has revived, as recent events, like the Yugoslav and other civil wars in the former Soviet republics, have unfortunately seemed to confirm it. The Germans were seen by rulers in the east as the people to build an infrastructure; since late medieval times they had been called in to help improve housing, farming, mining and business. North of Kysak is the town of Bardejov, whose German burghers controlled the salt monopoly on a trading route to the east. Though in far eastern Slovakia, it still looks like a German town, with its rathaus intact. The surname Schwab, common in Australian Rules football, comes from the lower Danube, where it was the local name given to Swabian Germans who settled there. In the absence of a compelling national or imperial power German cultural symbols filled the vacuum in the borderlands. In his acclaimed memoir *Memoirs of an Anti-Semite*, Gregor von Rezzori, who grew up in Chernowitz in the Bukovina, recalls how for many people of the east, German duelling and hunting rituals, baronial houses and drinking songs formed, in the absence of rivals, an admired culture.

Today the derogatory blanket term 'Easterner' lumps together Gypsies, refugees from strife-torn Romania, Bulgaria and former Soviet bloc countries, and Vietnamese left over from Cold War days. The German word *auslander* has the meaning of the English 'outlandish', a person from the outlands or badlands. The narrow end of eastern Slovakia is a funnel though which displaced persons are trying to get to the West. The border country between Kysak and Uzhgorod is dangerous, inhabited by bandits and smugglers; the Slovakian currency is worth much more than the Ukrainian one. Travel on trains coming from the east is tense, with constant identity paper inspections by suspicious guards. If they can get into Slovakia, people have a good chance of moving further west into the Czech Republic, with the prospect of eventual EC citizenship, everybody's goal. It is shocking to see these people sometimes treated like cattle or serfs at police and railway stations, and consulates. The British notion of internalised respect for the rights of people as individuals hardly exists. So the idea that the barbarians come from the east is becoming a self-fulfilling prophecy – the host nations are acting like Easterners to get rid of their Easterners.

The biggest concentration of Gypsies is in Eastern Europe, particularly in Romania and eastern Slovakia. The family of Isobel Fonseca, who wrote *Bury Me Standing*, a contemporary account of the Gypsies of Europe, came from Krompachy near Kosice in eastern Slovakia, though Fonseca herself is not a Gypsy. Since the Holocaust Gypsies have taken the Jews' place as scapegoats for society's ills. As Fonseca notes, Gypsies are 'mostly illiterate, mostly unemployed, and mostly without proper housing. Their lives are about a third shorter than those of their countrymen.' As itinerants often squatting in abandoned dwellings and living a tribalised life on the outskirts of society and treated badly by the rest of society, they resemble the role of Aborigines in our country, but when we tentatively made this comparison during at a talk at Presov University, the audience was quick to deny the parallel – 'But we got here first!' they indignantly replied. When Czechoslovakia split in 1994, individuals had to opt for one citizenship. For Czechs and Slovaks this was no problem, but people had forgotten about the Gypsies' status. Of the 400,000 Gypsies in eastern Slovakia, about half applied to be citizens of the Czech Republic, with prized potential EC status, though they had never lived there. In spite of Vaclav Havel's dictum that the treatment of Gypsies is a litmus test for a civil society, many have been denied Czech citizenship.

One notices a peculiar co-existence of anarchy and autocracy in the east. Train inspectors and passport clerks are officious, even brutal, towards tourists, shopkeepers can be surly and rude to customers, bureaucrats enjoy wielding power over citizens. The writ of authority hardly runs here. Governments pass laws all the time, but they do not necessarily have effect. Life runs on below the level of official society, through the suitcase economy and backyard vegetable plot. Another peculiar mixture is that of sophistication and simplicity. Modern business conglomerates exist side by side with a barter economy. People cut grass on the roadside with hand-shears to feed animals tethered in backyards or flats. After corn is harvested by huge modern machines, the locals come out to grub about for seconds to eat themselves. In Presov services had collapsed when we were there. The local council did not pay workers to remove black ice from the streets. As a result many people were in hospital with broken limbs, which cost the community more than the ice-clearing operation.

In *Exit into History* Eva Hoffman laments the 'shortage of a usable past' in these lands, by which she means the attempt to link back to the time before Communism. Its grey panel buildings are already crumbling, in contrast to the solid edifices of the Habsburgs. Some people devote themselves to retrieving from the debris the world of the past, like goyim who in the absence of Jews set up museums of Jewish history. In many places there has been little modernity, industrialisation, or enlightenment; in some there has been a counter-reformation, but no reformation. To be successful, these societies will have to coalesce the sophisticated secular modernists, who run the technology and business sector, with the traditionalist believers, whose numbers increase as you move into the countryside or travel east.

Quadrant, January-February, 2001

THE RUTHENIANS

(1996)

The Ruthenians are a Slavic people who have never achieved nationhood. In 1994 we visited a group of old Ruthenian churches in far eastern Slovakia, and in 2014 we viewed a display of Ruthenian icons and iconostasis in Lvov.

Reading Eamon Duffy's book *The Stripping of the Altars* while teaching in Prague in 1994, I was intrigued by his description of medieval English Catholicism: the rood lofts, the cult of local saints, the revering of the Roman virgins and martyrs, the focus on the dead, the intervention of religion in all spheres of life, and its public manifestations. Then it dawned on me that I was seeing much the same all around me in central and eastern Europe: the cathedral of the Roman martyr St Barbara at Kutna Hora (the silver mountain), statues of St Agatha holding her severed breasts, icons of St. George and the dragon, ossuaries, wayside shrines, multiple liturgies, public Corpus Christi ceremonies, remnants of a religious way of life which was once Europe-wide. Religion as public life becomes more noticeable and more intense as one moves east from Bohemia through Moravia into Slovakia.

In the furthest part of east Slovakia and in west Ukraine live the Ruthenians. Ruthenia is an old region which, though torn by boundary changes and political and religious clashes, still has an identity. The Slavic people called Rusyns, or Ruthenians, live mainly in the north-west corner of Ukraine west of Lvov, but also over the border in Slovakia, Poland, Romania and Hungary, which abut this area. The language of the various Slavic groups like the Belorussians and Ruthenians merged into each other, especially in the border regions, so they became like dialects of each other. The Ruthenian name comes from the original Rus, and they are a much older people than the Muscovites who much later appropriated the claim to be 'Russian'. In medieval times their existence was recognized by area called the 'Rus Palatinate'. By 1900 there were about a million Ruysns, but their numbers have been depleted by repression, assimilation and emigration.

Between the two world wars much of Ruthenia was in Czechoslovakia, but in 1945 the easternmost section of Slovakia was moved across to the Ukraine, so the Ruthenians in this region have since that time been split between the two countries: those in Slovakia have race, religion, customs and language in common with their fellow Ruthenians in western Ukraine, and not with the Slovaks among whom they live. The Ruthenians are poor mountain villagers under pressure from all sides. It is a region which has never ruled itself, always a suppressed, tension-filled borderland controlled by others. Here race, religion, politics and culture have rarely corresponded with national boundaries.

Czechoslovakia is a Slavic wedge into German-speaking lands. This is the region of the furthest penetration west of Orthodoxy and Slavic influences, and a battleground between Orthodoxy and western Christianity. The region came under Austrian rule from the mid eighteenth century, and the Ruthenians were among those converted to the Uniate religion, with allegiance to the Pope, though in other matters (for example liturgy, married priests, iconostasis in their churches), they retained their eastern, Slavic orientation. So they have divided loyalties – in their religious allegiance they face west, but culturally they still face east. Here three religions – Catholicism, Uniates (Greek Catholics), and Orthodoxy (Russian and Ukrainian) – contend.

The Ruthenian communities of north-east Slovakia are known for their distinctive small wooden churches, built by local carpenters about 250 years ago out of red spruce with shingle roofs. There are not many left. They are often set slightly apart from the village in a wooded area. Originally the churches were barn-like, with a dominant horizontal line. They evolved in a characteristic tripartite shape: a vestibule with bell tower above, a rectangular nave in the middle, and a sanctuary or shrine, each a separate unit, but connected to form a whole. All three parts eventually had a tower or dome. But though basically eastern onion dome in style, Baroque and even Gothic influences from the Austrian empire influenced their design. The churches face eastwards, with the turrets sloping down from the west, that is, the bell tower is the highest. The churches have few windows and are dark in the interior.

Inside these churches have an iconostasis built by peasant carpenters and artists – the wooden background is rudimentary. The iconostasis usually has five tiers. At the top is the rood (the cross), the second has religious scenes with foliage surrounds, the third tier has in the centre an icon of Christ as Pantocrator, with six of the apostles on each side of him. Below are scenes from Christ's life, with a mandylion in the centre, an image of Christ's face imprinted on a cloth 'not painted by human hands'. The lowest (floor) level has three doors, on each side of which are further icons of the patron saint of the church and other favourite figures (evangelists, prophets, fathers of the church) like the Archangel Michael and St. Nicholas (Svaty Mikulas), or more localized saints around which a cult may form, like St. Paraskieva or St. John of Suceava, saints not known in the Western tradition. The walls are sometimes painted with folk art. A common painting is that of the Last Judgment, with the damned going through the mouth of Hell to the infernal regions in Bosch-like detail, and the ladder of life going up to Heaven. The earthly rivals of the Ruthenians

– Calvinists, Turks, Jews, Tartars, Cossacks, Germans and others – are depicted to the side, perhaps being saved by the actions of divine providence. The interiors of the churches also have painted crosses and banners for processions, altogether an ensemble rich in colour and decoration.

Icons in the Ruthenian churches are not the separate images of the saints as we see in books or items for sale, but part of an elaborate, coherent assemblage of images, the iconostasis. The artist is proud to conform to a traditional standard, not, as in the West, to display his individuality and originality. However there is local variation, as some icons derive from a Galician tradition to the north. These Ruthenian icons are illustrated and explained in Vladislav Greslik's book *Icons of the Saris Museum at Bardejov* (1994), who was our guide when we visited the churches. Western influences reached here later than those from the east. The altar rails in churches in the West are all that is left of the iconostasis in our culture.

In 1918 Czechoslovakia was formed with almost all of Ruthenia in the new country; the Ruthenians were unified, though still with split allegiance in politics and culture. But their traditional life was in decline for economic reasons. In the late 1940s came two simultaneous disasters: they were divided between two countries (Czechoslovakia and Ukraine), and Communism, to which they were opposed, was imposed in both. So there were multiple tensions: Slavic versus West, Communism versus anti-Communism, and Ukraine versus Czechoslovakia. They were persecuted by the Communist authorities, and their churches pulled down or taken over by the Orthodox. Many had to choose between Slovak Catholicism and Orthodoxy. After the Velvet Revolution and freedom in 1989, Ruthenian Uniates were given back their churches, but so few were left they were told to worship together with the Orthodox who had recently been their persecutors. Since 1993, when Slovakia became separate, their situation has become more precarious, as they are seen as alien 'Ukrainians' or 'Russians' (an example of being named in a derogatory way by one's opponents), and are being subjected to Slovakization, without Prague to protect them. In spite of all this, Presov, the main university town in north east Slovakia, has two seminaries, Uniate and Orthodox, which are thriving at the moment.

Traditional Christian religion has been preserved in these regions. But as we move further east into Ukraine, something far more ancient and pre-Christian has been preserved. The Ruthenians are comprised of three groups: Lemkians in the west, Boikians around the border, and Hutsuls in the Carpathian mountains. The Hutsuls are the most remote group, protected by their mountain fastnesses; having made a conscious decision to keep to themselves and not to modernize, they have low education levels. They occupy themselves with cattle and sheep rearing, forestry and wood-carved handicrafts, being renowned for their decorated axes and colourful clothing. They have a tradition of being outsiders, and in the past bands of Hutsuls roaming in the woods were considered by others to be bandits or brigands, but the Hutsul people saw them as protectors, like Robin Hoods. The word 'Hutsul', a Romanian one meaning outlaw, is scorned by the Hutsuls themselves. In summer they take their herds to the uplands.

Generous, passionate but vindictive, they fascinate outsiders, particularly other Ukrainians, since they have preserved ancient folk customs, daily rituals and myths which once were common in the whole of the Ukraine. Outsiders describe them as deeply superstitious, but in reality they have kept as a living culture what others have lost. They are Christian, but mixed up with their religion are animist beliefs retained from an earlier time. They believe Nature, not God, was the origin of life. In everyday actions they believe the spells of their myriad nature gods have to be assuaged by charms and other means. A Kiev writer and former dissident Valentyn Moroz has described this process of blending:

The Hutsul has always accepted the new with great caution, and only that which could be merged with the old. Such was the case with Christianity. St. Ulas's day coincided with the day of the fox, the day of St Fokiy with the day of the fire. The new was assimilated into a framework which was built up over the centuries. Otherwise spirituality would consist of individual fragments. The figures on the Hutsul candle holders are not at all Christian. The pre-Christian deities are a force which is not yet divided into God and the Devil, a deity embodying both Good and Evil...Great cultural achievements do not come through the destruction of tradition, but through building layer on layer.

These beliefs have been preserved in literature, especially in the 19th century. The greatest writer of the time, Michael Kotsiubynsky, a non-Ruthenian from west Ukraine, visited them and decided to preserve in imaginative form their culture, which was threatened then by modernization. He commented:

I keep thinking about those wise people who built their churches, monasteries, and chapels in the best, the wildest places. They know what they are doing. They are addressing not so much us as the ancestors who are alive within us, ancestors who for centuries staged their sacred games in woods and groves.

His aim was to draw out 'the sleeping ancestral voice'. He did this in one of the greatest works of modern Ukrainian literature, the novella *Shadows of Forgotten Ancestors* – the title indicates his aim. It is the story of a young boy who is a throwback; his soul is preternaturally in tune with the faint and elusive music of nature. Its music sings within him as he plays his flute. He lives more within his head and in the world of infinite yearnings than in the present. He falls in love with a girl from a rival family, but his father dies in a blood feud with them. The impoverished youth is thereby forced to go to the uplands, which are inhabited by a variety of devil spirits, like wood and water nymphs, fauns and satyrs.

The trek to the mountains begins in spring. In winter the uplands have been the domain of the *maras*, ancient Slavic spirits of winter and death. These spirits are banished on the holiday of St. Iurii (St. George), which falls on the first day of spring, but the fertility rituals enacted have been taken over from the older fertility god, Iarylo. This is an example of Christianity talking over the old rites, but being unable to suppress them. Even in crucifix scenes on icons, the pagan sun and moon gods are depicted: the sky is a face, with the right cheek the sun and the left the moon. The chief shepherd is a shaman who keeps the eternal flame going all summer, and orders the daily tending of the flocks by elaborate, time-honoured rituals. Here the hero has a vision of the death of his beloved in the valley below. He returns to marry unhappily. The Hutsuls are partly pagan, sexual rules are relaxed and non-monogamous, and his wife has an open affair with another man who casts spells. The hero pines away and dies. This summary makes the story sound like a mixture of *Romeo and Juliet* and *Wuthering Heights*, but we can strip away the Romantic overlay and recognize that the narrative is basically a means of recounting Hutsul folk lore and myth. Every object around them is infused with spiritual values; the past comes alive in them.

In the 1960s artists and intellectuals came from all over Ukraine to visit the Hutsul region, as they realized the old ways were being destroyed by the forced collectivization of farms. One centre of attraction was the beautiful Hutsul town of Kosmach, a mecca of old Ukrainian and Hutsul arts, renowned for its musicians, embroidery, painted Easter eggs, sheepskin coats, and its church, whose bell was donated by Dovbush, the most famous Hutsul outlaw. People were interested in the living remains of the past, not in an increasingly homogenized future, where Hutsuls were being turned into Ukrainians, and into members of the Soviet Union. A film of the famous story *Shadows of Forgotten Ancestors* was made in 1963. The iconostasis was taken from the Dovbush church at Kosmach to Kiev for filming, but afterwards it was not returned, since the Communist government had a policy of making religious objects museum pieces or destroying them, so they could not be part of a living culture. Other village icons and crucifixes were wrecked, stolen or taken away at the same time. So a film designed to resurrect the past became an occasion for destroying it; the government's agents were literally iconoclasts. Not just religion but the people's life and culture were being taken away from them. The villagers said: 'They have orphaned us'. As Valentyn Moroz, who admired and defended the Hutsuls, put it: 'The church has become such an integral part of cultural life that it is not possible to destroy it without harming the spiritual structure of the nation'.

A talk given to a Literature and Religion Conference, Sydney, 1991, with additions c. 1996, unpublished.

THE BORDERLAND PEOPLES
OF EAST EUROPE

(2013)

Recent research on the nations and races of Eastern Europe.

The Idea of Galicia: History and Fantasy in Habsburg Political Culture, by Larry Wolff; Stanford University Press, 2010

The Politics of Language and Nationalism in Modern Central Europe, by Tomasz Kamusella; Palgrave Macmillan, 2008

Belarus: The Last Dictatorship in Europe, by Andrew Wilson; Yale University Press, 2011

These books circle around a conundrum: why in Central and East Europe didn't the inhabitants set up self-governing, independent states with defined borders as they did in Western Europe? Why were territories so shifting, why were the locals so dominated by others? In his *History of Europe* the renowned British historian Norman Davies sees Europe as a small peninsula of the vast Eurasian land mass. At its western end exist littoral states, whose shape is determined by the sea: England, Ireland, France, Spain/ Portugal, the Netherlands and the Scandinavian states. Coasts create defined borders which can't be changed. These countries formed themselves into reasonably homogenous nations some centuries ago. They were not as a rule successful in permanently subduing adjacent races, though not for want of trying. The littoral states were seafaring people who eventually put their expansionist energies into developing empires overseas.

Central and East European nations are principally situated on inland tracts of land, part of the vast Eurasian land mass; many have limited or no outlets to the sea. The eastern imperial powers [Russia, Germany. Austria and Ottoman] set up vast multi-lingual, multi-ethnic empires, which were, depending how you looked at them, the 'prison-house of nations' or the 'kindergarten of nations' (Ernst Gellner). The Russians use the phrase 'the near abroad' for their colonial possessions adjacent to the imperial heartland, a phrase hard to comprehend from our West European perspective.

Since the collapse of Communism a great outburst of scholarship re-examining the borderland areas of East Europe has been taking place. Now for the first time the past is becoming unfettered, less subject to national and imperial misinformation. Archives previously unavailable are being opened up by younger researchers not hung up by old grievances and ideological allegiances. The editorial director of Yale University Press's series on Soviet documents, Jonathan Brent, has described the many pitfalls awaiting the researcher in his book *Inside the Stalin Archives.* Jonathan Brent, Larry Wolff and Timothy Synder are all American university academics descended from Jewish families who emigrated to the United States a few generations ago from the border regions of Eastern Europe.

In his most recent book, *Vanished Kingdoms*, Norman Davies draws attention to the fact that nations periodically die or are assimilated by others. Non-existent nations are neglected not just because the victors write the history, but because, as Davies points out, an historian is naturally drawn into explaining the origins of what exists today. To remedy this gap in the historical record, Davies devotes substantial chapters in his book to sixteen important European realms which no longer exist. Some were in Western Europe, such as Burgundy, Savoy, Visigoth Toulouse and Aragon, but others were in the east: the Polish-Lithuanian Commonwealth, Baltic Prussia, Galicia, the kingdom of Montenegro, Ruthenia and the late unlamented Soviet Union.

Timothy Snyder is now justly famous for his book, *Bloodlands,* on how Stalin and Hitler operated their killing machines, not in Germany and Russia proper, but on the territory in between. In his earlier book *The Reconstruction of Nations* (2003) Snyder provides an interconnected history of five peoples since the joint Polish-Lithuanian Commonwealth was formed in 1569: Poles, Belorussians, Ruthenians, Ukrainians and the non-Slavic Lithuanians. The Commonwealth, which was ended in 1795 by the final partition of Poland, stretched at its most extensive from the Baltic to the Black Sea. Within it the Poles ruled the Ruthenian and Ukrainian lands, and the Lithuanians the Belarus ones. Like the later Austro-Hungarian empire, this vast kingdom contained many races and creeds who couldn't be moulded together into the unified state their Polish-Lithuanian rulers desired. Over the decades power in the Commonwealth gradually moved from the Lithuanians, who founded it, to the Poles, whose culture, being linked to Western Europe, had a higher status. Polish rulers acted like nobles, which angered the other races of the Commonwealth. At crucial junctures this prevented unity in the face of German, Russian and Austrian encroachments.

Belarus is the region between Poland and Russia. A people contiguous to the Ruthenians, the Belorussians achieved statehood only in 1921 and independence in 1991, though the name Belarus can be found on old maps. The area of Belarus is a large, flat plain with no mountains, coasts or other defining features, which makes it vulnerable to takeover, as many autocrats, including Hitler and Stalin, were quick to realize. The people and language of this area were originally called Ruthenian not Belarusian. Andrew Wilson in his book on Belarus says the name may also mean 'virgin' Ruthenia, the area never conquered by the Mongols. The Belarusians were ruled by Lithuanians, Poles and Russians at various stages. The old Commonwealth had six principal languages: Polish, Lithuanian, Old Slavonic, Latin, a Slavic peasant vernacular, and Yiddish. The Ruthenian language was a forerunner of Belorussian and Ukrainian. Peasants of Slavic provenance in these borderlands talked in a range of dialects which were intelligible to each other. A Ruthenian-Belarussian peasant vernacular existed from medieval times, but was gradually superseded by a Polish vernacular, which was understandable to most Commonwealth peoples, unlike the non-Slavic Lithuanian one.

In the countryside the peasants in the old Commonwealth were by and large Ruthenians, Belorussians and Ukrainians, whereas the Poles and Lithuanians were the ruling gentry, and the Jews the urban traders. Snyder shows that, remarkably, historic Vilnius, now the capital of Lithuania, had about 5% of its inhabitants as Lithuanians. The majority were Poles and Jews, with the Belarusians and Lithuanians living as peasants in the surrounding countryside. Lvov, now the main city of western Ukraine, had more Poles than Ukrainians. To complicate the picture further, some East Slavs moved from Orthodoxy to Western Christianity under Polish and Vatican influence. The Union of Brest 1596 created the Uniate Church, a half-way house between Catholicism and Orthodoxy. The Uniate Church was strong in borderland areas like Ruthenia and western Ukraine, and became a rallying point and carrier at certain stages of Ukrainian nationalism. But as a hybrid it did not help the growth of Belorussian nationalism.

Over time Ruthenian-Belorussian identity faded under pressure for increased Polishness. The Cossack uprising in the 1650s in Ukraine spelt the death knell of the Polish-Lithuanian Commonwealth. The ruling group in the Ukraine was split between Polish gentry, Ukrainian nobles and the Cossacks, the loose cannon in the arrangement. In this situation no political compromise was possible. In league with Muscovy, the Cossacks staged a devastating revolt, fomented by resentment against Polish overlords. When the dust cleared the only winners were the Muscovite Slavs, who from the 1670s got a grip on the eastern half of Ukraine. As Snyder shows, this event went a long way to determining the modern shape of Russia, Poland and the Ukraine. The Muscovites now claimed that the foundational Kievian Rus Slavic patrimony had been inherited by Moscow. They thus invented their version of 'Russian' history, claiming that most east Slavs were really Russians, to be ruled by them. Ukraine they renamed Malorossiya, Little Russia. Muscovite 'Russia' was founding its colonies at the same time as it was founding itself, so there was from the start a blurring between the two. Russian became the dominant Slav language. As the old riddle goes: What's the difference between a language and a dialect? A language is a dialect backed by an army and navy.

Poland was partitioned from 1772 to 1795. The tragedy of Poland being gobbled up by Prussia, Russia and Austria has been widely acknowledged, but it was just as tragic for adjacent borderland countries. Belorussia (including its high Jewish population), Lithuania and much of West Ukraine went to Russia. A large crescent-shaped swathe of Slav lands, which joined the territory of the Carpathian Rus to the Polish region around Cracow, was renamed Galicia and given to Austria. So the Slav peoples were now hopelessly divided on arbitrary imperial lines. Further border changes in subsequent centuries made the problems worse. Larry Wolff's book is on the history of Austrian-ruled Galicia, which existed from 1772 to 1918; Norman Davies also has a chapter on Galicia. When Prussia and Russia decided to dismember Poland in 1772, the Austrian Empress Maria Theresa at first protested bitterly against it, as the Poles were fellow Catholics, but she eventually took Galicia. As Frederick the Great acidly remarked of her hypocrisy: 'The more she weeps, the more she takes'. As Wolff shows, Galicia was an artificial construct, split between Catholic Poles in its west and Ruthenian Uniates in its east, with Lvov as its capital. Cracow was at this time smaller than Lvov.

The Austrian rulers in Vienna were German speakers with a quite different culture to the Slavs in the distant north, and their rule and style was never accepted there; Emperor Franz Joseph, a legendary figure to Austrians, was openly mocked in Galicia. Galicia sadly became a seat of inter-Slav rivalry. In peaceful times the Poles and Ruthenian Slavs of Galicia naturally allied themselves against their imposed Austrian overlords. But in revolutionary times such as 1846, when the Poles rose in insurrection seeking independence, Ruthenian peasants used the opportunity to slaughter their hated Polish landlords. Class triumphed over religion and their common Slav background. After the unsuccessful 1863 Polish rising against Russia, the Belarusian peasantry were torn between three unsatisfactory options: failed Polishness, Lithuania with its different language, and the Russians who by absorbing them had denied them national status. Galicia became a repository of the idea of a Uniate Ukraine, a notion not allowed in the Russian-controlled parts of Ukraine.

Snyder demonstrates the effect of these constant shifts of allegiance on the Galician town of Kolomya, which is today in Ukraine:

> In 1939-41 and 1945-91 Kolomya was a town in southwestern Soviet Ukraine, between 1941 and 1944 a town in the Nazi *Generalgouvernment*, before the Second World War a town in Poland's Stanislawow province, before the First World War a town in Austrian Galicia, before 1772 a town in the Polish Kingdom's Ruthenian province.

As a response to these changes many borderlands people had no larger regional or national identification. Territories did not exist in their own right.

In the nineteenth century, in order to overcome their historic disabilities, the various Slavic and other 'unhistoric' peoples of central and Eastern Europe became embryonically consciousness of being distinct entities, and pressed for statehood and independence.

They struggled for internal self-definition, tired of having their situation described by others. But there was a tension between nationalists' dreams and the reality on the ground at any time. They suffered from what historians call 'primordialism'. They looked back to the supposed medieval glories of their race, cancelling out the intervening period of subjugation, and tried to create new nations on exclusive ethnic-linguistic lines, without their historic enemies. Galicia disappeared as a separate region at the end of the First World War, going to Poland. After the Second World War this region was split once again, with the western part going to Poland and the east to Ukraine. The two world wars and the rise of Communism and Fascism greatly complicated the project of independent nationhood.

Tomasz Kamsuella is a Polish academic widely published on the connections between language and politics. His book on these problems is an encyclopaedic, 1,000 page survey which brings linguistic and historical enquiries together. Language he believes has been the crucial marker in this region, not religion as in the Balkans. Nineteenth century nationalists strove to break down the empires into their constituent nations which would be, on the West European model, constructs where race, language, territory and borders more or less coincided. This is called by today's researchers ethnic-linguistic homogeneity. Older transnational languages with prestige, such as Latin, German and Old Slavonic, which had been used for trading, administration and diplomacy, were now superseded by 'official' national languages in each country. Kamusella quotes a nineteenth century Czech nationalist, Karel Borovsky, expounding the effect of this:

> Wherever your language and nationhood are disregarded, you are oppressed, no matter how liberal the country may be. Where your language is excluded from schools and offices, freedom is taken away from you, from your nation, more than by police or censorship.

As Kamusella notes, it was ironic that those who pushed for this linguistic homogeneity were themselves multi-lingual: the first pan-

Slavic congress, held in Prague in 1848, conducted its proceedings in German.

From our West European perspective we see the First World War primarily as a struggle between England and Germany, but Kamusella explains its origins in the 'multidimensional instability' caused by the weakened empires and the rising nationalisms of the east:

> Seeking to weaken loyalty to the tsar in occupied areas of the Russian Empire, Berlin and Vienna encouraged local ethnolinguistic national movements. In the case of Austria-Hungary, it was like trying to put out a fire by dousing it with petrol and the national movements of the Dual Monarchy wasted no time in grasping this message.

At the end of the first world the empires of the east collapsed. The post-war settlement was based on Woodrow Wilsons's ideal of self-determination: smaller nations should have their day in the sun. But as Kamusella documents, the new nations ran into the old problems. Nationalism was in theory a noble aim, given the way the imperial autocracies had ruthlessly suppressed their captive nations. Czechoslovakia, formed in 1918, ran into the same problems as the Austro-Hungarian empire it has just escaped from. In the latter one country, Austria, had dominated; it had given a form of independence to Hungary, but the Hungarians, being nationalistic, did not bestow on the many minorities within their borders (eg. Croats, Slovaks, Romanians) the same rights to independence and self-expression they themselves had just been granted. This pattern was repeated in the new Czechoslovakia, where the Slovaks were granted a form of autonomy from Czech suzerainty, but neither they nor the Czechs fully respected the rights of their other minorities. Much the same thing happened in Poland and other newly liberated nations. These toxic paradoxes caused as many problems as they solved.

Between the wars rulers of the new states used a variety of administrative means short of terror and murder (such as forbidding minority languages in schools, transfer of populations and forced assimilation) to keep their own ethnic group firmly on top. Opposite pressures were at work: attempts to achieve homogeneity within neat borders coincided with the rise of dictators whose rabid ideologies were tearing the region apart. In the Second World War the previous rule book, which had imposed some restraints, was torn up. Early in their careers when they were not in power, both Hitler and Stalin were intensely interested in the nationalities/race question. They too were products of this striving for national homogeneity. In power they became imperialists with a nationalist cast of mind, though that sounds a contradiction. They carried out crude nationalistic polices on a grand scale, moving whole peoples around at will. We see the second world war primarily in terms of military strategy, but when Hitler looked at maps he saw no place in continental Europe for Jews, Gypsies or Slavs. Hitler and Stalin created a new type of multi-national, multi-ethnic empire, not content, like imperial rulers in the past, to oversee a diverse citizenry. They wished to achieve a new supranational purity by mass killings, expelling whole peoples and atomizing those which remained.

The Wilsonian settlement after the First World War set up small nations. The settlement after the Second World War, in contrast, set up blocs of nations, the Soviet one and the Western one in response. The result, but not the aim, of the two world wars, was to achieve the ethnic-linguistic alignments the earlier nationalists had desired, but at horrendous cost. After 1945 many nations were racially homogeneous. Between the wars more than one-third of Poland's population was non-Polish; after the war it was about 95% ethnically Polish, with its Jewish, German, Lithuanian, Ruthenian, Ukrainian and Belorussian minorities gone. Small ethnic groups, like the Ruthenians and Silesians, are re-emerging and striving for limited local autonomy: small and local is beautiful. There is now, apart from the treatment of the Gypsies, little overt persecution of minorities – multi-ethnicity and minority rights are in vogue. On the other hand Putin wishes to reassert Russian hegemony in the borderland regions. After all that suffering the wheel has turned full circle again.

Quadrant, January-February, 2013, abridged

COMMENTS ON THE AUTHOR'S WRITINGS

* Prof. Vincent O'Sullivan in *Australian Literary Studies*: 'Patrick Morgan's (chapter) seems to me exemplary of the *New Literary History of Australia* at its best, beginning with the kind of *apercu* that opens a fresh perspective. Those writers with something of Morgan's flair for apothegm and distillation produce a number of brilliant essays.'

* Victorian Community History Award Judges on *The Settling of Gippsland*: 'A brilliantly researched book with a cast of characters to rival the number in *War and Peace*...Equally impressive is the lean and easy style which Patrick Morgan has used to cram so many events together and give the story vivacity'.

* Peter Coleman in *Quadrant*, May, 1998: 'The most prophetic essay of all was by Patrick Morgan on the 'abuse and prevention' of literature by the intolerant, politicized 'mates' of Australian culture.'

* Prof. Henry Mayer in *The National Times*: 'Patrick Morgan, a perceptive and badly underestimated writer, analyses the Australian cultural type.'

* Michael Danby in *Quadrant*: 'The wide variety of viewpoints includes contributions from leading Australian academics like... Patrick Morgan.'

* Prof. Tom Griffiths in the *Victorian Historical Journal* on *The Literature of Gippsland*: 'His writing is both matter-of-fact and full wonder. It spills over with enthusiasm and ideas. This is a pioneering form of regional history showing the rich potential of fiction as an historical source.'

* Prof. Stuart Macintyre review in *Overland* on *Quadrant 25 Years*: 'Writers such as Patrick Morgan, represented here by his recent essay on 'The Paradox of Australian Literature', show that it [Australian cultural criticism] can be done.'

* Don Watson in *Overland*: 'Some time ago Patrick Morgan devised a literary taxonomy which reflected the widely differing experience of Gippslanders...It is an excellent brief introduction...an evocation of the place which is bravely wry and haunting'.

* Monash University Review Committee (1999): 'Mr Morgan has made a substantial contribution to the Gippsland Campus, and to the wider Gippsland community. He has a national reputation and a formidable publication record.'

* Cardinal George Pell review of B.A Santamaria *Running the Show, Quadrant,* October 2008: 'The introductions to each set of documents, written by the editor Paddy Morgan are... independent and judicious in their evaluations. His concluding section entitled 'Commentary', fewer than twenty pages, is a masterpiece, honest, shrewd and perceptive.'

* Brenda Niall review of *Melbourne Before Mannix* in the *Victorian Historical Journal* (2013): 'Patrick Morgan's immensely valuable new book…Morgan's examination of the political influence wielded by Catholics in Carr's time has special interest. Morgan's book is at its incisive best in the final section…Morgan's shrewd, fair-minded analysis of the impact of Mannix'.

* Lawrence Maher review of *Melbourne Before Mannix* in *Labor History* (2013): 'Morgan's book is a highly informative addition to the literature on the social and political history of early Melbourne Catholicism…Morgan has used to considerable effect the very detailed and clearly written accounts of public life involving the Catholic laity of Melbourne.'

* Doug Morrissey review of *The Vandemonian Trail*, *Victorian Historical Journal*, June 2018: 'Every now and then a book come along that indelibly stamps itself on a period of history. Patrick Morgan's *The Vandemonian Trail*, is one such book. The author has written an informative and fascinating account of the Tasmanian convict migration to Victoria…Thanks to the author's impressive knowledge and research, the Tichborne claimant and Bogong Jack narratives are no longer enmeshed in obscuring myth.'

* Mr. B.A. Santamaria, letter responding to a review of his *Australia at the Crossroads*: 'I am grateful…because it is about the only account I have read which shows intellectual understanding of the little I have tried to do.'

* Dr. John Ritchie, general editor of the *Australian Dictionary of Biography*, letter on an entry written for the *ADB*, 1991: 'The

article reads beautifully and I thank you for the time, care & thought you gave it. I hope that you will write more 'lives' for our future volumes'.

* Professor Patrick O'Farrell, letter on a review of his latest book, 1991: 'You have so accurately divined my overall purpose [in writing on Irish Australia] that I thought I should write to say thank you for your perception…It is both a joy and a consolation to encounter a mind as clear, penetrating and generous as your own'.

ACKNOWLEDGEMENTS

Grateful thanks are extended to publications in which these essays first appeared: the *Adelaide Review, Antipodes, The Bulletin, Farrago, Kunapipi, Meanjin, Quadrant, Táin* and *Tinteán*. Articles from symposia on the No Case and on Professor Patrick O'Brien are also included here. Over the years Donald Horne generously published my articles in *The Bulletin*, as did the Brian Buckley in *The Sun*, Stuart Sayers and Jennifer Byrne in *The Age*, Michael Costigan in *The Advocate*, Jennifer Campbell in *The Australian*, Christopher Pearson in the *Adelaide Review*, John Carmody and James Franklin in the *Journal of the Australian Catholic History Society*, Colin Coomber in *Catholic Life,* and Val Noone in *Táin* and Liz McKenzie in *Tinteán*. In *Quadrant*'s case I have been fortunate to work with James McAuley, Peter Coleman, Paddy McGuinness and Keith Windschuttle as editors, Richard Krygier as founding manager, Marie Gillis as secretary in the magazine's early days, and Robin Marsden and George Thomas as editorial assistants. The unspoken presence behind these articles is my wife Ann, to whom I am deeply indebted. Thanks once again to Connor Court and its Director Anthony Cappello for accepting this manuscript and publishing it so efficiently. Connor Court has filled a crucial gap in Australian publishing, for which many authors and readers, including myself, are grateful.

www.ingramcontent.com/pod-product-compliance
Lightning Source LLC
Chambersburg PA
CBHW051103030726
47504CB00006B/1759